T0271087

ROUTLEDGE LIBRARY EDITIONS:
COMMODITIES

Volume 2

AGRICULTURAL COMMODITY MARKETS

AGRICULTURAL COMMODITY MARKETS

A Guide to Futures Trading

MICHAEL ATKIN

Routledge
Taylor & Francis Group

LONDON AND NEW YORK

First published in 1989 by Routledge

This edition first published in 2024
by Routledge
4 Park Square, Milton Park, Abingdon, Oxon OX14 4RN

and by Routledge
605 Third Avenue, New York, NY 10158

Routledge is an imprint of the Taylor & Francis Group, an informa business

British Library Cataloguing in Publication Data
A catalogue record for this book is available from the British Library

ISBN: 978-1-032-69509-9 (Set)
ISBN: 978-1-032-68907-4 (Volume 2) (hbk)
ISBN: 978-1-032-68929-6 (Volume 2) (pbk)
ISBN: 978-1-032-68923-4 (Volume 2) (ebk)

DOI: 10.4324/9781032689234

Publisher's Note
The publisher has gone to great lengths to ensure the quality of this reprint but points out that some imperfections in the original copies may be apparent.

Disclaimer
The publisher has made every effort to trace copyright holders and would welcome correspondence from those they have been unable to trace.

Agricultural commodity markets
A Guide to Futures Trading

Michael Atkin

ROUTLEDGE
London and New York

First published 1989
by Routledge
11 New Fetter Lane, London EC4P 4EE
29 West 35th Street, New York, NY 10001

Typeset by Leaper and Gard Ltd,
Printed in Great Britain by
Billing & Sons Ltd, Worcester

British Library Cataloguing in Publication Data
Atkin, Michael
    Agricultural commodity markets: a guide
    to futures trading. – (Commodities series).
    1. Commodity markets.
    I. Title   II. Series
    332.64′4

    ISBN 0–415–01887–0

Library of Congress Cataloging in Publication Data
Atkin, Michael.
    Agricultural commodity markets: a guide to futures trading/Michael Atkin
        p.   cm. – (Commodities series)
    Bibliography: p.
    Includes index.
    ISBN 0–415–01887–0
    1. Commodity exchanges.   I. Title.   II. Series.
    HG6046.A85   1988   88–23992
    332.64′4 – dc19   CIP

To the memory of
Ben Smithies

Contents

Contents

Contents

Figures

Tables

Preface

It could reasonably be argued that one needs a good excuse to add to the great quantity of writing about futures markets. The large amount of literature notwithstanding, there remains a remarkable degree of ignorance about the workings and purpose of the futures markets. They are still widely seen primarily as vehicles for gambling and carry the additional opprobrium of being seen to generate profits from the droughts and natural disasters which mean hardship and distress for many. These views misunderstand how markets work. That the ignorance of markets is widespread can be seen from the public debate over the role of financial futures markets in the stock market crash of October 1987; a debate characterized by a hostility to futures markets which could only be the product of minds unencumbered by understanding. Incidentally, even if futures markets were primarily about gambling, it is hard to see why this should cause comment; Britons spend £3 billion a year betting on horses, and they do so with odds and effective commission rates which make the occasional flutter on the pork belly market seem like a safe investment.

Futures markets are institutions with serious economic purposes, and the fact that this is not more widely appreciated is partly a result of the shortcomings of the available literature, which tends to fall into one of two camps. On the one hand, there are the academic publications which have advanced specialists' understanding of the markets considerably but which are impenetable to the broader community. On the other hand, there are the 'how to make a million dollars from the orange juice market' type of publications, which do little to change the view of the markets as a type of casino.

In seeking to fill the gap left by these two types of publication, this book is aimed at a broad audience of students, economists, traders, and the general public. In the first part of the book the futures and options markets are discussed and explained. There is also a detailed discussion of the ways of analysing and trading the markets. We then turn to the major agricultural commodities, describe their supply and demand characteristics, and give some indications of how professional traders operate in these markets. There will be many readers for whom one or other of these constituents is already well known but they will, I hope, find much that is interesting, nevertheless.

A comprehensive list of the colleagues and friends to whom thanks are due would be unwieldy. I do, however, owe special thanks to Charles Young and James Fry for everything they have taught me over the years. Errors and omissions are of course my responsibility.

Chapter one

Futures markets and agriculture

Commodities and futures markets

Commodities are bulk, unprocessed raw materials. Perhaps the key feature of commodities, however, is their fungibility, the fact that one load of a commodity is an extremely close substitute for another. Agricultural commodities, which can be further divided into raw materials, such as cotton, and foodstuffs, such as wheat, comprise a large part of the total commodity market; the other traditional groupings of commodities are metals and minerals, such as copper and iron ore, and energy, such as crude oil. Recently people have also started to think of money and financial instruments as commodities; after all, money, in the form of foreign exchange for example, satisfies the fungibility criterion and can be traded just like wheat or copper.

Another important feature of many, but not all, commodities is that their prices are extremely volatile. This volatility is caused by many factors, but perhaps the most important in the case of agricultural commodities is the weather. Fluctuations in rainfall and temperatures cause large fluctuations in agricultural production and these, in turn, affect prices. Of course, weather-related variations in production only have a major impact on prices because of the economic characteristics of supply and demand, but the weather is a key variable. It is this volatility in price which lies at the heart of the rationale for futures markets, and to understand it we need to understand the differences between spot, forward, and futures markets.

Spot markets, forward markets, and futures markets

All kinds of goods are exchanged every day on spot markets, which are also known as cash or prompt markets. On these markets a buyer and a seller agree a price and contract to exchange goods of specified quality and quantity for delivery in the immediate future. When spot markets are volatile, traders and merchants are exposed to large risks, because the value of their inventories can fluctuate widely. A merchant who has bought sugar at £100 per ton will sustain a large loss on the value of his inventory if sugar prices fall to £80 per ton. Conversely, he will make a large profit if prices rise to £120. A great deal of past trading activity took the form of traders and merchants taking the gamble that they could sell their inventories later or in a different place at a higher price than they paid.

In order to secure some protection from sudden changes in prices, however, buyers and sellers developed forward markets, in which contracts are exchanged for the delivery, at some agreed time in the future, of a specified quantity and quality of a good at an agreed price. Thus a forward market is just like a spot market, except that it calls for delivery in the more distant, rather than in the immediate future. By the nineteenth century rapid expansion in international trade in agricultural commodities had given forward contracting a major role in trading.

However, spot and forward markets suffer some disadvantages, especially from the point of view of those who wish to protect themselves against price volatility. These disadvantages stem from the fact that each forward contract is specific to the two contracting parties. It therefore specifies quantity, quality, delivery date, and delivery location; and the price in the contract will reflect these factors as well as the value of the commodity itself. These other factors limit the value of the contract to anyone other than the two contracting parties, thus making it difficult to establish a secondary market in forward contracts. For example, a contract calling for the delivery in Liverpool of 100 tonnes of top-quality Ghanaian cocoa beans in January is not worth a great deal to a Dutch chocolate maker who wants some low-quality Ivorian beans in April. Thus the forward market is always at risk from the default of one of the parties, which will leave the other with a less valuable contract. Futures markets differ from forward markets, in that although they are legal agreements between two parties to deliver a commodity at a future date, the quantity, quality, delivery date, and delivery point are all standardized, leaving only the price to be established by the contracting parties. They are therefore pure price markets, which free participants from worrying about the specific problems of delivering certain qualities of a commodity to certain locations, and allow them to concentrate on setting a price for the underlying commodity. While this does not entirely remove uncertainty from future prices, it does convey marked advantages, most notably in increasing the liquidity of trading.

Perhaps the key advantage of a futures market is that people can participate in it, even though they may have no intention of making or taking delivery of the underlying commodity. Because the contract is standardized, it can effectively be sold on to someone else. To understand how this operates, we need to look at the structure of a modern futures exchange.

The modern futures exchange

The modern futures exchange has a number of important features. The one which is its public face and which does little to inspire public confidence is the trading floor. This floor, or pit, is simply an area thronged by traders who shout and gesticulate at one another in a scene reminiscent of nothing so much as a medieval depiction of chaos. It is on this trading floor that prices are set: traders shout bids and offers at one another, and each completed trade is reported to a clerk, then fed into a computer and transmitted by electronic news services around the world. Floor traders buy and sell on the basis of the instructions they receive from people outside the pits, or for their own accounts. In this respect, a futures trading floor is like any other market-place where buyers and sellers congregate.

Futures markets are different, however, in a number of respects. First, there is no limit on the number of contracts which can be traded. Anyone can buy, as long as there is someone to sell. There is no finite stock of contracts which some people 'own' and wish to sell to others. Selling a soybean futures contract is promising to deliver soybeans at a date in the future, so it is not necessary to own soybeans in order to make the promise. Second, a futures exchange has a clearing-house, an institution whose role can be understood by referring back to the fact that a futures market does not require someone to make or take delivery of the underlying commodity. Imagine that a trader who had sold a March sugar futures contract for, say, £100 later bought another for, say, £80. He would have two obligations: one to sell sugar in March for £100, another to buy sugar in March for £80. The market could organize itself such that full settlement of each contract takes place, with the trader required to receive the first sum and pay the second sum in full on the appropriate delivery dates. This would impose a large financial burden on traders. Futures markets solve this problem by creating a clearing-house, which simplifies the process by restricting payments to the net sum and performing the job of settlement among traders. It does this by becoming the opposing party to each contract, assuming the selling position to each buyer and the buying position to each seller. Thus each bargain struck on the trading floor between two traders (one buyer and one seller) is instantly transformed into two contracts: the seller takes out a contract to sell to the clearing-house, and the buyer takes out a contract to buy from the clearing-house. Of course, the clearing-house's net position is zero.

It is the clearing-house which makes it so easy not to worry about having to deliver soybeans. A trader who has sold a soybean futures contract has an obligation to deliver to the clearing-house, not to another trader. Thus the first trader can cancel his obligation by buying a contract (i.e. undertaking to receive soybeans). It does not matter that these two obligations were struck with different traders on the floor. It is the net position with the clearing-house that matters.

The clearing-house also insists on the payment of a deposit as a performance bond; this is now called 'initial margin'. The operation of the margin system also removes the incentives to default, which can be powerful in the case of adverse price movements. Imagine that a merchant who has coffee in his warehouses sells 10 contracts, each of 5 tonnes, of September-delivery coffee on the London market at a price of £1,500 per tonne. The trader will make a payment to the clearing-house of the initial margin. (The precise amount is fixed by the exchange and depends on the contract, its volatility, and the type of customer, but is never more than 10 per cent of the total contract value.) If the price of coffee rises substantially, the trader will have an incentive to default, since although he would forfeit his deposit with the clearing-house, he could more than recoup his money from the appreciation in the value of his stocks of coffee. Thus the clearing-house would in such a case demand the payment of an extra sum, or 'variation margin' from the trader. Conversely, if prices move in a favourable way, there is no risk of default and the exchange will pay a 'credit margin' to the trader. One advantage of the margin system is that it makes futures markets highly geared. Since the prices of the underlying commodities are volatile, the value of a futures contract can increase or decrease dramatically. Since a futures contract can be controlled with a small deposit, it is very attractive to speculators. We return to this in the following sections.

Settlements by a clearing-house also reduces the number of contracts which result in actual delivery of the physical commodity. Traders are able to 'close out' their promises to sell by purchasing promises to buy, thus giving them a zero net position with the clearing-house. They are left with the net financial gain or loss from the change in prices. Typically this is easier than making or accepting physical delivery of the commodity under the terms specified by the contract. Delivery is possible; in a modern futures market typically fewer than 5 per cent of all contracts result in delivery. The advantage of the futures market is precisely that it allows its participants to concentrate on price alone.

Using a futures market

It is very easy to take a position on a futures market, but there is inevitably a certain amount of jargon which must be understood. It is also important to have an understanding of the way in which a futures market and its key participants operate.

The trading floor

The trading floor is where all trades are transacted. All orders therefore have to be communicated to the floor. Floor traders will either be employees of companies, or they will be 'locals', i.e. individuals who trade on their own account. Locals provide a substantial proportion of the liquidity in US futures markets, but they are less common outside the USA. The London Futures and Options Exchange, for example, only admitted locals in 1987; prior to that, all floor traders were employees of member companies. Locals can hold positions for as long as they wish; research in the USA has identified three quite separate types of local behaviour. Those who only hold positions for a few minutes, behaviour which in effect is arbitrage within the pit itself, are known as 'scalpers'; day traders are those who will hold a position for a few days at most; and position traders are those who hold open positions for a much longer time.

Large companies will have their own employees on the floor to execute their own orders at lower costs and to be able to offer a better service to their customers. The link between the trading floor and the outside world is provided by two types of company: trading companies, and commission houses.

Trading companies and commission houses

Trading companies are involved in the production, distribution, or utilization of commodities, and they are heavy users of futures markets because they hold inventories and are exposed to large potential losses on those inventories through price fluctuations. Some of these companies are extremely large, with trading interests extending around the world and across a wide range of commodities, whereas others are very small. A number of companies are simply the trading arm of a farmers' co-operative, for example, trading only one or two commodities. Generally only the larger companies will have their own employees on the trading floor of the exchanges they use.

Second, there are commission houses. These are brokerage companies which offer a service to anyone who wishes to use a futures market and make their money from the commissions they charge on their customers' transactions. The larger commission houses will employ their own floor brokers. The employees of commission houses who deal with customer accounts are known as 'account executives'. Again, commission houses vary enormously in size. Some are large, diversified international finance houses and offer futures trading facilities along with a range of other financial services from stockbroking to merchant banking. Others are small, entrepreneurial companies which may have only a handful of employees. All reputable commission houses, irrespective of size, will make an effort to find out about their customers and, in the case of private clients, will try to establish that they have the resources and temperament to trade. Different houses have different criteria for accepting clients; most have a minimum account size, but the minimum will vary greatly. Most will also wish to be satisfied that no clients are speculating with more than a certain percentage of their net worth.

Very large users of futures markets will tend to use more than one brokerage house, especially when they have large orders. This, then, prevents their activities from becoming too obvious and moving prices against themselves.

Hedgers and speculators

The ultimate users of futures markets can be divided into two categories: those who hedge and those who speculate. Hedging is the process whereby those engaged in physical transactions in commodities can protect themselves against adverse price movements. Consider the example of an exporting firm which buys grain from farmers in order to ship it overseas to customers. It takes time to buy the grain and transport it overseas; moreover, at the time of purchase the exporter will not know precisely to where, or exactly when, the grain will be exported. The firm is therefore exposed to the risk that selling prices will slump between the time of purchase from farmers and the time of final sale. (Even a small change in prices can be extremely serious for trading companies, given the small margins on which they operate.) To protect against this possibility, the firm will sell futures contracts equal to and at the same time as the purchases from farmers. This transaction makes it 'long of physicals' and 'short of futures', and it is protected against changes in the price of the commodity. If the price falls before the export sale is completed, the firm sustains a loss on its physical transaction; but the fall makes its futures position more valuable and the profit on this offsets the loss incurred in the physical transaction.

Another important example of hedging is provided by farmer selling of a crop. Farmers face uncertainty over the cash prices for their crops which will prevail at the time of harvest. To protect themselves against this uncertainty, they can sell futures contracts, approximately equal to the size of their expected crops; this gives them the obligation, and the right, to sell a fixed quantity of a crop at the agreed price. While this means they cannot profit from any increase in the price above the level of their futures sale, it does remove the fear of sharply lower prices at the time of harvest. A transaction of this type has a further advantage to farmers. A crop which has been hedged on a futures market has a more certain value than one which is unhedged; this value can be offered as collateral to a bank if the farmer needs to borrow money. Most rural banks in the USA accept futures contracts as security against loans, and the use of futures contracts in hedging production is growing in importance as a way of securing finance for investment projects, especially in the mining industry.

It is important to note that, for the hedger, the purpose of the futures transaction is to limit risk, not to make money. Hedging transactions limit the dangers of adverse price movements, but by the same token, remove the possibility of windfall profit. Imagine that in the case of the exporting company above, prices of grain had risen in the interval between their purchase from farmers and their sale to an overseas customer. In this case, they make a profit on their physical transaction, but lose money on their futures position. The company would have made money with an unhedged position. Because of this possibility, one finds that in the real world there is not the neat distinction between hedgers and speculators insisted upon by textbooks. Many firms involved in physical trade will choose not to hedge when they judge that price trends are moving in their favour, thereby effectively speculating on the future direction of price changes. (Of course, they may be wrong and end up losing money.)

Speculators are people who have no interest in the underlying physical commodity, but participate in the markets in order to make a profit from the changes in prices. They embrace the risk which hedgers seek to avoid, and do so in the hope of making money. Speculators trade markets, promising to make or take delivery of commodities, but they never allow those contracts to run to maturity; they always close out their positions by making an offsetting transaction. Consider a simple example, where soybeans are traded on the Chicago Board of Trade. The contract size is 5,000 bushels (60 lb each) and the market is priced in dollars per bushel. Imagine that the price is $6.00 per bushel. A speculator who thinks that prices for soybeans will go up to $6.25 per bushel can buy a contract at $6.00 by paying the margin demanded by the exchange. (This will be about 5 per cent of the total contract value: 5,000 bushels at $6.00 each is $30,000 and 5 per cent of this is $1,500.) Imagine that the speculator is right, and prices go up to $6.25. The contract is now worth $31,250. The speculator can realize this profit of $1,250 without bothering with trucks of soybeans: all that is needed is to take out a contract to sell. The speculator, then, has two positions with the clearing-house: one to buy at $6.00 and another to sell at $6.25. The net position is a profit of 25 cents per bushel, which is $1,250 because there are 5,000 bushels in the contract. Speculators like futures markets for a number of reasons.

The first is the comparative ease of futures trading. It is easy to enter a position in a futures market; moreover, because all obligations are held towards the clearing-house, it is easy to cancel a position by entering into the opposite obligation. An obligation to buy, represented by the purchase of a futures contract, can be cancelled by taking out an obligation to sell, represented by the sale of a futures contract. Since a futures market acts as a focus for flows of information, it also is far easier for someone to find out about a commodity which is traded on a futures market than one which is not.[1]

The second is the low level of margin required to control a futures contract, which makes them very highly geared. In this respect, they resemble the property market which, in the UK at any rate, is extremely attractive to investors. A £50,000 house can be purchased with a £5,000 deposit (and a £45,000 loan). If the price of the house goes up by only 10 per cent to £55,000, the value of the owner's stake has gone up by 100 per cent, from £5,000 to £10,000. Similarly, a futures contract in a commodity can be bought cheaply, with a margin which is never more than 10 per cent of the total contract value, but the entire amount of any increase in the value of the contract accrues to the owner. Since commodity prices are, in general, highly unstable, there is clearly the potential for huge profits. Because of the system of credit margins, interim profits can be withdrawn from a futures position which moves in a favourable way. Similarly, there is the potential for huge losses, for prices can, and do, move as quickly in an adverse direction as in a favourable one. For many participants in futures markets the possibility of profits outweighs the possibility of losses, but an awareness of the potential for losses and of strategies to limit losses is essential for those who wish to become involved. (These issues are discussed more fully later in this book.)

Third, in futures markets it is possible to make profits from increases or decreases in prices. This is not possible in other markets. If you believe the price of shares in a company is going to fall, there is little you can do to profit from that belief; you can sell any holdings you may have, but that merely prevents you from realizing a loss. In futures markets, if you believe a price is going to drop, you can sell a futures contract, and you can effect this with the same ease as buying a futures contract. Selling a futures contract, or 'going short', is simply to take on an obligation to sell the commodity on the delivery date at the agreed price.[2] If prices decline, that obligation to sell (which is, *ipso facto*, a right to sell) at a higher price is clearly a valuable one, and it can be exercised at a profit. The number of futures contracts which can be bought and sold is limited only by the willingness of someone to enter into the opposite side of the transaction.

The mechanics of trading

Initially a speculator who wishes to trade will need to open an account with a commission house which assigns an account executive to the account. The account executive will become the channel of communication between the client and the trading floor. Each order, agreed between account executive and client and then passed to floor trader, will specify five things: (a) whether it is to buy or sell, (b) the quantity, (c) the delivery month and year, (d) the commodity (and the exchange if necessary), and (e) the type of order. This last specification is important, because prices can fluctuate considerably during trading hours, and one's view of how profitable a trade will be depends on the price at which the opening order is transacted, or 'filled'. When markets are trading actively, the price that a customer sees on a screen as the last recorded price at the time he decides to trade may no longer be the price by the time his order reaches the trading floor. A very large order may cause prices to move. Accordingly, it is important to specify the price which the customer is prepared to pay. The most common types of order are as follows.

A *market order* is filled at the best available price as soon as it reaches the floor. A *limit order* sets the upper limit at which a buy order can be filled or the lower limit at which a sell order can be filled. Market and limit orders are the most common kinds of order in the markets. A *market-if-touched (MIT) order* becomes a market order when the market is bid or offered at or beyond the price specified. An MIT sell order is placed below the current market price, an MIT buy order above. A *spread order* is a combination buy–sell order for different delivery months of the same commodity. This type of order can be given without any absolute prices on either leg of the spread, but restrictions can be placed on the premium; e.g. 'spread buy 5 July wheat sell 5 March wheat, 6 cent premium or better'.

Obviously the time for which an order is to be held is important. Most orders are *day orders*, good only for the day on which they are entered. There are, however, also *fill or kill (FOK) orders*, which are to be filled immediately at the stated price or cancelled, and *good till cancelled (GTC) orders* whose meaning is obvious.

Another important part of trading is deciding what to do when the market goes against the original position and where to take profit when the market moves in its favour. In the case of an adverse movement, margination will be necessary, and the amount of money which is available for margin calls will be discussed with the account executive. It is also common practice to place a *stop*, or *stop-loss order* at an agreed level. This kind of order is designed to close out a trade which is going the wrong way; thus a *buy-stop* closes out a short position, and will be placed above the level at which the short was initiated, whereas a *sell-stop* closes out a long position and will be placed below the original buying price. A more sophisticated tool is a *trailing stop*, which is moved at the end of each day to a new level. Selecting the right place for a stop can be difficult, since it involves a judgement about the market and an assessment of how large a loss can be sustained, but as we shall see it is one of the keys to successful futures trading. When the price level specified in the stop is reached, it is treated like a market order; therefore, there is no guarantee that it will be filled at the specified level.

If a trade is initiated with a specific target in mind, a GTC order to close out the position at the target level can be placed along with the original order.

The role of futures markets in agriculture

As we have demonstrated in the previous section, futures markets can be understood as the outgrowth of forward contracting. Therefore, their rationale is normally seen in terms of risk management. A common analogy made is that between futures markets and insurance schemes: speculators are seen as underwriters, carrying the risks to which those engaged in physical commodity trade are exposed. In fact this analogy is rather limited in its usefulness; futures markets are much more complicated than insurance schemes, and play more than the risk management role. In this section the various roles are considered.

Price discovery and the provision of liquidity

One of the most important roles played by futures markets is that of providing an obvious, public source of prices for important commodities. As soon as a contract is agreed between a buyer and a seller, it is logged by the clearing-house and the price is fed into a computer and transmitted via electronic networks all around the world; summaries of price movements are also published in newspapers. The ease with which it is possible to find the price of, say, coffee contrasts greatly with the difficulty of finding the price of a commodity which is not traded on futures markets such as coal. Moreover, the futures price is a 'pure' price, in that all the details of delivery, quality, and so on, are standardized. A trader who wants to know the price of coal will find that it varies in a less than obvious way with quality, quantity, and delivery terms, and that a great deal of investigation is needed to find out the best price at a particular time.

Historically the idea of public price announcement was important in the establishment of what is now the world's largest futures market, the Chicago Board of Trade. In the late nineteenth century many of the traders in that city were concerned that unfair prices were being paid for agricultural commodities by certain unscrupulous traders; they therefore decided to establish a system whereby a central market-place was set up, where all traders would come and openly bid for the available supplies. This, then, provided the precursor of the modern futures trading 'pit', where buyers and sellers set prices by open outcry.

Essential to the performance of this role is liquidity. In order to establish fair prices, it is necessary that there is a large number of buyers and sellers in a market. Yet the number of producing, trading, and consuming companies in a particular commodity-using industry is likely to be small. Potentially this poses difficulties for sellers and buyers at certain times of the year: how could Ghana sell its cocoa if Rowntree, Cadbury, and the few other chocolate-producing companies happened not to want any cocoa at the time Ghana needed to sell (perhaps to buy some essential imports)? Ghana would particularly like to be able to sell without causing prices to move sharply downwards, but this will only be possible if there are large numbers of buyers available in the market. Liquidity is essential to the success of futures markets: many of the new contracts which are developed by commodity exchanges fail because they do not attract sufficient buying and selling interest. Generally a successful futures market needs both the support of the trade (i.e. hedgers) and the interest of the speculative community.

For most of the major agricultural commodities which are discussed in this book the price set on the futures market is the key reference price for world trade in the commodity. There are futures markets which are of purely local interest, but we shall be concerned primarily with commodities and markets for which the futures price has a broad economic significance. In the case of soybeans, for example, the world market price is effectively determined on the Chicago Board of Trade.

Hedging, the price of storage, and the relationship between spot and futures prices

It may seem obvious, but it is of considerable economic significance that agricultural commodities have pronounced seasonal fluctuations in supply, and considerably less pronounced seasonal fluctuations in demand. Grain is planted in one season, grows and ripens in another, and is harvested in a third; bread is consumed the year round in reasonably stable quantities. In an unsophisticated economy one would see grain prices very low at the time of harvest (when supply is large relative to demand), and very high at the end of the crop year (when supply is small relative to demand). This instability of prices would clearly be bad both for producers and consumers; moreover, it would be unnecessary since the provision of storage facilities for grain will effectively lower available supply for consumption at the time of harvest (since the demands of storers of grain as well as those of consumers have to be met) and increase supply later in the crop year. Thus the availability of storage facilities will reduce cash price volatility over the course of the crop year.

In a market economy, however, storage facilities will only be provided if there is a return to the resources invested in building and running them. If a merchant is to buy grain for storage, he will only do so (in the absence of a futures market) if he is reasonably confident that he will be able to sell the grain later in the crop year at a higher price than he paid for it, since he must cover the costs of his operations, including the opportunity cost of the capital used to buy the grain in the first place. This exposes the merchant to great risk, since the spot price may decline, or may stay constant, or may not rise by enough to compensate for the costs of storing. For centuries merchants were willing to absorb this risk, but the development of a futures market provided a mechanism whereby this risk could be diminished since it provides a way in which a price can be established in the present for the delivery of grain in the future. The difference between futures prices for different delivery dates will reflect the incentives available for holding goods from one period into the next.

Some of the earliest research by economists into the futures markets, and in particular the researches of Holbrook Working, emphasized the role of futures markets in setting a price for storage facilities. In a normal market the price, quoted today, of grain in two months time will be equal to the current spot price for grain plus the costs of storing grain from today for two months. Ordinarily, however, the premium is slightly lower than the full costs of storage because of hedging.

This difference between a nearby and a futures price (or between two distant futures prices) is called a 'contango' in the UK; but its American name, 'a carrying charge', gives us a clue to its economic meaning. Markets which show a 'full carry' are those where the full costs of storage are reflected in the structure of futures prices. Variations in the carrying charge are a way in which the market can encourage traders to perform inter-temporal arbitrage: if the futures prices show more than the full carry, then there is an incentive to forgo current consumption and store grain to earn this excess carrying charge (i.e. there is an incentive to buy cash grain and sell future grain).

In a normal futures market, prices of distant futures are higher than cash and nearby prices. This relationship reflects the plentiful availability of the commodity in the cash market and the incentive to store it into the future. In general, the value of a commodity in the future is equal to its value now (the cash price) plus the cost of storing it into the future.[3] Conversely, if the market shows an inverse carrying charge (called a 'backwardation' in the UK), then there is an incentive to remove grain from storage and make it available for current consumption. This situation often arises in the season following a bad harvest but when there is an expectation that the next harvest will be good. Futures prices will penalize the storing of grain into the next season, on the grounds that the next harvest will cover future needs and grain should not be stored from this season into the next.

Remember that although most futures contracts are closed out with no delivery taking place, it is possible to make or take physical delivery against a futures contract. That traders can deliver the commodity against futures maintains an economic relationship between cash and futures prices. If futures prices are too high, arbitrageurs will sell the futures, buy the cash commodity, and store and deliver it against their futures contract. If futures prices are too low, arbitrageurs buy the nearby futures, take delivery, and sell the commodity in the cash market. Both these actions serve to bring cash and futures prices closer together, and lead to the convergence of the two as the futures contract comes nearer to expiry, becoming, in effect, the cash market.

Because of this relationship between spot and futures prices, holders of commodity stocks can hedge their inventories by selling futures contracts. However, there is no such thing as a perfect hedge in the real world, a hedge in which a futures profit (loss) exactly offsets a physical loss (profit). All hedgers are exposed to what is called 'basis risk'. The basis is the difference between a nearby futures price and the price of the commodity in a particular spot market. In any given spot market prices will reflect local demands and supplies and transportation costs. An example of basis risk is that faced by a US grain exporter. The exporter may be interested in prices for grain in the Gulf of Mexico ports, which will not be the same as the prices in Chicago. In the longer term this difference will equal the cost of transportation down the Mississippi, but it could easily alter over the few weeks for which a company might hold a hedge. Or in the example of a farmer hedge selling his crop, there is clearly the risk that, because of unforeseen difficulties such as the weather, the size of the farmer's crop is not the same as the size of the futures position.

Thus futures markets are certainly not institutions which remove risk from physical dealings in commodities. None the less, there is a useful analytical distinction between hedging and speculating.[4] Hedgers can simply be defined as those who use futures markets in order to limit the risk attached to their present and future positions in the physical commodity. Hedgers can be long or short of the futures market, so they are defined not with respect to their positions, but to the usage to which they put the futures market. (In fact studies of futures markets show that, as a whole, hedgers tend to be short of the futures market since, as a whole, they tend to be long of physical commodities; this empirical feature of the markets, however, is irrelevant to the analytical distinction: many hedgers are routinely long of futures.) Speculators are those who have, and expect to have, no position in the physical commodity. They take positions in the futures market in the hope that they will profit from the very price fluctuations which hedgers seek to avoid. Thus a futures market provides a mechanism whereby the risk of price change is transferred from hedgers to speculators.

Clearly, a major difference between these two groups of participants is their attitude to risk. Hedgers avoid it since small variations in prices can dramatically affect their small operating margins. Speculators embrace it and carry large risks in the hope of large profits. This difference in risk profile is essential to the operations of the markets, and crucial to the liquidity which they provide. Since the participants in the markets have such varying attitudes to risk, the existence of a futures market means that it is almost always possible to buy or to sell. That is, it is almost always possible to find someone whose assessment of the probability of various future outcomes is different from one's own. It is not only that while you may think soybeans are going up in price someone else thinks they are going down, but also that a 10 per cent probability, for example, of prices going up is a good enough chance for a speculator to risk money (and go long of soybeans) and, at the same time, a remote enough possibility to encourage a hedger to go short. This difference in expectations and in attitudes is what makes markets work since for every buyer there must be a seller. Of course, there are occasions when everyone shares the same view, so that there are no buyers (or sellers) to take the opposite view of the market. On these occasions, prices move rapidly until they reach a level where someone will take the opposite side. (Most futures markets impose limits on the maximum daily price fluctuation. This restricts the ability of prices to move to a level where a new buyer (or seller) can be found. A market which is locked at its limit is one where no one can be found to take the opposite view. In extreme circumstances a market moves its limit on several successive days.)

The establishment of forward prices

By providing public price discovery, and by allowing hedging, futures markets clearly establish prices for dates in the future. It is important to recognize that these are not necessarily forecasts of future spot prices. Expectations of future supply and demand will affect spot prices as well as future prices, provided a commodity can be stored: if, for example, in January it comes to be widely expected that a large import order for wheat will be placed by the USSR in June, then the price of March wheat will rise as well as the price of June wheat since the futures market will have to ration the available wheat among those who wish to use it now and those who wish to export it later.

The existence of stocks, and the stock-rationing role of futures prices, is important even in the case of the establishment of prices for contracts for the new crop year. In the case of new crop contracts, there is information (i.e. the expected size of the new crop) which may appear to be relevant only to them; however, if a bad harvest is expected, nearby futures contracts will also rise in price, since the available stocks have to meet not only current demands, but also those future demands which would be left unsatisfied by the shortfall in the new crop. None the less, it is true that there is an expectational element in futures prices for commodities. (There is no expectational element in futures prices for currencies, however: these are simply determined by spot exchange rates and interest rate differentials.)

In the case of commodities which either cannot be stored at all or cannot be profitably stored from one season to the next, the futures markets cannot provide the same kind of inventory-guidance role. In these commodities futures prices are pure forecasts of future spot prices. An example of the first kind of commodity is livestock. Futures contracts are traded in live cattle and live hogs, and the animals which are specified by the contracts are animals which are ready for slaughter. They cannot be stored since keeping them beyond the point at which they are prime meat animals would incur feeding costs and lower the quality of their meat. An example of the second kind of commodity is potatoes. Once the new crop is available, the price of old potatoes falls so rapidly that it is not economical to use storage facilities to keep potatoes from one season to the next. Only in exceptional circumstances would potatoes be stored into the new season.

In these instances, however, futures markets are concerned to send signals to the economy about supply and demand decisions, just as they encourage or discourage inventory holding in the 'normal' kind of commodity. Farmers and others can respond to futures prices of non-storable goods by changing their production and marketing decisions, just as inventory holders respond by building up or running down their stocks of storable goods. The efficiency with which futures markets perform this role is discussed later in this chapter (see pp. 19–22).

The reduction of volatility and uncertainty

Commodity prices are notoriously unstable. Equally notorious are the problems generated by this instability such as the fluctuations in the incomes of commodity-producing countries (especially those in the underdeveloped world) and the difficulties of making short-term marketing and long-term investment decisions, to name only the more commonly stated. In fact futures markets help to diminish the impact of instability; unstable prices are a problem when the path of their instability is uncertain – it is only when no one knows what prices are going to do that marketing and invest-ment decisions are difficult. Since futures markets allow hedging to take place, they permit much of the uncertainty to disappear.

Second, and more important, futures markets should diminish the underlying level of instability. While instability is attractive to speculators (it is only the chance to make large profits from large price changes which entices speculators into the markets), the activities of speculators will serve to reduce volatility. Contrary to the image of speculation in popular discourse, it has long been recognized by most economists that it is usually stabilizing rather than destabilizing: speculators have every incentive to sell high and buy low – and this will tend to take the top off every peak and the bottom off every trough. In general, the more thinly traded a market, the greater will be its instability. Speculators, by increasing the volume of trade, will reduce the sensitivity of a market to small pieces of information. The extent to which futures markets achieve success in the performance of this role is considered in the next section.

The performance of futures markets

Futures markets are increasingly important in the world economy; the rapid growth of futures on financial instruments is testament to this. Yet the very nature of futures markets has generated scep-ticism about their reliability. There are also periodic, well-publicized scandals about the markets. It must be admitted that the way in which futures markets set prices encourages scepticism: traders (mostly young men) shout orders at one another across small pits, using hand signals because the noise is so great. More-over, futures markets (not unlike stock markets) are popularly perceived to be essentially vehicles for speculation, and sight is often lost of the underlying economic roles that they perform.

For the most part, futures exchanges are companies which, like other companies, have an interest in finding new products to trade, to enhance their market position. In the USA, in particular, new futures contracts are constantly being introduced: two recently launched contracts are futures in the Consumer Price Index on the New York Coffee Sugar and Cocoa Exchange, and in High

Fructose Corn Syrup (a sugar substitute) on the Minneapolis Grain Exchange. It can appear to the public that new contracts and new exchanges are being invented for no good reason.

Yet futures markets do have the serious economic purposes, outlined above, of permitting hedging and transferring risk; setting fair and open prices; reducing price volatility; and of establishing forward prices. A legitimate and indeed important question is: are futures markets successful in performing these economic roles?

Why are there futures markets for some commodities but not for others?

Before tackling this issue, it is useful to ask why, given the numerous benefits claimed for futures trading, there are not futures markets for a broader range of commodities? Although there is no definitive answer to this question, a broad measure of agreement exists on the conditions which are required for the establishment of futures trading.

First, there must be price volatility. Without such volatility, which can be caused by variability in production, consumption or stockholding, there is no risk to those involved in the trade and no possibility of speculative profit. In the majority of agricultural commodities price volatility is the result of the impact on supply of the inherently variable weather, but not all commodities are sufficiently volatile.

Second, the commodity itself must be reasonably homogeneous, allowing a satisfactory contract to be defined. It must be possible sensibly to standardize the quality and delivery conditions for the futures market, and this factor more than any other has prevented the establishment of a futures market in coal. The quality of coal and its suitability for different uses vary greatly from mine to mine, making it very difficult for one customer to switch sources.

Third, there must be a competitive underlying market structure. There are several aspects to this requirement. There must be a large number of producers, consumers, and traders since under monopolistic or monopsonistic conditions there would be insufficient price volatility; there would also be opportunities for those controlling production or consumption to manipulate the market. There must be a volume or value of trade in the physical commodity which is large enough to support a futures market. There must also be support for a futures market from the trade; opposition from those who deal in the underlying commodity will starve the market of hedging demand and doom it to failure. An example of a market failing for this reason is provided by tea. It is often claimed that the heterogeneity of tea makes it an unsuitable candidate for futures trading. In the early 1970s, however, a feasibility study concluded that the establishment of a tea futures market was possible and both a contract and trading rules were designed. The market failed to get off the ground because of opposition from the producers and the blenders. This opposition arose more from conservatism than from any appreciation of the nature of futures trading: that price risks exist in tea can be seen from the existence of forward contracting.

These considerations do not constitute necessary and sufficient conditions for the existence of futures trading; it is unlikely that such conditions could be found. They do, however, provide useful clues for explaining the absence of futures trading in a large number of goods.

Do futures markets work?

How well do futures markets perform their economic functions, already listed in this section? Let us consider them in turn.

Futures trading provides a location for the exchange of information and increases the number of market participants who require (and have incentives to obtain) a flow of accurate and timely information about the traded commodity. This improvement in the quantity and quality of information, which reduces uncertainty, should lead to prices which more accurately reflect the state of supply and demand. Empirical studies indicate that futures trading improves the quality and quantity of information about a commodity, and does lead to more efficient price formation.[5] Moreover, the prices which are established in futures markets are often used in physical commodity trade: for example, a Japanese company buying sugar from Thailand will typically pay a price which is tied to the New York futures price. In a case such as this one, the attraction of the futures market price both for the buyer and the seller is that it is a price which the two parties can accept as being free from distortion. The usefulness of futures markets for physical commodity trade can hardly be understated and extends from international trade, on the one hand, to the farm gate in the USA, on the other hand. When an American grain or soybean farmer sells his crop to the local elevator or merchant, he will normally receive a price directly related to the relevant futures market. The merchant will quote his buying price not as, say, $5.00 per bushel, but as '5 cents under Chicago', meaning 5 cents lower than the nearest contract month on the Chicago Board of Trade.

Futures markets also play a valuable role in physical commodity trade through the provision of hedging facilities. Clearly, futures markets work in this sense since a large volume of hedging does take place. It is reasonable to conclude that physical commodity traders would not hedge if they did not find it useful to do so, yet futures markets do not provide as good a set of opportunities to hedgers as they might wish. Each futures market transaction requires two parties, a buyer and a seller; moreover, each buyer and seller would rather participate in a liquid market, where their purchases and sales will not have a large impact on the market price. The liquidity in most futures markets is heavily concentrated in nearby contract months, which makes it difficult for hedgers to effect large hedges in distant months. Of course, positions in nearby months can be rolled forward, but this increases transactions costs and requires very large orders to be placed in a single contract, running the risk that prices will be affected by the orders. Futures markets need liquidity to perform their function, and many of them lack this liquidity. It is often difficult to understand why some markets are illiquid, and it is therefore hard to know what might be done to rectify this. Yet it remains a constraint on the ability of the markets to provide hedging facilities for many producers in many commodities. (This is a particular problem for the parastatal commodity-exporting organizations in developing countries, which control large volumes of commodities.)

Another important role of agricultural futures markets is price forecasting. This is particularly important in the case of non-storable commodities, such as live cattle and live hogs, and in the case of contracts for new-crop months, such as November Soybeans or December Corn. How well do futures markets forecast future spot prices?

Simple though this issue may appear, it is hard to assess. Performance is only relative, and futures markets would be doing a valuable service if they were to forecast prices better than any other available method. Comprehensive statistical analyses of the futures markets for corn, wheat, soybeans, soybean oil, soybean meal, cotton, and live cattle and live hogs indicate that there is no great difference between them and econometric price forecasts over the time period for which there are actively traded futures contracts.[6] Possible exceptions, where the futures markets do not appear to forecast prices well, are live cattle and live hogs; but this may be because producers are able to alter their production decisions in response to futures prices, thus undoing the forecasts. This illustrates a possible dilemma with public forecasts of the future. Contracts in futures markets are only actively traded, and thus can only be expected to provide good forecasts, for up to eight months ahead, a time period which is not really large enough to allow producers and consumers to use these forecasts in making their planning and investment decisions. Yet if the markets did provide forecasts on which producers and consumers could act, the forecasts could be undone by that action.

The final major benefit which it was claimed for futures markets was that of price stabilization. It is a popular belief, frequently encouraged by journalists and politicians, that speculation is destabilizing, and the word itself carries some negative connotations. A US Congressman, in 1973, expressed this view:

> Both producers and consumers have suffered as a result of
> huge price fluctuation. I am convinced that someone,
> somewhere is profiting from all this. And I suspect that in some
> cases at least, the people responsible for the price fluctuations
> are among those benefiting from them.[7]

In the USA political concern over the effects of speculation reached a peak in 1958, when futures trading in onions was prohibited.

Futures markets, because they only exist when prices are volatile anyway, and because they require active speculation, may not seem to provide good ground on which to establish the proposition that speculation in futures markets stabilizes prices. In fact three kinds of evidence strongly support this proposition.

In the first place, there have been numerous studies comparing the price behaviour of commodities during periods when they have been traded on futures markets and periods when they have not. These studies have been carried out on wheat, onions, cotton, pork bellies, and live cattle.[8]

The earliest studies were published in 1896, and they show that cash market volatility is generally lower during times when active futures markets exist. Individually each of these studies would establish little since they establish a statistical association, not a causal relationship, between futures trading and reduced volatility. Taken together, however, they make attempts to find out explanations of reduced volatility sound rather implausible and constitute a powerful case for the proposition.

A second type of evidence has been provided in a recent study by Rutledge.[9] In economics there is a theory which holds that if one variable is followed with a high degree of probability by another variable, and if there is no third variable which can be used to factor out the probability relationship, then we can say the first variable causes the second. (This is a rather restrictive notion of

21

causality, but it has the great advantage that it can be empirically tested.) Using this theory, Rutledge examined trading volumes and price movements for thirteen commodities over three time periods, each of approximately four months' length. His study was designed to ascertain whether changes in the volume of trading 'cause' changes in prices, or vice versa. Of a total of 136 contracts examined, it was only in two that the data indicated causality running from trading volume to price volatility. Rutledge states, 'the results provide remarkably strong support for the hypothesis that movements in trading volume represent a response to, rather than a cause of, movements in price variability', and that the study 'forms the basis for rejecting the . . . view that speculative activity destabilizes price'. (Rutledge 1978: 164.)

Finally, a study of the three major wheat markets in the USA, i.e. Chicago, Kansas City, and Minneapolis, found that hedging costs were lower in markets where there was active speculation, and that the less liquid exchanges were only able to accommodate hedgers by spreading contracts against the Chicago market.[10] This is an important result because the mechanism whereby futures markets lower price volatility is through the inter-temporal allocation of stocks, and it is hedgers who actually carry commodities. The results by Gray indicate that active speculation makes it easier for hedgers to perform this role.

It would be unwise to put too much weight on the findings of a comparatively small number of academic studies, yet it is worth stating that these studies have covered a number of commodities in a number of time periods and provide remarkably little evidence to support the view that futures markets increase price variability. The reasonable view is that futures markets not only reduce market volatility, but through their provision of opportunities to hedge, they also allow market participants to reduce the uncertainty attached to price movements.

Is it possible to make money trading futures?

Futures markets represent an important possible use for funds which individuals and institutions do not need for their immediate purposes. The range of uses for surplus cash is wide, from bank deposit accounts, government bonds, shares and unit-trusts, and works of art through to commodities. From the perspective of the investor, the problem is to build a portfolio of investments which, in terms of risk, capital growth, and income and tax liability, match the individual's requirements.

Seen in this light, speculating in commodities is an attractive part of an investment portfolio since the potential gains are high. Moreover, not only do futures markets allow one to short the market more easily than other investment vehicles (thus allowing one to profit from price falls as well as price rises), but the degree of commodity price volatility and the lack of correlation between changes in commodity prices and those in the prices of other investments allow one to find profitable opportunities in commodities at a time when, say, stock markets are distinctly lacklustre.

Some people make large sums of money from futures – the stories of great wealth coming from a position on the coffee or pork belly market are not all fictional. The high potential profits in commodity markets are of course associated with high risks: people can and do lose extremely large sums of money in futures markets. For this reason, speculation in futures should never comprise more than a small part of the portfolio of any but the most clear-headed, risk-loving investor. But leaving aside the spectacular gains and losses, what can be expected on the whole and in the long run from participation in futures markets?

The first point which needs to be made is that futures trading is a zero-sum game. Because there is a long for every short (giving the clearing-house a net position of zero), one person's gain is another person's loss. What is more, it is a zero-sum gain before commissions are paid. The fact that commissions have to paid increases one person's loss and reduces another's gain. From the point of view of the economy as a whole, the sum of all commissions is the price which the economy pays for the broader economic benefits of having the markets.

In one of the earliest pieces of writing by an economist on futures markets, Keynes suggested that this process could work to the advantage of speculators. Keynes's view, elaborated by the eminent British economist John Hicks, is the following.[11] Hedgers, who use futures markets to avoid risk, sell forward their current deliveries at a price which covers their storage costs. Because they are risk averse, they are only able to do this if speculators absorb the risk; since this risk bearing is of value to the economy, it receives an economic return. This return is exacted by speculators by buying the hedger's contract at a price which is lower than that which they expect to receive when the hedge is lifted. On this theory, a futures market is like an insurance scheme in which speculators earn a risk premium.

A completely opposite view was provided by Hardy, who saw speculators as gamblers.[12] They do not demand any compensation for their risk-bearing role since their reward is entirely psychic:

they enjoy the thrill of gambling. Indeed they are prepared to pay for this pleasure by their losses (which amount at least to the commissions they pay). The markets are ensured a steady flow of speculative money by new entrants joining in and replacing those who have lost all they can afford to lose.

It is important to stress that it is not necessarily irrational for speculators to participate in futures markets, even if it is true that as a class and over time they lose money. This is for three reasons: in the first place, given the price path of commodities over time, it is highly probable that there will be times when investments in commodities make money while other investments do not. Thus any balanced portfolio may include commodities, and the job for the speculator is to capitalize on these times. Second, given that the possible profits from the futures trading lottery – if such it be – are huge, it can be rational to participate in the lottery, even if the probability of winning the prize is small. Third, if speculators derive pleasure from the excitement of futures trading, then the question of financial return is largely irrelevant.

These two competing theories of the returns to speculators have been examined empirically, in two main ways. One approach is to concentrate on the behaviour of prices, testing the logical conclusion from the Keynes–Hicks view that futures prices tend to rise until expiry, providing a net return to speculators (who are long in the market). In general, this body of research has tended to suggest that speculators do not earn a risk premium.[13] For example, research by Dusak considered a sample of wheat, corn, and soybean futures contracts over the period 1952–67 and found that average returns on the contracts over this period were close to zero (before commissions).[14]

More recently, however, this result has been challenged by Bodie and Rosansky.[15] Their research considered the results from a simple strategy of buying futures contracts, holding them for a three-month period, then liquidating them. This strategy was simulated for 23 commodities over the period 1950 to 1976 and found that the returns from such an investment strategy in commodities differed remarkably little from the returns available from the US stock market (measured by the Standard and Poor's 500). The mean annual average nomimal rates of return over this period were 13.05 per cent from the stock market and 13.83 per cent from commodities, or 9.58 and 9.81 per cent respectively in inflated-adjusted terms. Moreover, the authors found little year-to-year correlation between the behaviour of the stock and commodity portfolios, and found that commodities were a much better hedge against inflation. Commodities performed far better than stocks in years of high inflation, suggesting that commodities have a valuable place in an investor's portfolio.

The importance of this study should not be overstated, however. The authors also found that, by confining their data to the three commodities and the shorter time period examined by Dusak, their methodology produced the result of returns which were close to zero. What is more, by excluding 1973 from their analysis (the year in which commodity prices rose dramatically), the average return on commodities dropped from over 9 to 6.6 per cent. Close inspection of their results suggests that the returns are concentrated in a small number of commodities, indicating that the naïve trading strategy of simply buying-and-holding generates a favourable result over time only because a large enough number of markets are held for a long enough time period to benefit from profitable moves in some of them.

The second way of examining the returns to speculators uses the data collected by the Commodity Futures Trading Commission (CFTC) and its predecessor, the Commodity Exchange Authority (CEA), on positions held by hedgers and speculators in the US markets. The CFTC (before it the CEA) is the statutory body charged with the regulation of US futures markets. Among its duties is monitoring the open positions held on the markets, a duty which is supposed to enable it to prevent artificial squeezes being placed on any contract. These commitments are divided into three: hedgers, large speculators, and non-reporting traders. This division arises because any trader whose open position in any market exceeds a limit set by the authorities must report that position to the CFTC, which classifies it as hedging or speculative. The remaining commitments are held by small traders and it is generally assumed that they are speculative.

With the aid of some assumptions about the length of time for which these positions are held, it is possible to approximate the flows of profits and losses among these three groups. There have been two attempts at this, by Houthakker,[16] who examined wheat, corn, and cotton over the period 1937–52 (giving a total of 324 monthly observations), and by Rockwell,[17] who examined twenty-five commodities over the period 1947–65. Although there are some differences between these two studies and questions have been raised about some of the assumptions made, both reach the same fundamental conclusions, that it is rare for small speculators to make profits but normal for large speculators to make substantial profits.

Houthakker found that small speculators made small profits in cotton, but their losses in wheat and corn made their net returns about zero. He found that large speculators, however, made large profits, and that hedgers made losses. (Of course, for hedgers any losses in futures are likely to be counterbalanced by profits in cash market transactions.) Rockwell found that, in his eighteen-year sample, speculators lost money in 11 years and made profits in the other 5 years, leaving them with small overall losses. Conversely, large speculators made profits in 15 years, leaving them with large overall profits. Again, these profits come largely from hedgers, who lost money consistently.

All of these studies present the results of an analysis of aggregate behaviour and so tell us little about the returns to individual traders. There have been two studies of the accounts held by speculators with trading firms which examine the results actually achieved by individuals. The first of these, by Blair Stewart,[18] published in 1949, examined the results of clients of a bankrupt firm; the fact that he found a large number of clients to have lost money has been thought to be unrepresentative on the grounds that the firm's subsequent bankruptcy cast doubts on the quality of the recommendations it gave its clients. The second study of this type, by Ross,[19] examined all the accounts of a major US brokerage house, opened in 1967, and a random sample of those opened in 1968. The trading performance of a total of 380 accounts was followed until records ceased, or for five years, whichever came first. Overall, these 380 accounts lost $670,878, after commissions, with the profits earned by some accounts more than offset by others' losses.

To check that the results of this small sample were not unrepresentative, Ross also examined 2,367 accounts active during 1970 and 1971. Again, he found losses; these accounts lost a total of $5,399,267 in two years. They did show gross trading profits, but their profits from the markets of nearly $2.6 million were outweighed by the $8 million paid in commissions. Average losses in commodity trading are small: 57 per cent of Ross's sample lost less than $1,000 each. A small number, who apparently became addicted to speculating, lost a large amount of money. A small number earned substantial profits.

Clearly, futures markets do not present an easy route to large trading profits. They are institutions with a serious economic purpose, and that purpose is not to give speculators large profits. The evidence, combined with the experience of those in the markets, suggests the following conclusions. First, losses tend to be many, profits few: but profits can be extremely large. (In other words, the distribution of losses and gains is highly skewed.) Therefore, to a large extent the key to futures trading is to keep each loss small, so that the profits outweigh the total loss. Alternatively, one only should try to participate in the large movements. Second, speculator behaviour seems to indicate that they trade too frequently, suggesting a compulsive form of trading. This is especially true of small speculators, who may well regard their ventures into commodity markets as gambles. Both of these conclusions lead to a third: that speculators would do better if they knew more about the behaviour of markets in general, and about the characteristics of the commodities which are traded. One of the purposes of this book is to provide this information.

Chapter two

Agricultural options

Options – an introduction

If the notion of futures markets appears somewhat strange to many, options appear even more difficult. The enormous increase in options trading during the 1980s has resulted in the rapid development of trading techniques which appear hopelessly complex to the outsider. Yet even though modern agricultural options trading dates only from 1983 – when the USA enacted legislation permitting it after a ban which had been in place for almost fifty years – options date from the Middle Ages and options on securities have existed since the seventeenth century. What is more, options are conceptually quite straightforward instruments. Like futures contracts, they convey rights; but unlike futures contracts, they do not convey a symmetrical set of obligations. How options work can be readily understood by a simple example.

Imagine that a property development company, Industrial Developments, is building a new industrial estate. A local manufacturer, Combined Widgets, would like to buy one of the units on the estate, but cannot afford to do so now. They are, however, optimistic that they will have a good enough year to justify and pay for expansion. The new development is well placed for their expansion plans. Therefore, Combined Widgets ask Industrial Developments to give them the right to buy one of the new units at a price of £10 per square foot in a year's time. Industrial Developments are worried that prices will rise and that they will lose out, so they ask for a payment of £1 per square foot. Combined Widgets pay this sum. This straightforward transaction illustrates many of the important features of options. In effect, Combined Widgets have bought an option to buy the unit. Note that they have *not* bought the new property, nor have Industrial Developments sold it. Combined Widgets may exercise this option, or may abandon it; if they do exercise it, Industrial Developments will be obliged to sell them the land.

To use the modern terminology, Combined Widgets have bought a 'call option' (an option to buy is a *call*, and an option to sell is a *put*). Industrial Developments, who sold the option, are the grantor, or writer, of the option. The price at which the option can be exercised (in this example, £10 per square foot) is the 'strike' or 'exercise price'. The option has a given duration (in this case, a year), and if Combined Widgets do not exercise it within this time, it expires worthless. The price paid for this right (again in this example, £1 per square foot) is the premium.

The different positions of grantors and purchasers of options can be illustrated by considering a range of outcomes for this transaction. First, imagine that the price of industrial units rises to £13 per square foot over the life of the option. In this case, Combined Widgets will exercise the option, realizing a gain of £2 per square foot. (This is the price of the unit, £13, minus the strike price, £10, minus the premium which has already been paid, £1.) Industrial Developments make a loss of £3, but this is partially offset by the £1 premium received a year ago.

Second, imagine that the price of units falls to £8 per square foot. In this case, Combined Widgets will abandon the option, thus limiting the loss to the £1 premium paid. Industrial Developments' loss of £2 per square foot is partially offset by the premium received, making a net implied loss of £1.

Finally, imagine that the price of units does not change. In this case, Combined Widgets may either exercise or abandon the option – but in either case they have made an effective loss of £1 per square foot, the premium. However, Industrial Developments, have made a profit, since the premium received a year ago is a clear profit.

The rights and obligations carried by options are not symmetrical. In a futures market transaction, losses and profits are realized in equal measure by the buyer and seller of each contract, since each futures position is both a right and an obligation to buy or sell at the contracted price. In an option transaction, the option taker has a right to buy (or sell) but no obligation to do so if the market moves unfavourably; the option writer has only an obligation to sell (or buy) at the contracted price but no right to do so if the market moves favourably. Accordingly, the profit and loss potential for Combined Widgets is not the same as for Industrial Developments. Combined Widgets' potential profit is unlimited, whereas their maximum loss is the premium, which is forfeit if the option expires worthless. Industrial Developments' potential loss is unlimited, whereas their profit is limited to the amount of the premium. The best outcome for an option grantor is that the option is never exercised, turning the premium into clear profit. Clearly, the option grantor bears greater risk, and it is for this reason that the premium is demanded.

The above example does have some shortcomings: for instance, one could imagine that the new unit is worth more to Combined Widgets than to anyone else. Moreover, in the event that the option is exercised Industrial Developments' losses are only paper losses, since they do not have to go out on to the market to buy the unit to meet the obligation. Even so, we have made clear the essentials.

In the case of options on traded commodity futures, grantors and purchasers are no more known to each other than are buyers and sellers of futures contracts. These options also differ from the above example in two other respects, neither of which is crucial to the understanding of options. First, they are options on futures contracts, *not* options on the underlying commodity. A November 550 strike soybean call option gives the purchaser the right to buy a November soybean futures contract, not the right to buy soybeans in November. For that reason, it expires rather sooner than one might think, typically in the month before that of its name. Second, because they are options on a freely traded instrument, they are themselves freely traded. There are options which cannot be traded, but which can be exercised only by the original taker against the original grantor – these are called 'conventional options', to distinguish them from traded options. Most of the options on commodities traded in London are conventional options, but those on US futures contracts are traded options. Since they are freely traded, they can be closed out in exactly the same way as futures positions; thus an option grantor can close out his position by buying back from someone else an identical option.

In order to ensure liquidity in traded options, they are only available at predetermined strike prices, which are established by the Commodity Exchange. Thus soybean options are available at 25 cent intervals (e.g. 475 c. 500 c. and 525 c. per bushel), even though soybean futures contracts obviously can trade at intermediate prices. The limited number of strike prices leads to some more important terminology: in-the-money, at-the-money, and out-of-the-money. Options (both calls and puts) with a strike price the same as the currently prevailing price of the underlying futures contract are said to be 'at-the-money'; calls with strike prices higher, and puts with strike prices lower, than the current futures price are said to be 'out-of-the-money'; and conversely, calls with strike prices lower, and puts with strike prices higher, than the current futures price are said to be 'in-the-money'. Exactly which series are at, in, or out of the money depends on the market price of the underlying future, which of course can vary. (In other words, whether an option can be said to be in-the-money on a given date does not depend on the relationship between its strike price and the market price of the future at the time that the option is granted; an option which is in-the-money when granted can easily be out-of-the-money a few days later.)

Like anything else, options are traded at a price (i.e. a premium) which reflects the relative strength of supply and demand. There is a great deal of literature on options which devotes itself to the mathematics of options prices, and indeed there is much that is interesting in this topic. Yet we should not lose sight of the fact that option prices are determined by buyers and sellers, each of whom is faced by the same question: does the market valuation of the option differ sufficiently from my own to make the option a good investment? In order to assess this, we need to know more about the valuation of options.

Option premium determination

Option premia consist of two elements: the intrinsic value and the extrinsic value. Extrinsic value is sometimes called 'time value', yet this is misleading as it is not only time until expiration which determines it. Properly speaking, time value is one constituent of extrinsic value. Intrinsic value simply reflects the difference between the option strike price and the current price of the underlying futures contract. Thus if July soybeans are trading at $6.00 per bushel, a July 550 cent soybean call option will have an intrinsic value of 50 cents. The price at which the option trades, then, will never be lower, and will generally be greater, than 50 cents since the option can be exercised in the market and yield a 50 cent return. Clearly, options which have a positive instrinsic value are in-the-money.

On the expiration date of an option, its value will simply be its instrinsic value. Further away from this date, however, its value will generally be greater since there is a chance that before the expiration date, the price of the underlying futures contract will rise to a level at which it will be extremely profitable to exercise the option. The grantor of the option needs to be compensated for this possibility. Accordingly, there are four factors which determine this probability and thereby influence the extrinsic value of an option: first, the relationship between the option strike price and the underlying futures price; second, the time remaining before expiration; third, the volatility of the underlying futures price and the risk to which grantors are as a result exposed; and fourth, the level of interest rates. Together these factors can be used mathematically to derive a theoretical value for an option premium. The appendix to this chapter illustrates how this is done in the case of the commonest formula used, the Black-Scholes method. However, it is possible to understand these factors without recourse to the mathematics; let us consider each factor in turn.

The relationship between the strike price and the futures price

Options which are deep in-the-money or deep out-of-the-money will have a lower extrinsic value than options which are close to being at-the-money. A deep in-the-money option has a large intrinsic value and is highly likely to be exercised; but it offers little leverage potential, since the large premium (reflecting the large intrinsic value) has to be paid and profits have to be related to this invested money. When an option is only a little in-the-money, it offers much better leverage, because the premium is lower. At the opposite extreme, an option which is deep out-of-the-money will have a very low premium since its intrinsic value is zero, and the chance that it could ever be exercised at a profit is remote. Yet the premium (which of course is entirely extrinsic value) will increase as it becomes closer to being at-the-money.

The time remaining until expiration

The more time there is before an option expires, the greater the probability that the price of the underlying future will move and make the exercise of the option profitable. Thus extrinsic value diminishes with time. However, the relationship is not linear. Generally, the time value of an option is a function of the square root of the time remaining until expiration (this means that time value erodes very slowly when there is still a long time to go before expiration, but erodes very quickly in the final days).

Interest rates

Buying an option represents a use of capital; accordingly, it has to compete with other possible investments and should be affected by interest rates. Higher interest rates will lead to lower prices for put options. They have an ambiguous impact on call options since on the one hand the yield has to rise to keep pace with other investments (pushing premiums down), but on the other hand the higher interest rates will push up the storage costs of commodities, widen the carrying charges, and thus push up the value of the futures contracts against which existing call options are held. In practice, the impact of interest rate changes on option premiums is very small; moreover, the fact that short-term interest rates do not fluctuate greatly means that the bulk of option trading decisions can be made without reference to interest rates.

Volatility and risk

If the market price for a commodity never changed, then an out-of-the-money option would be valueless; the unchanging nature of the underlying commodity price means that there would never be a time when the option could be profitably exercised. It seems reasonable therefore that the price of an option will reflect the market's assessment of the probability that the option will be profitable at some point during its life. Therefore, one would expect options on highly volatile commodities to be more expensive than those on less volatile commodities. The grantor of an option on a more volatile commodity bears more risk; hence the premium will be higher as compensation for this risk.

The problem with volatility is assessing it: an option's premium will be related to market expectations about future volatility. Clearly, this cannot be known. Historical volatility can be calculated, but it turns out that any measurement of historical volatility is sensitive to the time period over which volatility is measured. The problem is knowing what weight to attach to different periods in the past: if a commodity price fluctuates in a reasonably regular manner and then experiences a month of violent fluctuation, how much importance is to be attached to that month? Does it represent a new pattern, or simply an aberration? Clearly, this cannot be known in advance and, as a result, most mathematical models which calculate 'fair' option prices use historical volatility. The interplay between historical and expected future volatilities generates trading opportunities which can be exploited (this issue is taken up in Chapter 5).

The fact that future volatilities cannot be known with certainty generates one source of risk which is reflected in an option's premium. A second problem, however, arises from the different attitudes to risk that are held by potential grantors of options. A risk-loving grantor will be willing to grant options at a low premium – perhaps at the premium implied by a low estimate of the recent volatility of the underlying commodity. But as more option buyers come into the market they may exhaust the willingness of risk-loving grantors to grant options. Therefore, they will need to find other option grantors who are slightly less risk-loving:

the more risk averse an option grantor, the higher will be the premium which is demanded as a compensation for risk-bearing. Thus one can see option premiums rising even if there is no change in the volatility of the underlying commodity, simply because of the strong demand for options and varying attitudes to risk in the option-granting community.

The delta of an option

Taken together, the above factors can be used to assess the responsiveness of an option premium to the changes in the underlying futures contract as time progresses. This responsiveness is called the 'delta' (that is, simply the elasticity of the option premium with respect to the underlying futures price). The delta is a number between zero and one; in general, in actively traded markets deltas behave in the following way:

(1) Deltas for at-the-money options are close to 0.5: this is because there is only a 50 per cent chance that the next price move will be favourable for the option.
(2) Deltas for out-of-the-money options are low since any likely change in the value of the underlying future will have only a low probability of moving the option into profit.
(3) Deltas for in-the-money options are high, and are asymptotically close to 1 as their intrinsic value increases and the time remaining to expiration decreases. Theoretically they will not be unity for as long as there is a chance that an adverse price movement could occur. (In fact in thinly traded option markets deltas for deep-in-the-money options often are unity.)
(4) Deltas for out-of-the-money options are higher, the longer there is before the expiration of the option.

For anyone considering the use of options in an investment or hedging strategy, the delta will affect the number of options and the strike price series which best fit the desired exposure to a movement in the underlying commodity.

Option premiums – an example

A simple example from two days' trading in October 1987 will illustrate the above features of option premiums. The example is drawn from options on soybeans, traded on the Chicago Board of Trade in a contract size of 5,000 bushels (one bushel being equal to 60 lb of soybeans), quoted in cents per bushel. It is a convention of option premiums that they are quoted in the same units as the underlying futures contract; thus a soybean option quoted at 25 cents would cost $1,250 (i.e. 25 times $50, each cent of price movement of the futures contract being equal to a $50 dollar movement in the total value of the 5,000 bushel contract).

On Friday, 16 October 1987, November soybeans closed at $5.43³/₄ per bushel; March 1988 soybeans closed at $5.62. When trading resumed on Monday, 19 October, the market was extremely weak because of a record fall in the New York Stock Exchange; at the close of trading on the 19th, November soybeans were $5.24 per bushel, down almost 20 cents, and the March contract closed at $5.42, down exactly 20 cents. In somewhat calmer trading conditions on Tuesday, the market recovered some of its losses; November closed at $5.35, up 11 cents, and March closed at $4.51¹/₂, up 9¹/₂ cents. Options on soybeans are available in 25 cent strike price intervals and the following were the closing prices for a small number of options on these two contracts:

November put options

strike	close on 19 October	close on 20 October
550	25.0	15.0
575	50.0	40.0

November call options

strike	close on 19 October	close on 20 October
525	7.0	13.25
550	1.25	2.0

March put options

strike	close on 19 October	close on 20 October
550	21.0	21.0
575	42.0	38.0

March call options

strike	close on 19 October	close on 20 October
525	29.0	33.0
550	18.0	23.0

These price quotations illustrate intrinsic value, extrinsic value, and the behaviour of these in response to changes in the price of the underlying future (i.e. the delta). Options on November futures had very little time value on these days, since they were to expire on Friday, 23 October; hence they display less extrinsic value than the March options, which had several months to run. Note also that as a result of the low extrinsic value of the November options, they have a high delta if they are in-the-money; the in-the-money puts declined in value by 10 points following the 11-point increase in the future.

Conversely, there is much more extrinsic value in the March options. However, it should be noted that these option premiums do not move in exactly the way that theory suggests. This is because of the comparative thinness of trade in options on 20 October; indeed the March 550 puts did not trade at all, and so the closing premium of 21 is a purely nominal quotation. In part, this was the result of the extreme uncertainty in the soybean trading pit, with traders nervous about the implications of the wild movements in the US stock markets; but in part also, it does reflect the fact that options are not traded with anything like the liquidity of futures markets. This has important implications for trading options (discussed in Chapter 5).

The advantages and disadvantages of options

It is frequently said that options are an attractive medium for less experienced investors, because a purchased option has a high profit potential and low risk: in the event of an adverse price move in the underlying commodity, there are no margin calls to be met, so the money at risk is confined to the initial premium paid. Conversely, a favourable price move yields profits.

This feature of options – that unlike the double-edged futures market they are a single-edged sword – is what makes them attractive for both hedgers and speculators. A speculator who, in August, feels that soybean prices will move higher by the New Year but is worried that there may be a period of price weakness during the harvest can buy a long-dated call option in August. This saves him the worry of having to take a futures market position at the right time. If he takes out a long futures position too soon, he may have to marginate that position in the event of a setback in the market, whereas if he waits for the setback, he will have to judge carefully when the market has reached bottom, apart from running the risk that there may be no setback. The long-dated option saves him from these worries, while leaving him free to benefit from an upswing in prices.

The relative attractiveness of call options and long futures can be seen with the aid of a simple diagram.[2] Imagine that a speculator thinks soybean prices will rise from $7.00 per bushel to $8.50, but he is worried about the heavy losses he could make if prices fell to $6.00. He sees that a $7.00 call option will cost him

$0.50 per bushel. If he buys this option, his maximum loss is the money spent to buy the option, because the worst that can happen to him is that the option expires worthless. (The option will be worthless if, at the time of the expiry of the option, soybeans are $7.00, or less, per bushel.) If soybeans go up in price, he will make a profit, but he must deduct from the profits the cost of the option; hence the breakeven price for soybeans at the option's expiry is $7.50 per bushel. Conversely, if he goes long of soybean futures, his breakeven point is lower, but his losses will be much more than 50 cents per bushel in the event that the price falls sharply. Figure 1 illustrates these possibilities.

It should be noted that there is a third possibility: that the speculator grants, or writes, a call option. As we saw above, the risk profile of buying an option is not the same as granting one. Figure 1 illustrates that the maximum profit for an option grantor is the premium; the best outcome for the grantor is that the option expires worthless and the premium is all profit. Conversely, the grantor faces unlimited losses in the event that prices rise to the point where the option can be exercised at a profit. The grantor faces losses equal to the buyer's profits.

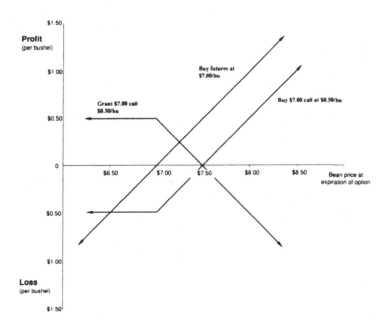

Figure 1. Risks and returns of call options and long futures

Options not only benefit speculators; they offer opportunities to hedgers as well. Imagine that a soybean farmer expects to harvest 40,000 bushels of soybeans, and that his costs of production are $6.50 per bushel. Imagine that new-crop soybean prices are currently $7.50 per bushel. Clearly, the farmer could sell his crop on the futures market, giving himself a price of $7.50 per bushel. If he thinks, however, that there is a chance prices could rise further, he can buy put options to guarantee a floor price while not ruling out the chance for increased profits. Let us say that he buys $7.50 strike price put options, for a premium of 50 cents per bushel. If prices rise to $8.50 at the time of harvest, the farmer will abandon the puts and sell soybeans for $8.50. His average selling price, therefore, will be $8.00 (i.e. $8.50, minus the 50 cent option premium). This is higher than the $7.50 he would have received by selling futures at the time the options were bought, but lower than the $8.50 he would have received had he just taken his chances. Conversely, if the price falls to $6.50 and he has to sell his crop at this low price, he can exercise the puts for $7.50, making a 50 cent profit (i.e. $7.50, minus the $6.50 cash price minus the 50 cent premium). In this case, his average selling price is $7.00 per

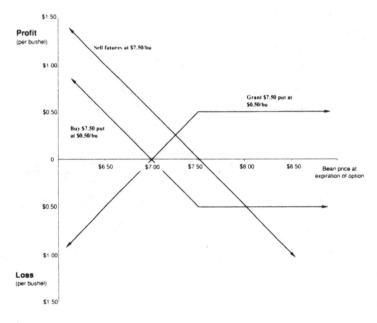

Figure 2. Risks and returns of put options and short futures

bushel. This is worse than he would have received from selling his crop at the futures price of $7.50 at the time he bought the options, but better than the $6.50 he would have received had he just taken his chances.

Again, these two possibilities are illustrated in Figure 2. The diagram shows that the maximum loss on a bought put option is the premium paid, whereas profits can be large if prices fall substantially. Conversely, short futures positions can lead to large losses in the event of substantial price rises.

The final possibility, that of granting a put option, is also illustrated on Figure 2. As in the case of a granted call, the maximum profit which can be made is the premium. With a granted put potential losses are limited only by the inability of prices to fall to zero.

Interestingly, there is always an outcome which, with the benefit of hindsight, is better than buying options, but equally interestingly, there is no outcome which makes the option purchase appear to be the worst decision. For this reason, options can be a sensible investment for the risk-averse. Since people have different risk preferences, there will always be some people for whom this feature of options – that even on the most favourable outcome they underperform a straight futures position – will be a disadvantage. Apart from this, however, it is as well to ask the question at this stage, what are the disadvantages of options?

We saw earlier that the three essential components in the price of an option are the price of the underlying commodity, the time remaining until its expiry, and the volatility of the underlying futures price. Anyone who buys (or writes) an option is, obviously, taking a view on its price; therefore, option traders are exposed to risk not only on the underlying futures price, but also on time and volatility. How important these are can be seen from the following examples.

First, if a price movement in a futures market occurs at a time different from that originally envisaged, options can simply expire worthless. For example, you may have held the view in the spring of 1987 that sugar prices would rise at some time over the summer, from their level of around 6 cents per pound to around 8 cents per pound. The sugar market is volatile, however, and the chance of a downward move in prices to around 5 cents could not be ruled out. The purchase of 6 cent call options on the October sugar futures contract would, therefore, appear to be an ideal way of profiting from the upturn, without the risk of a margin call on a futures position. In the event, sugar prices did decline a little, to just under 6 cents, but they remained at this lower level through

September, and the call options expired worthless. In early October, however, shortly after the options' expiry, sugar prices did begin to increase, reaching 7.5 cents per pound by the end of the month. By this time, however, the option purchaser had lost money. Trading on futures markets does not run the risk that the anticipated price movement will take place at a different time; contracts can be rolled forward from one contract month to another at little cost until the price movement materializes. One can buy long-dated options, of course, to benefit from a price move which may be delayed, but they have a high time value and consequently are expensive. When trading options, therefore, it is important to have a view on the likely timing of futures price movements since this will critically affect the profitability of the trade.

Second, a change in the volatility of the futures price will affect the price of an option. Imagine that you buy a put option, hoping to profit from a fall in the futures price and a rise in the value of the option premium. However, if the volatility of the futures price drops, then all options will decline in value and this fall may offset any rise in value from the level of the futures price. The twin effects of declining volatility and eroding time value as an option approaches expiry can result in rapid falls in the value of options, leaving the option holder with only the intrinsic value. It is useful, therefore, to look carefully at volatilities before beginning an option trade and to be sure that a reasonable profit can be made from the expected change in intrinsic value.

Claims that options are less risky instruments than futures contracts should be taken with a large pinch of salt. Trading futures implies exposure to a change in the price of the commodity. Trading options implies exposure to that risk, plus an additional risk that any change will take place at the 'wrong' time, plus the risk that the volatility of the price will change.

It should be clear by now, however, that one person's risk is another person's chance for profit; hence there are ways of trading options which allow one to benefit from changes in volatility and the unpredictable timing of price changes. We return to these later in the book.

Appendix: the determination of option prices

Option premiums are determined by the forces of supply and demand in the competitive environment of the trading pit. None the less, there are a number of mathematical formulae which can be used to determine the 'fair value' of an option premium. The commonest formula is the Black–Scholes option pricing model, named after its two originators. The formula for determining the fair value of a call option is as follows:

$$C = \exp -rt\{UN(x) - EN(y)\}$$

where $r =$ the short-term interest rate;
$\quad\quad t =$ the term to option expiration;
$\quad\quad E =$ the option exercise price;
$\quad\quad U =$ the price of the underlying commodity future;
$\quad\quad N(i) =$ the value of the cumulative normal probability distribution for the operand i. Mathematically,

$$N(i) = 1/(\sqrt{2\pi}) \int_{-\infty}^{i} \exp(-0.5z^2) \, dz$$
$$x = [\ln(U/E) + (sd^2t)/2]/sd\sqrt{t}$$
$$y = [\ln(U/E) - (sd^2t)/2]/sd\sqrt{t}$$

In these two latter expressions, ln is the natural logarithm and *sd* is the historical market volatility.

Market volatility is calculated as follows. Take a daily price series for n days, $P1, P2, \ldots, Pn$. Take the log of the ratio of one day's price to the previous day's price:

$$Ri = \ln(Pi/Pi - 1)$$

Then the standard deviation, *sd*, is given as:

$$sd = \sqrt{\frac{365}{n-1} \sum_{i=1}^{n} (R_i - \bar{R})^2}$$

where $\bar{R} = \dfrac{1}{n} \sum_{i=1}^{n} R_i$

There is an analogous formula for determining the fair value of a put premium.

The most important use for this formula is in inverse. Given the market price of an option, the formula can be used to determine the level of volatility implied by that market price. This, in turn, can be compared with the historical level of volatility, and the judgement can be made whether the option is 'expensive' or 'cheap'. This information allows one to trade options by comparing the market's expectations for future volatility with one's own.

The most obvious trading opportunity is to short an option premium (i.e. grant an option) if the current implied volatility is high, but one expects that volatility to diminish in future.

It cannot be stressed too much, however, that option prices are determined by the market, not by mathematical formulae. The decision to trade an option necessitates taking a view on future volatility, and this cannot be known in advance by computers any more than by human traders.

Chapter three

Commodity futures exchanges

There are in the world approximately 100 commodity exchanges, but not all of them trade futures contracts. No precise listing of commodity futures exchanges has ever been compiled – partly because of the difficulty of establishing a list of necessary and sufficient characteristics for an exchange to satisfy. It is not clear, for example, that the London Metal Exchange is a futures market; its contracts are more like forward delivery contracts than the standardized delivery-month contracts traded in fully fledged futures markets. In this chapter we attempt to provide a complete listing of exchanges trading futures contracts in agricultural commodities, but two caveats are in order. First, exchanges are constantly adding new contracts and winding down old ones. The list of commodities traded in 1986 is different from that for 1985. The approach adopted here is to include contracts that were actively traded at the end of 1986, although mention is made where relevant of new and previously active contracts. Second, the decision to exclude some exchanges may appear to be arbitrary; there is something closely resembling futures trading in India and Argentina, but neither country is included. The final decision on inclusion was made in the light of the wider significance of the exchange. There are also a large number of exchanges trading futures but no agricultural futures; these have also been excluded.

The volume of futures trading – an overview

First of all, it is useful to have an overall view of the size of futures trading as a whole and the importance of agricultural commodity trading within the total; the tables in this chapter are designed to provide this overview. Table 1 presents the ten largest futures exchanges, ranked by volume of trade on all futures transactions (i.e. including non-agricultural futures). It is normal to measure futures activity by number of contracts traded, even though

Table 1   The world's ten most active futures exchanges, 1986

Exchange	Contracts traded
Chicago Board of Trade	81,135,634
Chicago Mercantile Exchange	59,831,171
New York Mercantile Exchange	14,644,413
Comex	14,174,698
Tokyo Stock Exchange	9,395,829
Liffe	6,471,389
Coffee, Sugar and Cocoa Exchange	5,535,081
Tokyo Grain Exchange	5,220,680
New York Futures Exchange	3,182,992
London Commodity Exchange	3,055,588

Source: Futures Industry Association.
Notes: Liffe is the standard acronym for the London International Financial Futures Exchange. The London Commodity Exchange has been renamed the London Futures and Options Exchange, or London Fox. Comex, or the Commodity Exchange Inc., is based in New York, as is the Coffee, Sugar and Cocoa Exchange (CSCE).

contract sizes vary greatly. For example, the New York coffee contract, at 37,500 lb, is three times larger than London's 5-tonne contract. But measuring the total value of trade in a common currency would be difficult, because of the different prices at which deals are struck and variations in exchange rates, and misleading, because of the leverage inherent in trading futures contracts with small margins.

The table reveals several important features of futures trading: all of the top ten are in Chicago, New York, Tokyo, or London, and the position of Chicago is dominant; its two exchanges are by far the largest in the world. There is a huge gap between the volume of futures trading in Chicago and that elsewhere in the world; the Chicago Board of Trade (CBOT) alone is twenty-five times busier than the London Fox, even though the Fox is the tenth largest exchange in the world. The volume on both Fox and Liffe together is only 12 per cent of the volume on the CBOT.

For a century now, Chicago has been the dominant futures trading centre, but the scale of trading has expanded dramatically in recent years. Comprehensive figures are only available for the USA, but they show that the total volume of trade on all US exchanges has grown from 3.9 million contracts in 1960, to 13.6 million in 1970, to 92.1 million in 1980 and to 184.4 million in 1986. Growth outside the USA has been rapid, if not quite as spectacular; Liffe, which opened its doors for business only in 1982, was the world's sixth largest exchange by 1985.

How do agricultural commodities fit into this context? Both the

CBOT and the Chicago Mercantile Exchange (CME) have a number of active agricultural futures contracts; and the London Fox and the Coffee, Sugar and Cocoa Exchange (CSCE) are both agricultural commodity exchanges. (The CSCE does have one non-agricultural contract, which traded fewer than 9,000 lots in 1986.) Obviously the bulk of the growth in futures trading is the result of the growth of financial futures, but as Table 2 shows, agricultural contracts account for over 20 per cent of the total volume of US futures trading. Unfortunately, comparable figures are not available on a global basis, but industry estimates suggest that agricultural commodities account for rather more than 20 per cent of world futures trading.

This pattern has changed enormously in the past two decades; as recently as 1974, 70 per cent of all US futures trading was in the grains/soybeans/meat complex contracts. The volume of trading in this complex simply has been overtaken by the extraordinary growth in financial futures over this period.

Table 3 shows the ten most actively traded individual contracts. Again, it should be noted that the dominant position of Chicago is evident. Eight of the ten are financial instruments, with interest rate contracts (the US and Japanese bonds and the Eurodollar) in a dominant position. Trade is also active on the Standard and Poor's 500, a broadly based US stock market index. (The table excludes option contracts, which are also actively traded; indeed the traded volume of options on the Standard and Poor's 1986 was 113,151,085 contracts, more than double the turnover of the most active futures contract.) Agricultural contracts managed to hold eighth and ninth places, and the CME's live cattle contract was just edged from tenth place by the Swiss franc.

Table 2   US futures trading, by type of contract, 1986

	Contracts traded	*Percentage*
Interest rates	70,202,183	38
Agriculturals	38,276,714	21
Stock indices	26,462,813	14
Currencies	19,352,161	10
Precious metals	14,692,890	8
Energy	12,869,624	7
Metals	1,927,481	1
Others	570,630	<1
Total	184,354,496	100

Source: Futures Industry Association.

Table 3 The ten most actively traded futures contracts, 1986

Contract	Exchange	Volume
Treasury bond	CBOT	52,598,811
Standard and Poor's 500	CME	19,505,273
Eurodollar	CME	10,824,914
Japan government bond	Tokyo Stock Exchange	9,395,829
Gold	Comex	8,400,175
Crude oil	NYMEX	8,313,529
Deutschmark	CME	6,582,145
Corn	CBOT	6,160,298
Soybeans	CBOT	6,133,668
Swiss franc	CME	4,998,430

Source: Futures Industry Association.

Table 4 presents the ten most active agricultural contracts. Clearly, Chicago is the major centre for trading agricultural contracts, and no London contract makes an entry in the list. In 1986, London's most active contract was coffee, which traded 1,510,156 lots and was number 13. Interesting features of the table are also the high volume of the various soybean complex contracts and the large volumes traded on the Tokyo Grain Exchange. (The Tokyo Grain Exchange trades contracts on Chinese and domestic soybeans in addition to that on US soybeans; the volume of trade is heavy, but it should be noted that the contracts are small: 15 tonnes, compared to the 5,000 bushel, or approximately 136 tonnes, contract on the CBOT.) As we shall see, Japan has a large number of thriving exchanges trading agricultural futures.

Until the 1970s futures trading was confined to agricultural commodities and a small number of metals. The enormous upsurge in trading of financial contracts has had important implications for

Table 4 The ten most actively traded agricultural contracts, 1986

Contract	Exchange	Volume
Corn	CBOT	6,160,298
Soybeans	CBOT	6,133,668
Live cattle	CME	4,690,538
Sugar no. 11	CSCE	3,583,814
Soybean oil	CBOT	3,182,963
Soybean meal	CBOT	3,049,005
US soybeans	Tokyo Grain Exchange	2,997,827
Wheat	CBOT	2,090,316
Red beans	Tokyo Grain Exchange	2,045,635
Live hogs	CME	1,936,864

Source: Futures Industry Association.

exchanges, and for the firms and individuals who use them. Although agricultural commodities have taken a backseat over this period, they occupy still a central role in the whole business of futures. In the next section we take a more detailed look at the exchanges which trade agricultural commodities, beginning of course with Chicago.

Commodity exchanges

Chicago

The Chicago Board of Trade (CBOT) was founded in 1848, initially to promote the interests of commerce in the city. In 1859 it was authorized by the State of Illinois to develop quality standards for grain and futures trading was under way by 1865. Throughout its existence it has been the most important futures exchange in the world – although its neighbour and great rival, the Chicago Mercantile Exchange, can claim to be the most innovative. The CBOT is still the busiest exchange and boasts the most actively traded individual contract, the Treasury bond (a long-dated US government debt instrument). Its option-trading division, the Chicago Board Options Exchange, boasts the busiest options contract, that on the Standard and Poor 500.

Although agricultural commodities, which were the CBOT's only line of business for over 100 years, have taken a back-seat to financial futures, they still account for approximately 25 per cent of the exchange's business. Moreover, the figures for total turnover are affected by the great volume of trade in just one contract, the

Table 5 Agricultural commodities on the CBOT, 1986

| Contract | Volume: | |
	futures	*options*
Corn	6,160,298	575,634
Soybeans	6,133,668	775,139
Soybean oil	3,182,963	
Soybean meal	3,049,005	
Wheat	2,090,316	9,314
Oats	140,952	
All agricultural contracts	20,757,202	1,360,087
All CBOT contracts	81,135,634	19,678,199

Source: Chicago Board of Trade.

Note: Options contracts on soybean oil and soybean meal were introduced in 1987.

Treasury bond, which traded over 52 million lots in 1986. In that year, the corn contract was the second most active CBOT contract. Table 5 gives the volume of trade in both futures and options contracts on the agricultural commodities in 1986.

As the table illustrates, the five major agriculturals are all actively traded, a fact which makes them attractive to hedgers. The CBOT has been able to establish a virtuous circle, in which the liquidity of its markets makes them attractive to users, thus enhancing liquidity. An important reason for this is the presence of the locals on the trading floors, many of whom trade all the agricultural commodities and thus comprise a knowledgeable and effective group of speculators. Moreover, the fact that all the markets are liquid makes spread trading an attractive and feasible proposition for speculators.

This liquidity does not extend to options contracts to the same extent. Although CBOT options are very actively traded compared to options elsewhere, and especially outside the USA, options markets are still developing and will take many years to achieve a high volume of trade. Moreover, options are still coming on to the market-place; options on soybean oil and soybean meal were not available in 1986, but following approval by the Commodity Futures Trading Commission, they were introduced in spring 1987.

The Chicago Mercantile Exchange (CME, or Merc as it is sometimes known) was founded in 1919 and was, for a long time, looked upon rather as a poor relation of the CBOT; although it is still a smaller exchange, it has the reputation of being a more innovative and aggressive one than its neighbour and rival. For

Table 6 Agricultural commodities on the CME, 1986

Contract	Volume:	
	futures	*options*
Live cattle	4,690,538	718,099
Live hogs	1,936,864	105,516
Pork bellies	1,100,339	1,981
Feeder cattle	411,441	
Lumber	502,530	
All agricultural contracts	8,641,712	825,596
All CME contracts	59,831,171	8,944,353

Source: Chicago Mercantile Exchange.

Note: There were no options on feeder cattle or lumber in 1986.

example, it was the CME which first introduced livestock futures in the early 1960s, and financial futures in the early 1970s. Today the CME has three main divisions: the CME itself on which the agricultural commodities are traded; the International Monetary Market (IMM) on which foreign currency and interest rate contracts are traded; and the Index and Option Market (IOM) on which options on all the exchange's commodities are traded along with stock index futures. Agricultural commodities are rather less important to the CME than they are to the CBOT, but the liquidity and volatility of the livestock futures markets makes them attractive markets to trade; Table 6 gives the turnover figures for 1986.

Again, the table reveals the comparative illiquidity of option trading, although the figures are slightly misleading since options on pork bellies were introduced only in October 1986. Over the years a number of related commodities have been traded on the CME, including eggs and hams, but for one reason or another they have failed to generate the liquidity needed to survive. The failure of the ham contract is perhaps the most surprising, given the success of trading in hogs and pork bellies; after all, each hog has two hams and two bellies[1] and the existence of a ham contract would allow much better spreading opportunities. Yet the existing meat complex contracts do provide many trading opportunities, as we shall see in Chapter 8.

For the sake of completeness, we should mention the Mid-America Commodity Exchange and the Chicago Rice and Cotton Exchange. The MidAm, which is an affiliate of the CBOT, was established to trade contracts the same as those on the CBOT in all respects except size, which is smaller. Thus its corn, wheat, and soybean contracts are 1,000-bushel contracts, compared to the 5,000-bushel contracts of the CBOT. This step was taken to make it easier for smaller grain trade participants, particularly smaller farmers and elevator operators, to tailor their hedging programmes to the size of their cash market exposure. Because the contracts are, in all other respects, fungible with those of the CBOT, trading companies can group together MidAm contracts and run them along with their CBOT trades. The MidAm also trades small versions of the CME's contracts. It is reasonably active, as can be judged by the data on traded volumes presented in Table 7, but it should be remembered that these contracts are small.

The Chicago Rice and Cotton Exchange is a comparative newcomer to futures trading in Chicago. Its only active contract, namely rough rice, has been trading since August 1986, and it

Table 7 Agricultural commodities on MidAm, 1986

	Volume:	
Contract	futures	options
Wheat	344,749	7,492
Corn	406,694	
Oats	2,169	
Soybeans	843,231	6,635
Soybean meal	5,487	
Live cattle	58,752	
Live hogs	80,818	
All agricultural contracts	1,741,900	14,127
All MidAm contracts	2,368,547	14,218

Source: Mid-America Commodity Exchange.

trades on the floor of the CBOT. The volume of trade has been growing steadily since its inception. It is the only rice futures contract available, and it remains to be seen whether it will come to play a significant role in the marketing of rice.

New York

New York has been trading futures contracts for almost as long as Chicago. Certainly, by 1872, when the rules of the New York Cotton Exchange (NYCE) were written, cotton futures contracts were being traded. Despite the fact that New York is no longer a particularly important centre for physical trade in cotton, the New York cotton futures market is the only active one in the world. In an attempt to consolidate its position in world textile material markets, the exchange has traded wool contracts in the past, but the volume of trade has declined to the point where the contracts were suspended. The most successful innovation by the NYCE was the introduction of a contract on frozen concentrated orange-juice (FCOJ) (see Table 8).

Table 8 New York Cotton Exchange: traded volumes, 1986

	Volume:	
Contract	futures	options
Cotton	1,015,392	60,507
Orange juice	211,543	3,354

Source: New York Cotton Exchange.

Contracts on propane, the European Currency Unit and a weighted index of the international value of the dollar are also traded on NYCE, but of its total volume of trade in 1986 of 1,477,590 lots, over 80 per cent was in its two major agricultural contracts, cotton and FCOJ.

In the late nineteenth and early twentieth centuries, New York was the natural port of entry for the USA's tropical product imports. Therefore, in 1882, it was in New York that coffee futures trading began, when the Coffee Exchange of the City of New York was established. Following the closing of the London and Hamburg sugar exchanges at the outbreak of war in 1914, a sugar contract was added. It was so successful that in 1916 the exchange was renamed the New York Coffee and Sugar Exchange. In 1925 the New York Cocoa Exchange was established, and over fifty years later, in 1979, the two exchanges merged to become the Coffee, Sugar and Cocoa Exchange (CSCE) (see Table 9).

The only non-agricultural futures contract traded on the CSCE is the CPI-W contract, which is on the Consumer Price Index; hence it is a futures contract on inflation. Despite the obvious attractiveness of this as a hedging medium, it has not proved to be very successful and in 1986 traded fewer than 9,000 lots.

The New York Mercantile Exchange (NYMEX) has a potato contract, but its turnover of some 16,558 lots accounted for less than one-quarter of 1 per cent of its total turnover in 1986 of over 14 million lots, and in 1987 it ceased trading. Its most active contracts are in crude oil, heating oil, and platinum. New York is also home to the Commodity Exchange Inc., widely known as Comex, where base and precious metals are traded. These four New York exchanges share premises in the Commodity Exchange Center in Manhattan's World Trade Center, and they are examining plans for closer co-operation which may result in full merger.

Table 9 Coffee, Sugar and Cocoa Exchange: volume of trade, 1986

| Contract | Volume: | |
	futures	*options*
Coffee	1,073,142	5,319
Sugar no. 11	3,583,814	254,491
Cocoa	777,765	999

Source: CSCE.

Note: The CSCE also has two other sugar contracts, nos 12 and 14, which differ in important respects from the no. 11 contract; it is the no. 11, however, which is the most important, in terms both of volume traded and wider economic significance.

Agricultural Commodity Markets

The New York Futures Exchange, the youngest futures market in the city, is best known for its contract on the New York Stock Exchange Composite Index, but it also has a contract on an index of commodity prices. This index, compiled by the Commodity Research Bureau, a private company, measures price movements in a wide range of raw materials and is often used as a leading indicator of inflation.

Other North American exchanges

Moving out of the major North American financial centres into the continent's agricultural heartland, there are three other important commodity exchanges. Founded in 1881, the Minneapolis Grain Exchange, like the CBOT, began life as something akin to a modern Chamber of Commerce, but quickly became an important centre for both cash and futures marketing of grain. To this day, it remains the world's largest cash grain market, and both cash and futures trading are conducted on the same trading floor. Its principal activities are in marketing the grains grown in the Upper Midwest, but it does have an active wheat futures market. The wheat traded in Minneapolis (i.e. hard spring wheat) is high-protein, bread-making wheat, which normally sells at a premium to other grades of wheat. In 1986 this contract traded 283,900 lots, and options on the futures contract traded 3,259 lots. There is also a white wheat contract, and durum wheat has been traded in the past (an explanation of these different types of wheat is given in Chapter 6). In an attempt to broaden its futures trading activities, the exchange introduced a contract on sunflowerseed in 1980, but it was not a success. Futures trading in high-fructose corn syrup, a sugar substitute made from corn, began in 1987, but early trading volumes have not been encouraging.

The Kansas City Board of Trade (KCBT), which was founded in 1856 and began trading futures in 1876, has an active futures market in hard red winter wheat, which normally sells at a premium to Chicago's soft red winter and at a discount to the hard spring traded in Minneapolis. The Kansas and Minneapolis contracts are useful to hedgers (both farmers and users) because they correspond more closely to the types of wheat which they grow and use, and because the premiums over Chicago which they command are variable. It is the Chicago wheat contract, however, which attracts the bulk of speculative interest. In 1986 the Kansas market traded 744,023 lots of wheat futures and 18,302 lots of options. The KCBT was the first exchange to trade a stock index future, the Value Line Index, but it has never expanded its coverage of agricultural commodity markets.

Over the border, in Canada, is the Winnipeg Commodity Exchange, which began life in 1887 trading cash grains as the Winnipeg Grain and Produce Exchange. Its first futures contract in wheat was introduced in 1904, quickly followed by other grain contracts. The growth of the exchange was inhibited by the establishment of the Canadian Wheat Board (CWB) in 1935, which still has monopoly selling rights for many Canadian grains on world markets. This limits the degree of price volatility for a number of grains; however, the exchange has successfully developed contracts in many of the grains which are not regulated by the CWB.

The Winnipeg market has a tradition of innovation; its futures contract on rapeseed, introduced in 1963, is now one of the world's most actively traded agricultural futures and its gold contract, introduced in 1972, was the world's first. It established a new division in 1981, the Canadian Financial Futures Market, recognizing the growing importance of financial futures. Its major interest from the point of view of world agricultural developments is the rapeseed contract (see Table 10).

There are a number of other exchanges in North America where futures contracts on financial instruments are traded; the Philadelphia Stock Exchange, the Vancouver Stock Exchange, the Montreal Exchange, the Toronto Futures Exchange, and the Pacific Stock Exchange all trade futures or options on financial instrments. They do not, however, trade agricultural commodities.

Brazil

Brazil has a long history of trading commodity futures, although the contracts have been primarily geared to the needs of the domestic market. The Bolsa de Mercadorias de São Paulo was founded in 1917, and ever since has been trading a wide range of futures contracts. It has enjoyed rapid growth in recent years,

Table 10 Volume of trade on the Winnipeg Commodity Exchange, 1986

Contract	Volume
Feed wheat	178,368
Oats	26,632
Barley	285,766
Rye	120,938
Flaxseed	260,965
Rapeseed	1,082,845

Source: Winnipeg Commodity Exchange.

Agricultural Commodity Markets

Table 11 Volume of trade on the Bolsa de Mercadorias de São Paulo, 1986

Contract	Volume
Cotton	118
Fat cattle	162,524
Feeder cattle	1,087
Coffee (arabica)	157,667
Coffee (conillon)	408
Soybeans	744
Cocoa	3,227

Source: Bolsa de Mercadorias de São Paulo.

expanding its coverage from cotton, coffee, and soybeans in 1978 to the current range of commodities (see Table 11).

The São Paulo Exchange also trades futures on gold and exchange rates. In 1986 agricultural contracts accounted for 55 per cent of the total futures trading volume on the exchange. Options on coffee and gold are also available and, in 1986, 3,621 lots of coffee options were traded.

These contracts are primarily of domestic interest, although the two coffee contracts have a wider significance. The expansion of the exchange into financial futures, however, seems likely to result in its growing role in the Brazilian economy. In Brazil there are three smaller futures exchanges: the Bolsa de Mercadorias e Cereais de Santa Catarina, the Bolsa Mineira de Mercadorias, and the Bolsa de Mercadorias da Bahia. Of these, the Bahia Exchange, located in the major cocoa-growing region of Brazil, has a cocoa contract followed by many analysts: turnover on the market is small, but its price movements do reflect the availability of cocoa for export, and it is therefore of wider significance.

European exchanges

Like North America, Europe has a long tradition of futures trading. From the point of view of agricultural commodities, however, its importance is reduced by virtue of the operations of the European Community's Common Agricultural Policy (CAP). The CAP subsidizes European farm production and restricts imports of farm commodities which can be produced in Europe; the mechanisms which effect this also reduce price volatility and thus undermine the entire rationale for futures markets. Accordingly, the agricultural commodities which are actively traded on European futures markets are those which either cannot be

54

produced in Europe, such as coffee and cocoa, or those which, for one reason or another, fall outside the CAP's price-supporting mechanisms; there is also sugar, actively traded in London and Paris.

As befits its status as one of the world's major financial centres, London is a major futures trading centre. The London International Financial Futures Exchange (known as Liffe) is one of the world's most active markets. London also has a long history of trading agricultural futures, with the first markets set up towards the end of the nineteenth century.

The Cocoa Association of London was formed in 1926, but the London Cocoa Terminal Market Association was not opened until 1928. Apart from the period 1940–50, when the price and distribution of cocoa were controlled by the government, the futures market has continued to trade. Futures trading in sugar began in London in 1888, closed during the First World War, and then reopened in 1921; the market closed again in 1939, and government control over sugar was not relinquished until 1956. The United Sugar Terminal Market Association was formed in 1957, and has traded raw sugar futures since then. The details of the contract have changed several times, and repeated attempts have been made to introduce white sugar futures. Currently the market trades a raws contract which is, to all intents and purposes, identical to that of New York and is denominated in dollars per tonne. The most recent white sugar contract was introduced in 1987 – and it was, innovatively, a contract traded on screens by traders with computer terminals rather than on a conventional floor.

A Coffee Trade Association was formed in London, in the late 1880s, but no futures market was started until 1958, when the Coffee Terminal Market Association of London began trading its current robusta coffee contract. Robusta is strong coffee, generally grown in Africa and Asia, and normally sells at a discount to the milder arabica coffee grown in Latin America. The New York coffee market trades arabica, and in 1973 the London market introduced an arabica contract. However, it was unsuccessful and withdrawn in 1979.

The three markets, together with the now inactive rubber futures market, were loosely grouped together as the London Commodity Exchange (LCE). In 1986, as part of an attempt to increase its business, the LCE restructured itself, moved to new premises, and in 1987 was renamed the London Futures and Options Exchange, or London Fox. Shortly after its inception, this new organization launched the new white sugar contract and traded options on coffee, cocoa, and sugar. While it is too early to

Table 12 Turnover on the London agricultural markets, 1986

Contract	Volume
London Fox:	
Cocoa	837,085
Coffee	1,510,156
Sugar, f.o.b.	706,953
Sugar, c.i.f.	93,830
Other markets:	
Barley	30,827
Wheat	75,223
Potatoes	259,788
Pigmeat	5,041
Soybean meal	78,304

Source: London Fox; GAFTA.

Note: The year 1986 was a transitional one for London's sugar market; its older c.i.f. contract has now been replaced by the f.o.b. contract, but the two were being traded simultaneously in 1986; they have both been included here to give an idea of the total volume of sugar trading.

assess the success of the restructured exchange, it is certainly making a strong effort to boost London's profile in international commodity trading (see Table 12).

In the UK futures trading in grain began, in Liverpool, in 1883; in 1897 the Baltic Exchange in London began trading grain futures as well. The London Grain Futures Exchange was established in 1929, but closed down during the Second World War; the London market reopened in 1954, trading imported feedgrains. Despite the importance of the UK as a grain importer, however, the market has never become an especially active one. Since the accession of the UK to the European Community, and the incorporation of the UK into the Common Agricultural Policy, grain price volatility has been greatly lessened, reducing the need for a futures market. Although the market has continued to trade, it is small and of only local significance.

The other markets are all loosely grouped under the umbrella of the Grain and Feed Trade Association (GAFTA). The potato, meat, and soybean meal exchanges, however, together with BIFFEX, a futures market in freight rates, are contained in the same legal entity, the Baltic Futures Exchange, and they share trading premises. Discussions are under way to bring the wheat and barley markets into the same organization. Apart from the grain futures market, they are comparatively new and the meat exchange, in particular, has been active in developing new contracts in an attempt to generate increased business; during

1986, for example, contracts on live pigs, early pigs, beef, early beef, and cattle were introduced, but none was successful. Of the GAFTA markets, only soybean meal is a commodity of more than domestic interest. Although soybean meal is freely traded internationally, London's market has been unable to attract the volumes of business which its proximity to Rotterdam (where there is a large spot and forward market in soybean meal) would suggest should be forthcoming. The other markets trade commodities where the European Community (EEC) regulation is either non-existent, as in the case of potatoes, or very limited, as in the case of pigmeat.

London is also the home of the London Metal Exchange, the world's most important centre for base metal trading; the International Petroleum Exchange, where energy futures are traded; and the London International Financial Futures Exchange, which is London's largest futures market.

Futures trading in a range of agricultural commodities began in Paris in 1885, and by the 1930s there were fifteen futures markets in France. These were all closed during the Second World War and there was no futures trading until the cocoa futures market was opened in 1963. Trading in white sugar began in 1963, and the coffee market opened in 1970. Difficulties with foreign exchange controls limited the international appeal of the Paris markets, so in 1983 a facility was established allowing non-residents to convert their sugar transactions into US dollars, and their cocoa transactions into sterling.

As Table 13 indicates, it is the white sugar contract which accounts for most activity on the Paris exchange. Other contracts have been introduced – soybean meal in 1976, and cocoa butter in 1986 – but did not generate a large volume of trade. Options on white sugar futures are scheduled to be introduced in late 1987.

For a long time the Paris Futures Exchange enjoyed a privileged position, providing the only white sugar futures market in the western hemisphere. The need for a white sugar futures contract arises because of the increasing volume of world sugar trade which

Table 13 Agricultural futures in Paris, 1986

Contract	Volume
White sugar	520,812
Coffee	37,469
Cocoa beans	4,483

Source: Paris Futures Exchange.

is accounted for by white, rather than raw, sugar. The difficulty currently facing Paris is that both the London Fox and New York's CSCE recognized this and launched white sugar futures contracts in 1987. Since New York is such an active raw sugar trading centre, its contract is likely to be successful, but it is likely that only one of the European contracts will survive. The Paris market is taking steps in an attempt to improve its competitive position, and since previous attempts to introduce white sugar futures in London have not been successful, there would appear to be some reason for expecting the Paris market to survive. The existence of French exchange controls and the somewhat higher costs of dealing on the Paris market, however, would appear to favour London; unfortunately, at the time of writing, it is too early to judge.

France has another active agricultural futures market, the Lille-Roubaix-Tourcoing Potato Futures Exchange, where locally produced potatoes are traded. The market was founded in 1984, and traded 27,819 lots in 1986. There are also active markets in financial futures in Paris.

The Netherlands is one of the world's most important centres for the physical trade in agricultural commodities, and there have been a number of futures markets there in the past. Without the restrictions of the CAP, it is certain that Rotterdam would be an important grains and oilseed futures trading centre. As it is, however, although the country does have active financial futures markets, there are only two small agricultural futures markets, both in Amsterdam, trading domestic products. The Amsterdam Potato Terminal Market was established in 1958 and traded 140,060 lots on its potato contract in 1986. The Amsterdam Porker Terminal Market was established in 1980, and its live porker contract traded 19,718 lots in 1986. Neither of these markets has any wider international significance.

Japan

Japan has a long history of futures trading, the Dojima Rice Exchange having been founded in 1730. This was the world's first futures exchange, predating the development of futures markets in Chicago by over 100 years. Over the past 100 years there have been two main phases in the development of Japanese futures trading. The first of these began with the 1893 Exchange Law, which reversed the Meiji government's earlier ban on futures and provided a legal framework under which exchanges, trading a variety of commodities, flourished until the outbreak of the Second World War. The second phase began with the reconstruction of the economy after the war. The 1950 Commodity Exchange Law established a legal framework similar to that in force in the USA, and most of the sixteen commodity exchanges currently trading agricultural futures in Japan were founded in the early 1950s. As we shall see, there is a high level of activity in Japanese futures trading, but this is spread across a large number of specialized exchanges in a number of locations throughout Japan. Before looking at the individual exchanges, however, we should examine the method of price determination on Japanese exchanges, which differs from that in Europe and the USA.

Price determination on Japanese exchanges

In Europe and the USA prices vary continuously during trading hours, as individual buyers and sellers strike deals and report the agreed prices to the exchange. This gives rise to one of the commonest complaints about futures trading: that individual orders get filled at what, in the light of the entire day's price movements, appear to be disadvantageous prices. Stories are rife on the exchanges about floor brokers who give the best fills to their favoured clients, or keep them for their own positions, and although this practice is illegal, most people who have had close involvement in futures trading are aware of instances where dishonourable – if not illegal – practice has occurred. The problem arises because of the continuously variable nature of prices. Defenders of the system argue that everyone's best interests are served by prices which are set by open competition between large numbers of buyers and sellers, and claim that complaints are simply the result of 'hindsight trading', i.e. judging a fill on the basis of subsequent price movement. On the other hand, it is certainly true that there are days, and times within a day, when many markets are rather illiquid, and on these occasions it is difficult to justify the claim that the prices quoted are the result of competitive buying and selling.

Japanese futures markets, however, are much fairer, since they concentrated all buying and selling into fixed periods, and execute all trades at a single price. This system – known as the One Price Group Trading system – operates as follows.

Trading sessions are held at fixed times throughout the day, with the number of sessions determined by the exchange and varying between two and five per day. As each session nears, the floor brokers gather in front of a raised platform, on which are seated officials of the exchange. A clerk indicates a provisional price, and the floor brokers respond to this by indicating their bids and offers at that price. These bids and offers are recorded by other clerks; if

Agricultural Commodity Markets

Table 14 Japanese futures exchanges: volume of trade, 1986 (in contracts)

Tokyo Grain Exchange:	
US soybeans	2,997,827
Chinese soybeans	177,218
Red beans	2,045,635
Tokyo Sugar Exchange:	
Raw sugar	1,780,127
Refined sugar	4,266
Yokohama Raw Silk Exchange:	
Raw silk	217,110
Tokyo Commodity Exchange for Industry:	
Rubber (RSS no. 3)	1,097,351
Cotton yarn	325,275
Woollen yarn	9,181
Osaka Grain Exchange:	
Red beans	1,736,440
Imported soybeans	1,154,590
Osaka Sugar Exchange:	
Raw sugar	629,257
Refined sugar	5,912
Osaka Textile Exchange:	
Staple fibre yarn	6,318
Cotton yarn (3 contracts)	317,535
Wool yarn	226,712
Nagoya Grain Exchange:	
Red beans	624,366
Imported soybeans	529,391
Refined sugar	9,565
Nagoya Textile Exchange:	
Cotton yarn	333,427
Staple fibre yarn	74,867
Wool yarn	17,602
Kobe Grain Exchange:	
Red beans	197,029
Imported soybeans	455,156
Kobe Raw Silk Exchange:	
Raw silk	110,960
Kobe Rubber Exchange:	
Rubber (RSS no. 3)	1,044,648
Hokkaido Grain Exchange:	
Red beans	436,762
Imported soybeans	207,198
Kanmon Commodity Exchange:	
Red beans	217,047
Imported soybeans	372,330
Refined sugar	4,288

Toyahashi Dried Cocoon Exchange:	
Dried cocoons	1,270,431
Maebashi Dried Cocoon Exchange:	
Dried cocoons	1,052,417

Source: Japanese Federation of Commodity Exchanges; all Japan Grain Exchange Association; individual exchanges.

Note: Only major contracts are illustrated. Minor contracts include Potato Starch and White Beans on the Tokyo, Hokkaido, and Nagoya Grain Exchanges and Raw Sugar on the Kanmon Commodity Exchange. The Tokyo Commodity Exchange for Industry also trades precious metal contracts.

the totals of bids and offers are not equal, the clerk alters the price, raising it to encourage selling or lowering it to encourage buying. Several iterations may be needed before a price is found at which bids and offers are equal, but when this price is established the clerk indicates that the fix price has been arrived at and all existing bids and offers are executed at that price. The trading floor then moves to the next delivery month or the next commodity. This procedure is repeated at each fixing, up to five times per day. At the end of each business day positions are marginated against the prices fixed in the last trading session, and then margination takes place daily as on a western exchange. Therefore, at any one price fixing, all customers get the same fill, although prices at subsequent fixings may prove to be more or less advantageous.

From the economist's point of view, this procedure is fascinating because it conforms to the theoretical model of price determination in a competitive market which was advanced by one of the founders of neo-classical economics, Leon Walras. Walras explained how supply and demand are matched by market clearing prices with the aid of a hypothetical auctioneer, who calls out successive prices, co-ordinating supplies and demands and by this process finds the price which clears the market. He described the process as one of *tâtonnement*, or groping towards equilibrium. The auctioneer was intended merely as a heuristic device, but it is exactly this task which is performed by the clerk in a Japanese futures exchange.[2]

Currently this type of trading method is used throughout Japan, in the Philippines, and also in some of the trading pits on the Hong Kong Futures Exchange. Despite its obvious attractions, it has never extended outside East Asia for futures trading, although an analogous method is used to determine spot prices at the daily fixings in certain metal and currency markets.

61

Japanese futures markets

The extent of agricultural commodity futures trading in Japan is illustrated in Table 14. The range of commodities traded is impressive, including textile fibres from wool to dried cocoons (the raw material for silk production), rubber, red (azuki) beans, soybeans, and sugar. These are all actively traded on a number of exchanges, although it should be added that contract sizes are small: soybean contracts are 15 tonnes, rubber 5 tonnes, and sugar 10 tonnes. Clearly, this tends to inflate the turnover figures. Most of the exchanges are small and specialized, but there are several instances of co-operation and even merger. The Tokyo Commodity Exchange for Industry was formed in 1984 by the merger of the Tokyo Gold, Rubber, and Textile Exchanges, and the Osaka Sugar and Textile Exchanges share premises, trading on the same floor.

A number of the prices set by these Japanese exchanges are of international significance. The increasing involvement of Japanese trading companies in physical commodity trade between third-party countries means that Japanese exchanges sometimes obtain information in advance of other markets; for example, this often happens in the case of Chinese sugar imports. In the case of rubber, Japanese prices are of growing significance since the closure of New York's futures market, and the dormancy of London's, mean that the Japanese market is the only large market in a consuming country. Moreover, Japan is growing in importance as an importer of rubber. In the case of dried cocoons/silk, Japanese prices are effectively world market prices, since Japan is an extremely large silk producer and importer, and it is only in Japan that there exists a formal silk market. Finally, red beans, which are used in a variety of foodstuffs, especially sweets, are a favoured commodity for speculators in Japan. They have a volatile price, thanks to inelastic demand and a supply which can vary greatly with the weather. Since this market responds primarily to developments within Japan, it is difficult for those outside the country to gain access to the information flow which is necessary for successful trading.

Other Asian/Pacific exchanges

The Hong Kong Futures Exchange (HKFE) was incorporated in December 1976, reflecting the growing importance of Hong Kong's role in the international financial community; and the exchange's first contract in cotton began trading in May 1977. The now inactive cotton contract was quickly followed by sugar, soybeans, and gold. A contract on the local stock market index,

Table 15 Traded volume on the Hong Kong Futures Exchange, 1986

Contract	Turnover
Sugar	273,800
Soybeans	330,524

Source: Hong Kong Futures Exchange.

the Hang Seng Index, was introduced in 1986. Interestingly, the soybean contract, priced in Hong Kong dollars, is traded using the Japanese One Price Group Trading method, and the sugar contract, priced in US dollars, is traded using both this system and open outcry. Gold and the Hang Seng Index, however, are traded using only open outcry. Turnover, in 1986, on the sugar and soybean contracts is given in Table 15.

Given the role of Hong Kong in commodity trade in general, and given the economic expansion taking place in the Asia/Pacific region, it would seem that the HKFE would tend to grow in importance. Apart from the general uncertainty affecting Hong Kong because of the reversion to Chinese sovereignty in 1997, however, a serious cloud hangs over the HKFE as a result of the collapse in, October 1987, of world stock markets.

The rise in the Hang Seng stock market index throughout the first nine months of 1987 gave speculators large returns on long positions on the Hang Seng Index futures contract. On Monday, 19 October, the Hang Seng Index closed at 3,362, but later that day, when the US stock markets opened, the Dow-Jones 30 share index fell by over 500 points, its largest fall on record. At that time, there were about 80,000 open futures market contracts on the index, with institutional investors holding the bulk of the short positions as hedges against their stock market portfolios and with the long positions held by local brokers and speculators. There were fears that when the Hong Kong markets re-opened on Tuesday, 20 October, they would fall sharply; estimates suggested that the Hang Seng Index would fall to around 2,600. This would have resulted in huge losses for the holders of long positions; it was also feared that, in order to meet these losses, the holders would be forced to sell shares heavily, prompting an even sharper fall in the stock market. Faced with this prospect, the ruling bodies of the HKFE and the Hong Kong Stock Exchange, comprised mostly of the local broking community, suspended the opening of the markets on Tuesday, the 20th.

Their initial proposal, to impose a market settlement price on the index, would have limited the losses for the longs (who were

63

heavily represented on the ruling bodies) and imposed losses on the shorts (who had very limited representation since they were largely from the international investment community). Naturally the shorts were outraged by this proposal since they had been using the market for its economic purpose, hedging. Eventually the government arranged a HK$2 billion compensation fund (later increased to HK$4 bn), provided by all the components of the broking community, local banks, and the government, and the market re-opened on Monday, 26 October. A number of local brokerages went bankrupt, to be taken over by the larger companies which had contributed to the compensation fund. The government also launched an inquiry into the operations of the two exchanges, with a view to strengthening the controls of their operations.

As a result of this episode, international confidence in the HKFE has been severely shakened. Futures markets can work only if speculators are willing to accept risk. They do this in the hope of high profits, but it is essential that they be able and willing to accept losses if these occur. The events of October 1987 indicated that the local broking community, which had taken out large speculative positions, was prepared to use its power in the exchange's governing body to limit its losses. While this may be understandable behaviour, it is not compatible with the successful operation of an internationally credible market. It remains to be seen whether the government will introduce reforms in the rules of the market which will re-establish confidence in the market.

The Manila International Futures Exchange (MIFE) was incorporated in October 1984 and licensed to trade sugar and soybean futures in January 1986, and actually began trading these two commodities in October 1986. By December 1986 these contracts were trading over 4,000 contracts per month each, and although it is far too early to assess the success of the exchange, it appears to have got off to a good start. Trading is conducted under the Japanese one price group trading method.

In October 1987 approval was granted by the Philippine regulatory authorities for contracts to be introduced in coffee, copra, and coconut oil. The fate of the copra and coconut oil contracts (both are products of the coconut) will be interesting to watch since the Philippines account for about 70 per cent of the world's coconut product exports. Coconut oil has not been traded successfully on a futures exchange; a contract on the Pacific Commodities Exchange in California, which was introduced in 1972, failed to generate viable levels of trading interest.

Although it cannot be safely predicted that the MIFE will flourish in the years ahead, it does provide an example of the growing importance of futures markets in developing countries, and the increasing use being made by traders in these countries of the facilities which futures offer. This is a trend which is likely to continue, and we return to it in Chapter 11.

An older example of a futures exchange in a developing country is provided by the Kuala Lumpur Commodity Exchange (KLCE), which began trading crude palm oil futures contracts in October 1980. Palm-oil is a vegetable oil, produced from the oil palm. In the past fifteen years, cultivation of these trees has expanded enormously throughout South-east Asia, and palm-oil is now an extremely important export commodity for Malaysia. The KLCE provides the only futures contracts on palm-oil, and it has been a successful contract: turnover, in 1986, was 41,303 lots.

The exchange has had its difficulties: a major default in 1984 led to a restructuring of the exchange and to a tightening of the rules under which it operates. It has expanded steadily over the years, introducing contracts on RSS no. 1 rubber in 1983 and SMR 20 rubber in 1986. A palm-kernel contract was introduced in December 1986 and, in 1987, the first non-agricultural contract was launched when tin futures began trading. Earlier, there had been plans to introduce tin futures, but delays were imposed by the difficulties in the tin market following the collapse of the International Tin Agreement in 1985 and the subsequent closure of the tin market on the London Metal Exchange. The KLCE plans to introduce a cocoa contract in 1988 and is discussing the introduction of a contract on refined palm-oil.

The Sydney Greasy Wool Futures Exchange was founded in 1960, and by 1964 when its wool contract traded over 130,000 lots, it was the world's leading wool exchange. Its name was changed to the Sydney Futures Exchange in 1972, and a number of new contracts were introduced in the following years. Live cattle began trading in 1975, followed in 1976 by a wide range of financial futures.

Its agricultural contracts have been rather eclipsed by the growth in financial futures trading; the live cattle contract has been changed several times in an attempt to generate more turnover, but in 1986, it only traded 2,666 contracts. There have been similar problems with wool, which traded 363 lots in 1986. A contract on fat lambs was introduced in 1981, but trading volume failed to grow and the contract was suspended in 1985.

The exchange itself has grown in importance to the point where it was the eleventh most active in the world in 1986. The great bulk of its trading, however, is in financial instruments. In these markets the exchange has two key advantages, namely, its time zone and its native language, which combined with its willingness to introduce new contracts and experiment with their details, will ensure its importance in world futures trading. In terms of agricultural commodities, the history and outlook for the future are less encouraging.

A futures market in New Zealand wool has been in existence in one form or another since 1953, usually in London. For a time in the early 1980s, there was the unusual situation of the contract being traded in both London and New Zealand, with each day's New Zealand trades being cleared in London the next day. The New Zealand Futures Exchange (NZFE) formally began in early 1985, its first contract in wool being taken over from the London Wool Terminal Market Association.

The volume of trade in wool on the NZFE has never been large, amounting in 1986 to 13,555 contracts. A contract on New Zealand grown wheat was introduced in 1986, but suspended in 1987 because of low volume. As in Sydney, the largest area of growth has been financial futures; contracts on domestic interest rates, the US dollar, and the local stock market index are very actively traded.

By world standards the NZFE is a small exchange, but it has an importance greater than its size would warrant because of its trading method. There is no trading floor, or pit, in which buying and selling are conducted. Instead traders in Auckland, Wellington, Christchurch, and Napier are linked by computer terminals into which they input bids and offers. All trades are executed by this system, which closely resembles that used by London's Stock Exchange. This system, known as the Automated Trading System, or ATS, is well suited to New Zealand's low, scattered population, but it is also being taken up elsewhere; on London's Fox the ATS has been used for trading white sugar futures since 1987 when the contract was launched. In all likelihood, screen-based trading will become increasingly important in futures trading in years to come.

The regulation of futures trading: US and UK approaches

There are many levels and types of regulation necessary to ensure the fair and effective operation of a futures market. Many of the most important regulations in futures trading are contained in the details of the futures contract itself. For example, all futures contracts contain clauses dealing with the terms of arbitration in the event of dispute. Accordingly, most regulating is done by the clearing-house, the exchange itself, or by associations of exchanges and their users. The powers invested in these organizations are considerable: for example, in the USA floor traders can be fined large sums if they are found to be processing their orders in an improper manner. The importance of regulation by these bodies should not be underestimated; the system of margination, which protects against financial problems of one member leading to the bankruptcy of others, is administered by the clearing-house. For the most part, this type of regulation is not conducted under the terms of specific statutes and is known as 'self-regulation'. It can plausibly be held that most disputes are most easily resolved if exchanges are left to run themselves.

However, a different problem arises with the interests of society as a whole. Clearly, commodity exchanges cannot be expected to be given the authority to regulate on behalf of the public interest. Yet there is no clear dividing-line between those activities which can be handled by self-regulation and those properly the concern of statutory regulation.

A wide range of approaches to the statutory regulation of futures trading has been taken in different countries where, and at different times in history, there has been futures trading. Often futures trading has been prohibited by law: for example, in Germany all futures trading was banned in 1896, only to be permitted four years later. In Japan, where futures trading began in 1730, it was prohibited in 1868, although the ban was not in force for long. Perhaps most bizarre, futures trading in onions in the USA was prohibited in 1958 and the ban remains in force.

Legislators' frequent desire to prohibit futures trading arises because of ignorance, and their suspicion of markets they do not fully understand may be activated by interest groups suffering from the consequences of futures trading. Here the first such group is formed of traders in the physical commodity who believe that their profits are greater in the absence of futures trading (they are probably correct in this belief since futures markets appear to bring greater efficiency to spot markets). These traders are often able to prevent the establishment of a futures market, as they have done in the case of tea, for example. The American ban on futures trading in onions resulted from the onion traders' ability to link their dislike of the futures market to Congressmen's suspicion of the wide price swings which occur towards the end of the crop year in a market where the product cannot be stored from one season to the next. There has also been a concerted political attack on potato futures trading.[3] The attitude to futures markets of those involved in the production, marketing, and consumption of a commodity has varied over the years. Usually the trade is a vigorous defender of existing futures markets, and agrarian populist opposition to futures markets has almost entirely disappeared from the USA. Only live cattle futures markets are still the subject of periodic political campaigns. Conversely, many vested interests in the trade resist the introduction of new markets, and take a long time to become convinced of their benefits; although the fact that the benefits are widely spread throughout the economy does mean that certain groups inevitably see a net loss when futures trading is introduced.

The second interest group is the general public, who have two concerns about futures markets. First, they are concerned that futures markets should improve (or at least not interfere with) the movement of commodities through the economy at prices which reflect the economic value of those commodities. Thus society has an interest in ensuring that the attempt to put a squeeze on markets does not succeed, for a successful squeeze would push up prices to an artificially high level. Second, the general public is concerned to avoid losing when participating in the markets as speculators; and since they do not like losing (even when they have lost fairly), they may use their political influence to restrict their liability. Thus futures trading in France was only able to develop after the passing of the 1885 Naquet Law, disallowing losing speculators from invoking gaming laws to limit their liability. To this day, West German laws allow losing speculators to recover their losses under quite broad conditions and futures markets simply cannot operate unless people are willing to accept losses as well as profits.

On the other hand, the scope for fraud in futures trading is as great as in any other area, and there is a widespread feeling that a regulatory framework is required to protect against fraudulence. Always of particular concern has been the treatment of individual speculators – and there are many examples of individuals being badly mistreated by companies which offer facilities to 'invest' in futures markets. Among the earliest frauds were the US 'bucket shops', which took money from customers but did not put the money on the market. Instead they ran their own books, making large amounts of money when the markets moved against their clients. The reason why this concern has been greater in the case of futures markets (compared to, say, the stock market) is that, it is felt, speculators are seduced by the prospect of large profits and do not give sufficient weight to the prospects of losses; thus they are easy prey to unscrupulous 'investment advisors'.

Therefore, regulation of futures markets needs to be strict enough to prevent fraud and mistreatment of participants, but it should be loose enough to allow the markets to flourish and provide wider economic benefits, which they can do only if people are willing to take a loss as well as a profit. One particular danger is that an unholy alliance of trade interests and the general public will develop and impose a very strict regulatory regime, which protects individuals from the consequences of their own actions and allows the trade to continue to secure profits from a too cosy, non-competitive market-place.

The approaches adopted by the UK and US authorities to this problem are rather different, and provide an interesting contrast. Since the US regime has been in force for longer, let us look at it first.

Regulation in the USA

In the USA the key organization is the Commodity Futures Trading Commission, or the CFTC, which came into existence in 1975. The Commodity Exchange Act 1936, amended in 1968, had established the Department of Agriculture as the regulatory authority, but the growth in financial futures trading in the early 1970s made this rather inappropriate. The CFTC has a wide range of powers, supported by its ability to issue injunctions and levy fines. Principally these powers are of two kinds: first, the Commission is charged to ensure that futures trading meets its underlying economic purpose. Thus all contracts have to be approved by it before they can begin trading, and the operating rules of an exchange must also be approved. The Commission can also prosecute cases of manipulation and impose position limits. As part of this set of functions, it monitors the size of positions held by both speculators and hedgers once they exceed a certain level.

Second, the Commission regulates the interface between futures trading and the general public. It enforces minimum standards of both finance and staff competence for brokerage firms, and requires that clients' funds be kept separate from the funds of the house itself. (This is important since it protects a client's profits in the event that the brokerage company becomes bankrupt.)

Interestingly, the budget of the CFTC has never been very large, certainly not large enough to monitor the extent to which exchanges comply with its regulations. The day-to-day regulation of trading is the responsibility of the exchanges, and their own trade association also plays an active role in maintaining standards. None the less, the CFTC does not rely solely on the threat of action, for it does frequently impose restrictions on trading when it is concerned about the possibility of manipulation.

69

There have been many occasions on which the actions of the CFTC have been challenged by the exchanges, but it is for the most part an accepted and respected organization. It has the great virtue that it is a statutory body, operating within a clear legal framework and answerable under the law. Anyone who thinks its actions are unfair can take it to court.

Regulation in the UK

The situation in the UK is rather different. Traditionally futures exchanges were self-regulating, and viewed themselves principally as devoted to the interests both of their members and members' trade clients. One important consequence of this has been that the London exchanges have been unable to attract the volume of trade which can be observed on futures markets in the USA and Japan. Although the Bank of England has a great deal of informal authority over the exchanges and their member firms, the only legislation which, until recently, was relevant to futures markets was the Prevention of Fraud (Investments) Act 1958, under which it is an offence to mislead anyone in a futures market transaction. Under the Act there has so far been only one successful prosecution of a commodity futures case, and both the Bank of England and the Department of Trade and Industry appear to have been reluctant to act against many suspected frauds; there was no legislation designed to ensure that the futures markets make certain that their activities encourage greater efficiency in the economy as a whole.

In response to a widespread dissatisfaction with the state of legislation on investor protection, and as part of a general attempt to improve the efficiency of London's financial markets, the government commissioned the Gower Report on Investor Protection, which formed the basis for the Financial Services Act 1986.[4] The Act established the Securities and Investment Board (SIB) as the main instrument of regulation of all financial markets. True to the London tradition of self-regulation, however, the SIB's principal role is to establish self-regulatory organizations (SROs) for each of the major sections of the financial services industry, and to approve the rules to which the members of SROs must adhere. One of the SROs is the Association of Futures Brokers and Dealers (AFBD), and, after the implementation of the Financial Services Act in April 1988, it became illegal for any company to operate as a futures broker without being a member of the AFBD. Hence the AFBD's rulebook became the key element of regulation of the UK futures markets.

The AFBD rulebook is, of necessity, rather complicated. It

establishes financial standards for member firms, including minimum solvency requirements and the segregation of clients' funds. Complete records of all transactions must be kept for three years. It is supplemented by the code of conduct, which enjoins brokers to act in their clients' best interests; thus it forbids 'churning', or the practice of trading an account too often in order to generate commission, and requires brokers to inform clients fully about the risks of trading.

Two criticisms have been levied at the AFBD, and the SRO system in general. In the first place, there have been objections to the inclusion of a clause in the AFBD rulebook which allows it to exclude from membership anyone it deems not to be a 'fit and proper' person. Of course, the difficulty here is that no objective standard of 'fit and proper' can exist, and the effect of this clause is to make the AFBD seem more like a gentlemen's club than an effective agency for the establishment of good business practices. If there are objective criteria, they should be spelled out; if there are not, then the clause should be abolished, making the procedure for membership fair (and seen to be fair).

A second objection raised against SROs as a whole is that they generate an oligopoly by imposing artificially high costs of entering the industry. If the costs of meeting regulatory standards are too high, then new entrants to the industry will be discouraged and existing participants will be able to make excess profits. Given the existence of the 'fit and proper' clause, then it is all too easy to see how the effect of the regulations is to protect a cosy gentlemen's establishment from the consequences of open competition. What makes this argument all the more compelling is the fact that the SRO rulebook has been drawn up by existing participants, who can scarcely be credited with having an interest in seeing more open competition in their industry.

This argument actually exposes a fundamental problem with the SIB's entire rationale. Its principal responsibility is that of investor protection; it does not seek to advance the interests of the economy as a whole in having efficient financial markets. Therefore, it is highly vulnerable to the 'unholy alliance' of existing profitable participants and the risk-averse investing public, who combine to impose tight regulation at the expense of the open markets which benefit the whole economy. To achieve this open competition, it must be possible for new companies easily to enter a market-place. They should not be deemed unfit and improper merely because they threaten an established oligopoly, an eventuality all too likely while the AFBD rulebook is written by industry participants without the chance for protection of the general interest.

With the current UK regulatory framework in its infancy, it is hard to compare it properly with that in the USA.[5] The most that one can say is that it certainly represents an improvement, in terms of investor protection, over the former situation. In so far as the new environment does not affect the broader issue of futures markets delivering the economic benefits they promise, however, it is possible to compare the USA and UK in terms of their ability to prevent the manipulation of markets.

Preventing manipulation – the USA and UK compared

History is replete with examples of attempts to put corners on markets. The idea behind this is simple: someone takes a large long futures position and also gains control of a large proportion of the large deliverable stocks. As the long contracts approach maturity, the longs insist on delivery, thus generating a scramble on the part of the shorts for the available stocks. This drives up the price sharply, and allows the longs to make substantial profits. Theory suggests that such an operation is unlikely to be successful, since the longs will be left with large stocks which they will at some point be forced to liquidate, thus depressing the price. Nevertheless, the idea of putting a corner on markets is sufficiently attractive for it to have been attempted many times, and the consequential movements in prices are clearly disruptive to the underlying business of producing, distributing, and using the commodity concerned.

Perhaps the most famous recent attempted corner was that of the Hunt brothers, who attempted to corner the world silver market between August 1979 and March 1980. They planned to buy futures, take delivery and so build up their stocks, and then to squeeze a later contract. The CFTC was able to monitor the positions held by the Hunts on both Comex and the CBOT – and when these positions had grown to the point where they were causing concern, it pressed Comex to raise the margin requirement on silver and to restrict trading in silver to liquidation only. This caused the price of silver to fall. The Hunts, in late March, were unable to meet their margin calls and the brokers left with their long positions sold them out, generating widespread losses for the brokering community. The consequences of this affair lasted for many years: it was as late as 1987 when one major brokerage house reached an out-of-court settlement of over $20 million with the Peruvian state mining company which had sold silver short into the squeezed market, thus losing money. The Peruvians alleged breach of fiduciary duty by the broker who, they alleged, was advising the Peruvians to sell short at the same time as advising the

Hunts on their long position. The role of the CFTC was important in this affair in identifying the positions held by the Hunts, in pressing the exchanges to act more speedily than they might otherwise have done, and in providing a public forum in which the case could be discussed and measures to prevent a recurrence could be considered.

In the UK a comparable case is provided by the attempt by Malaysian interests to squeeze the London Metal Exchange's (LME) tin market during late 1981 and early 1982. The Malaysians began buying three-month tin, then switched to buying the metal in the cash market in November. By December they held a large proportion of the outstanding long forward contracts and about three-quarters of the deliverable supply. During December and January there was heavy shipment of tin to London, but it seemed inevitable that some holders of short positions would default. To counteract this, the LME Committee changed the rules in February 1983, limiting the liability of those shorts and extending the period over which delivery could be made. Throughout this episode the Bank of England was kept abreast of developments on an informal basis, but no formal public inquiry into this abuse of the market was ever conducted; full details are still not available. How effective the LME was in protecting its tin contract against abuse, and ensuring that hedgers enjoy the benefit of an operating tin market, may be judged by the fact that the tin market was forced to close in 1985 after the International Tin Council ran out of money to finance its price-supporting purchases.

Overall, attempted squeezes on markets are common enough for them to constitute a serious constraint on the ability of futures markets to inspire confidence in their economic purpose. Within the USA this problem has been explicitly recognized, and the protection of the markets' integrity is a central role of the CFTC. This is in marked contrast to the current regulatory environment in the UK.

Chapter Four

Approaches to price analysis

As we have seen in the preceding chapters, futures markets are an important part of the agricultural economy, an exciting vehicle for speculation, and are comparatively easy to use. But how does one decide whether prices are going up or down, and by how much? Where should stops be placed to limit losses? Broadly, there are two approaches to the analysis of price movements, and although each school has its enthusiastic adherents, most traders rely on both approaches for most of their trades. The two approaches are, first, the fundamental; and second, the technical. The fundamental trader believes that prices are the outcome of an understandable and rational economic process, and that to forecast prices one must consider the underlying supplies of and demands for the commodity itself. The technical trader believes that prices are simply statistical variables, which obey patterns like other variables, and which can be treated as though they were wholly internal to the market itself. Therefore, to forecast prices, one simply analyses the past behaviour of the market itself, searching for regularities.

Fundamental analysis

Fundamental analysis starts from the economist's proposition that prices are determined by supply and demand. Thus, if a drought in Brazil reduces the country's coffee crop, coffee prices can be expected to go up. Economists have a variety of tools to help them answer the important questions – such as by how much will coffee prices go up for any given shortfall in production – but before we look at the application of these tools to analysis of future prices, let us examine briefly the longer-term economics of commodity prices.

Much has been written on commodity price instability, and there is little point in adding to that literature here. If one examines the prices for commodities as a whole, including energy, minerals, and agricultural products, then two distinct features of prices are discernible. The first is a steady decline, since the end of the Second World War, in real (i.e. inflation-adjusted) prices.[1] An important corollary of this is the diminishing use of commodities as economies get richer. At certain stages of economic development, an increment to a country's gross national product (GNP) will generate a large level of demand for basic commodities, but as countries get richer, each increment of GNP leads to smaller and smaller demands for commodities. This is nothing more than an implication of the growing importance of services, rather than manufacturing, in both the total of global economic activity and its growth.

This is also a feature of agriculture. People's demands for food are finite, and as they get richer they spend a smaller and smaller proportion of their incomes on food. This means that the income which is earned by agricultural producers will tend to decline relative to the other sectors of the economy. This inherent feature of demand, coupled with the use of cost-reducing technology, makes the conditions under which agricultural prices can rise in real terms of little more than theoretical interest.

This longer-term trend notwithstanding, one important cause of fluctuations in commodity prices as a whole is those fluctuations in the level of global economic activity. When activity increases commodity prices increase, but when it slackens, commodity prices fall. Analysis of the markets shows that commodity prices are considerably more unstable than overall economic activity. Commodity prices are flexible in both directions, and are less prone to periods of stability. The most important feature of prices, however, is the high degree of instability of agricultural commodities and the fact that a great deal of this instability is uncorrelated with the level of economic activity (i.e. with demand). Agricultural product prices can fluctuate by almost 30 per cent from one year to the next, whereas economic activity rarely fluctuates by more than 10 per cent. Moreover, commodity prices can rise sharply, as in 1978–80, at a time when industrial production is falling. The reasons for this are rooted in the features of supply and demand for agricultural commodities.

In the first place, agricultural production is subject to periodic shocks caused by abnormal weather patterns: frosts, heavy rains, droughts, and hurricanes – all these can, and do, seriously affect crop yields in all major producers both in tropical and temperate zones. As a result, production of certain crops can fluctuate widely from one year to the next without major changes in planted areas.

To give one example, Brazilian coffee production was reduced from 29.6 million bags in the 1985–6 season to 11.2 million bags the next year by a severe drought in the summer of 1985–6. When climatic variability is combined with serious policy mismanagement, as in the USSR, the results can be spectacular: Soviet grain production was 185 million tonnes in 1983, 160 million in 1984, 178 million in 1985, and 199 million in 1986, giving an average fluctuation in production of over 10 per cent.

Second, the supply of agricultural commodities is inelastic with respect to price in the short run, but more elastic in the long run. Once a farmer has planted and harvested his crop, there is little he can do to increase production in response to high prices until next planting season. Hence any kind of shortfall in production cannot be made good very quickly. Of course, by the time next season comes along production can increase, but in the case of many agricultural commodities – such as, for example, cocoa, coffee and cattle – it takes many years before an initial farmer decision to expand production actually results in that increased production coming to the market. By the same token, once the investment to expand production has been made, it is uneconomic for farmers to cut back unless prices are very low. Given the inherent uncertainties over weather patterns and their impact on crops, farmers' limited ability to respond quickly to price incentives inevitably generates instability.

Third, demand for agricultural commodities is rather inelastic, with respect to both income and price. Providing people have sufficient income, they will buy food no matter what its price; conversely, reductions in the price of foodstuffs and, for that matter, increases in consumer income, do little to stimulate demand for food. This inelasticity of demand exacerbates the swings in price which arise from supply disruptions.

The relationship between price and consumption does vary from commodity to commodity. Broadly speaking, this relationship is a function of the availability of substitutes and the proportion of income which is spent on the commodity. Thus consumption of wheat, for which there is no ready substitute and which accounts for a tiny proportion of people's expenditure, is very unresponsive to price.[2] However, consumption of beef is somewhat more elastic, since there are ready substitutes in the form of other meats, and it accounts for a larger share of consumer income.

The relationship with income is quite important for understanding commodity price movements. An income–consumption curve shows that, as income rises, there is initially an increase in consumption, but as income continues to grow the response is smaller and smaller. The shape and height of this curve is not the same for all commodities, however; for staple goods, such as bread, the rises take place very early on in the phase of income growth, and consumption even declines as people's incomes increase further. Hence the main source of increased demand for a commodity like wheat is world population growth and economic growth in the poorest countries. The income–consumption curve for staples is very low and to the left. At the other end of the scale, demand for meat is very responsive to increases in consumer income, but people have to be reasonably wealthy before they start on the phase of expanding meat consumption. Hence world demand for meat is concentrated in the world's richest countries, although consumption is growing rapidly in those countries, such as South Korea, where consumer incomes have reached the critical level. The income–consumption curve for meat is very high and to the right. In between these two extremes are a range of commodities, such as sugar and vegetable oil, which are very responsive to income changes when income is at an intermediate level. Hence when a country like Pakistan enjoys good economic conditions, its demand for sugar and vegetable oil will grow faster than its demand for meat.

This kind of information is used by economists in developing analyses of the long-term behaviour of a commodity market. For the most part, it is also the kind of information which is used by futures market analysts, but it is extremely important to realize that futures trading is concerned with a comparatively short time horizon; few futures markets even provide contracts more than eighteen months ahead, and the actively traded contracts are rarely more than six months ahead. This means that, in addition to being concerned with patterns of supply and demand, we need to concern ourselves, too, with the level of stocks. This is especially important within the agricultural economy, where production is inherently seasonal.

Consider the following identity:

Beginning stocks + production + imports = consumption + exports + ending stocks

This simply states that the amount of a commodity which is on hand after the harvest and which is brought into the country must either be used by consumers at home and abroad or stored into next year. One year's ending stocks of course are next year's beginning stocks. It is an *ex post* identity, and leaves price unmentioned. Obviously the variables in the identity will be affected by price; this year's production, for example, is affected by farmers' earlier expectations of what the price will be, and consumption will also be (somewhat) affected by prices. Perhaps more important, however, the identity tells us that the impact on price of any disruption to production (perhaps the result of adverse weather) will be greater when stocks are low and demand is strong, and will be smaller when stocks are high and demand is weak. The most important function of price within the crop year, however, is to allocate the available supply between stocks and consumption.

One variable which is widely used to forecast prices is the stock–consumption ratio, the amount of a good which is available relative to the level of demand. This has to be interpreted with care, however, since it will naturally fluctuate over a crop year: stocks will be high immediately after the harvest, and inevitably lower just before the harvest. This feature of a seasonally produced commodity draws our attention to the crucial significance of stocks. In fact to understand short-term price movements we have to understand stockholding behaviour.

Why hold stocks?

The most important reason for holding stocks is to be able to meet demand over the period when there is no production. They effectively even out the seasonal fluctuations in supply, and therefore will be drawn down over the period up to the next harvest. Therefore, an important function of those who hold stocks is to assess the likely size of demands from different users over the coming year and ensure their stocks can satisfy these demands. Secondary reasons for holding stocks are as insurance against unexpected developments which may emerge over the year, as a speculative vehicle, to profit from any changes in price and as a safety net for next year. One external variable which will affect the willingness of people to hold stocks is the interest rate; high interest rates push up the cost of the capital tied up in inventory, thus reducing the level of stocks which people will be willing to carry.

Futures prices allocate the available supply between immediate demands and the future demands represented by stocks. Accordingly, they adjust in response to any factors which change the balance between stocks and demands.

First of all, once the size of a harvest is known, they adjust to reflect current expectations about the level of demand over the coming year. To the extent that subsequent demands by certain consumers represent merely the confirmation of expectations, there will be no price effect. At the beginning of the year, for example, it may be expected that Mexico will buy 100,000 tonnes of US corn per month over the course of the year. If a Mexican purchase of 100,000 tonnes is announced, prices will not alter, since stocks are on hand precisely to meet this eventuality. On the other hand, if at the end of six months the Mexicans have only bought 300,000 tonnes, stockholders will have to consider whether the programme of purchases has either been reduced or simply delayed. Whether prices go down will depend on the answer to this question.

In other words, prices respond to the unexpected (not to that which has already been anticipated). Uncertainty on the demand side comes from two main sources. The first is the import requirements of communist countries, particularly the USSR. These are uncertain, partly because information about the Soviet economy is hard to obtain and partly because the decision to import reflects political as well as economic factors. Information about communist economies is either unavailable (this is typically the case in China, where procedures for gathering statistics about the economy are rudimentary) or is regarded by the authorities as secret and not to be passed to the west; this makes it difficult for people in the west to assess the size of the import requirements. We do not know enough about domestic production levels and qualities, nor do we know enough about commodity-using industries. Analysts pore over the available information and extract an extraordinary amount from the few data, but it is rarely enough. Moreover, decisions to import are made politically at a high level; until the early 1970s whenever the Soviet Union had a bad grain crop, it was absorbed by the economy in the form of shortages rather than being supplemented by imports. Political relaxation in both China and the USSR, and determined efforts by the governments to improve the living standards of their citizens, are changing this situation, but important uncertainties remain. This explains the degree of attention given by the markets (for commodities from rubber and cotton to soybeans and grains) to Soviet and Chinese purchases. In many markets other countries are considerably larger consumers, but get less attention. The point about Soviet and Chinese buying is that it is uncertain in scale and timing, thus cannot be completely allowed for in advance by stockholders, and by futures markets.

The second source of demand-side uncertainty is the performance of the economy as a whole. Better-than-expected growth in consumer income will boost demand for meat and therefore for feedgrains above the level envisaged at the start of the crop year.

This will push prices higher. An unexpected change in inflation will affect commodity prices, just like any other goods. A change in exchange rates will also affect the prices of commodities in different currencies. Of course, markets are changing every day in response to the flow of new information and changing expectations about demand.

Finally, prices respond to emerging information about the new crop or other supplies. If it appears that next year's crop will be a bad one, then prices must rise now, discouraging current consumption and allowing stocks to build up to help provide for next year's needs. Conversely, if next year's crop is going to be very large, then prices can fall now, encouraging consumption since only a small carryover stock will be needed. In any crop cycle there are certain periods which are more important than others in determining how large the next crop will be; farmer plantings provide the first indication of the next crop, but the weather has a major influence and is critically important at certain stages in crop development. Since many agricultural commodities are produced in both hemispheres, and therefore on different cycles, there are several times during the year when uncertainty over future supply is great; the market will be sensitive during this period, and prone to move dramatically at news about temperature and rainfall which would have no impact at other times of the year.

In short, the role of a futures market in allocating stocks over different time periods means that fully anticipated events do not affect prices. Uncertain events and changing expectations will change prices. Clearly, each market has its own uncertainties (these are described in the second half of this book, when we analyse the major traded commodities).

For some commodities, such as live animals, stocks cannot be held. Since these are also commodities in which international trade is very limited in extent, the above identity collapses to the following:

$$production = consumption$$

In markets like these, price can be very volatile – precisely because it has to equilibrate production and consumption in each period. For this reason, these are among the most exciting markets to trade (as discussed in Chapter 8).

Market imperfections

Outside economics textbooks, supply and demand do not act freely on prices, and it is important to be aware of market imperfections when trading. The most significant imperfections are those generated by national and international policy.

Agricultural policies tend to distort markets, whether or not that is the purpose for which they were designed. The European Community's Common Agricultural Policy, for instance, so limits the freedom of markets to operate that price volatility is almost non-existent for the products it regulates. Almost all governments regulate agriculture to some extent, and their policies have important implications for the flow of commodities from producer to market; again, to the extent that these factors are relevant, they are discussed in the commodity profiles in this book.

In addition to national policies, there have been a number of international attempts to regulate commodity markets. Most of these, ranging from co-ordinated price-fixing by producers to United Nations sponsored International Commodity Agreements, are of interest only because of the different reasons for which they have failed. There are, however, three operational international agreements – covering coffee, cocoa, and rubber – which have provisions for intervening in markets to raise or lower prices. One consequence of these agreements is that they affect the willingness of private organizations to carry stocks, thus they have a major impact on the futures markets (detailed discussion of their operation is deferred here to the relevant commodity profiles).

Importance of seasonal factors

Clearly, seasonal patterns are of great importance in agricultural commodity markets, and they are closely studied by analysts. The need for account to be taken of seasonal fluctuations is obvious: a stock–consumption ratio will be higher just after a harvest than just before it; grain consumption by livestock will be higher during the winter months when there is no pasture available; and the use of cotton by textile factories will be lower during the summer months when they are closed for the holidays. Some markets have seasonal characteristics which are less obviously linked to understandable behaviour; for example, statistical analysis shows that during years when the sugar price is declining, the bulk of that decline tends to take place between February and September.

Procedures for the statistical adjustment of seasonal data, however, are rather complicated, and justice cannot be done to them in this book. Yet seasonal price patterns do repay close study, especially since the failure of markets to conform to their normal seasonal pattern provides a strong indication that there is a serious supply–demand imbalance. Perhaps the most interesting example is that of coffee. For reasons which are explained in Chapter 9, a key influence on the coffee price is the weather in Brazil and, in particular, whether there is a frost during the winter months of June, July, and August. Given that the crop is at risk from frost over this period and that a frost produces a sharp upward price movement, there are important implications for seasonal price movements. During April and May one would normally expect prices to rise as traders cover their short positions and establish long positions ahead of the danger season. By the beginning of the frost season, therefore, the price reflects this additional buying pressure and is higher than it would be if there were no threat of frost. As the frost season passes, however, prices will decline *if there is no frost* because of the erosion of the frost-expectation premium.

Therefore, one would expect to see rising prices in April and May, and either a steadily falling price over June, July, and August or, if there is a frost, sharp price increases in this latter period. Recently there have been several years in which this pattern was not followed by the market, and in each case further large price movements have occurred: in 1974 and 1977 prices declined in April and May, and went on to fall even more sharply once the frost danger had passed. In 1981 prices also fell in April and May, but there was a frost in late July, sending prices higher. What is more, in 1976 when there was no frost, prices rose in June, fell in the first two weeks of July but then rose steadily until the end of August. This example of strength in a period of seasonal weakness was followed by a sustained bull market in coffee, in which prices rose from the end-August level of 150 cents per pound to 320 cents per pound in April 1977. Clearly, contra-seasonal price movements can be viewed as signals to initiate trades.

Building models

Prices go up when supply is declining, or is expected to decline, relative to demand; they go down when it is rising, or is expected to rise, relative to demand. Often this is enough for a futures market trader, but one important problem does remain: exactly how far will prices move in response to a change in the supply–demand balance? To answer this, it is necessary to examine something about econometric approaches to price analysis.

It is possible to build mathematical models of commodity markets – these are no more than equations which attempt to capture the underlying relationships between economic variables. In order to quantify the strength of these relationships, they can be estimated using statistical techniques. The estimated relationships can then be used to forecast prices. A typical simple model of a commodity market is the following in the hog market.

Supply:

$$S(t) = a + bSF(t-6) + cHC(t-24) + w$$

Demand:

$$P(t) = g + hS(t) + fI(t) + z$$

where S is hog slaughter, SF is sow farrowings, HC is the hog–corn price ratio, P is price, I is consumer disposable income, and w and z are error terms.

This model simply states that supply of hogs is a function of the hog–corn price ratio two years ago and the number of sows farrowed six months ago. In the absence of stocks, the market must clear, hence price must be set to ensure that all the meat is consumed. Price is asserted to be a function of slaughter and consumer income. This is an extremely simple model, but can be easily estimated and used with the kind of statistical software available for a personal computer.

Using this model, an estimate of the price and income elasticities can be obtained – and these could also be used as a simple forecasting tool. A slightly more sophisticated version of this model, with dummy variables to reflect the seasonality of slaughter and sow farrowings, has been used in the analysis of futures prices over the period 1964 to 1978, and the study's authors claimed that 'using the econometric model to indicate the direction of futures market price changes . . . substantial trading profits could have been generated between 1971 and 1978 in the hog futures market'.[3]

It is therefore comparatively easy to build an econometric model, although considerable skill is involved in defining one which accurately captures the underlying market behaviour. While it is beyond the scope of this book to attempt a thorough description and analysis of econometric techniques for forecasting prices,[4] a number of observations are appropriate.

It should be remembered that econometric techniques are most usefully applied to longer-term price analysis. Indeed some of the most fruitful applications of econometrics have little to do with forecasting prices at all. Their record in short-term price projection is, on the whole, poor. Their usefulness, from the point of view of the futures market analyst, lies in their ability to detect trends in a market, and to detect periods when because of a delicate balance between supply and demand the market is vulnerable to a large movement in price one way or the other. Any econometric estimate of the specific size of a price change is likely to be far wide of the mark. From this, four important conclusions about model design and estimation follow.

First, the use of revised or final data should be avoided: if you are interested in how the soybean price will respond to the prospect of a crop of a certain size, then it is clearly pointless to estimate an equation containing past years' actual crop sizes. Over the summer months soybean prices can move sharply merely on fears that the weather will reduce crop yields; regressing those prices on data showing the final crop outturn seriously distorts the estimation of the relationship between price and production. One should always use the relevant estimate: this is all the more important when the estimate proves to be incorrect.

Second, a model which catches turning-points in a market is preferable to one which shows a better fit to the data but misses turning-points. It is quite common for econometric models to show a high degree of multiple correlation, but major changes in price direction only with a lag. Since one would only use a model for predicting price direction, it is obviously better to have a model which predicts price changes too early rather than one which 'predicts' them after they have actually happened.

Third, while it is important to have a model which is not overly sensitive to the data period in which it is estimated, and which yields consistent estimates of the important elasticities, it is equally important to recognize that economic behaviour changes, and this will call for models to be revised. An excellent example of this is provided by stockholding behaviour. Because stocks play a vital role in price movements, it is important to include them in any model of a storable commodity. But the willingness of people to hold stocks is not constant; apart from being affected by changes in interest rates, it is also affected by changes in manufacturing technologies and by the composition of stockholders. This last is extremely important in agricultural commodities because governments are often large holders of stocks. When the government holds large stocks, private citizens may be willing to run down their own stocks, secure in the knowledge that the government reserves will meet unexpected future needs. Since the government does not, in general, behave like a profit-maximizing stockholder, prices can behave differently when they control a large proportion of the available stock.

Finally, a model which is designed to forecast price (rather than, say, to give insights into market interlinkages) should be judged on its ability to predict price. Its theoretical elegance is neither here nor there, from a trading point of view. Economists who trade futures markets are too prone to believe that the 'market gets it wrong' when their models' forecasts are not borne out. Models which are used for policy-making can afford to sacrifice some predictive accuracy in return for other benefits, those used for trading cannot.

Using fundamentals to trade

The application of economic information to futures trading is, in large part, merely a refinement of the obvious relationships between supply, demand, and price, using knowledge of particular commodity markets. However, since elasticities do vary from market to market, and since the timing of interlinkages among commodities is often very complicated, it is important to develop an understanding of the commodities themselves (the second half of this book is devoted to the commodities, to facilitate the development of this understanding).

This type of knowledge helps to guard against the greatest pitfall facing fundamental traders: that of failing to appreciate to what extent the market has already discounted the traders' views about the supply–demand balance. Prices do not rise or fall indefinitely; that is to say, that there is a price level at which fundamentals which may appear to be bullish are actually bearish. Newspaper stories are particularly misleading in this respect, in that they tend always to report on developments well after the markets have already digested the news. For example, if the International Wheat Council issues a press-release, saying that world wheat production will be 15 per cent lower this year than last, this may not mean that prices will rise. The previous IWC estimate may have been for a 25 per cent reduction; or the market may not place much weight on what the IWC says.

There are also two other important pitfalls which can trap the unwary analyst. The first is to ignore the impact of exchange rate fluctuations on commodity prices. The prices of internationally traded commodities will be affected by the ups and downs of the currency markets. The exact effects of dollar appreciation or depreciation depend on the supply and demand elasticities and the share of the USA in consumption,[5] but, in general terms, if the dollar goes down in value against other currencies, then the dollar prices of commodities will go up and their prices in other currencies will go down. This has implications for trading; for example, the profitability of a long cocoa position in London (i.e. in sterling) will be adversely affected by a weakening in the value of the dollar against sterling. If this happens, and if nothing happens in terms of the supply and demand for cocoa, London (sterling) prices will go down and New York (dollar) prices will go up. In the case of cocoa, one has a choice about trading in sterling or dollars, but in the case of many other commodities this choice does not exist, and one should be careful to avoid the profits on a position being eroded by an adverse currency move.

The second pitfall is to pay insufficient attention to cash market developments. Futures prices are of course closely linked to cash market prices. Although the basis can and does vary, it is rare to see the two markets diverge sharply. None the less, futures markets are prone to waves of buying and selling which may have little to do with what is actually going on in the supply of and demand for the cash commodity, and it is not prudent to get caught up in these movements. If soybean prices are increasing rapidly on rumours of large Russian purchases, it is important to check cash prices for soybeans in the major soybean ports such as Rotterdam and the Gulf of Mexico. If they are not increasing, the futures price will be more vulnerable to a sharp setback. In the sugar market cash prices are particularly valuable. The major futures exchanges – New York, London, and Paris – tend to reflect developments in the western hemisphere, and important news in the east, such as Chinese buying from Thailand, may well be signalled in the cash market before the main futures markets respond. The sugar contract on the new Manila International Futures Exchange may come to serve this important role in reflecting the Pacific region developments, but until its value is proven the cash market should be closely followed.

We shall return to consider the strengths of fundamental analysis at the end of this chapter, after having considered technical analysis.

Technical analysis

A large number of technical systems are in use for the analysis of futures prices, many of which are operated by fund managers who invest large sums on the basis of buy and sell signals generated by their own (usually computer-based) systems. Most of these are based on price movements alone; but before looking at these, we need to understand the volume and open interest statistics and the other basic tools of technical trading.

Volume and open interest

Every day, after the close of trading, each exchange counts the volume of trade in each commodity, by contract month. This is simply the number of contracts which were traded on that day. Each trade is counted only once, even though the role of the clearing-house means that it ends up with one contract with each seller and an opposite contract with each buyer. These numbers will be published that day or the next. Also computed is the open interest, which is the number of open futures contracts which have not been closed out by an offsetting futures trade or by delivery. Thus open interest does not change when an old long sells his position to a new long, or a new short buys from an old short, since the sum of open positions will not have altered. Open interest increases when a new long sells to a new short, and it decreases when an old long closes his position by selling to a liquidating short.

Combining these figures with changes in prices provides valuable information about what is happening in the market. For any price change from one day's close to the next, it is possible that volume and open interest will have gone up or down. Making sense of these numbers rests on the view that there is only a finite number of people who will be interested in taking out positions on the market, and that the decisions of these people, in aggregate, give indications about when price movements are about to change direction. Thus, if prices and open interest rise together, buying pressure is coming from new longs. This is a technically strong market, and it is taken as a signal that prices will continue to rise at least until volume begins to fall. At that point, there is no one left to buy into the market, and this will indicate that prices have reached at least a temporary peak. Very high levels of open interest make markets vulnerable to sharp corrections, since many holders of open positions will have stops close to the market, and any profit-taking will move the market to those stops. When prices rise and open interest declines, it means that the buying pressure is coming from liquidating shorts; thus it is likely that prices will cease rising once the shorts are out of the market.

Exactly the same analysis can be applied to a falling market. When prices and open interest fall together, the selling pressure is coming from liquidating longs. It will subside once they are out of the market. This is a technically sound market and does not indicate that prices will continue to fall. Conversely, when prices fall and open interest rises, new shorts are driving the market down, and this will continue until volume begins to fall.

Two things should be noted about this. First, each unit of open interest consists of one long and one short; therefore, the total number of open longs must be equal to the number of open shorts. We can only make deductions about who is moving the market from the direction of price change. If prices are going up, what this means is that some people want to buy and they have to bid up prices to a level at which others are willing to sell. Thus, if prices and open interest rise, it is not that there are more longs than shorts (for that would be impossible), but rather that it is the longs who are making the running in the market. Second, volume and open interest can only be assessed in relation to the history of the market itself and, as we have seen, the levels of trade vary considerably from market to market. Thus a level of volume and open interest which would seem low for one commodity, for instance, soybeans, would be very high for another, for instance, cocoa.

Bullish consensus indicators

An important idea underlying the use of volume and open interest is that there are only a finite number of people who are likely to take a position on a market. From this, it follows that once everyone who thinks the market will move up has taken out a long position, there will be no more buying pressure, and prices have nowhere to go but down. This idea lies behind '*contrarian*' trading, whose devotees wait until a predominant view has emerged and then do the opposite. The best indication of the state of majority opinion is provided by the US weekly, *Consensus*. This magazine surveys the attitudes of the major professional commodity brokers and advisers, and sums these attitudes in the Index of Bullish Market Opinion. This index is bounded between zero and 100. High values indicate that a predominant number of people are bullish towards a market, and low numbers that a predominant number are bearish. These situations are termed 'overbought' and 'oversold' respectively. Contrarian traders see extreme levels of this index as implying that a move in prices is running out of steam and will shortly be corrected, simply because if everyone agrees on price direction there is no fresh money available to move the market.

This kind of trading would work very well if the pool of traders (and money) were exactly fixed, which of course it is not. The index can make no allowance for how bullish people are; if a number of traders are extremely bullish (or bearish), presumably they will be willing to commit more resources to the trade and may be able to draw new traders into the market. Thus for a long time it is possible for a market to appear 'overbought' as these new resources enter the market. None the less, markets rarely keep moving uninterruptedly in one direction for long; if prices move down sharply, many people will hold large profits on short positions entered before the move. If the trading community becomes bearish, a very low, oversold level will appear on the Consensus Index. As profitable shorts take their profits and close out these positions, the market will register buying pressure, but in order to get other traders to sell in an oversold market, the shorts will need to bid up prices. Thus the simple process of profit-taking prevents a market from moving monotonically, a rather important fact which speculators would do well to note.

Commitments of traders

The volume and open interest statistics and the Index of Bullish Market Opinion help us to draw conclusions about the activities of all traders. Yet it is often helpful to know in more detail what the various types of traders are doing since some of them are more likely to be right than others. For example, if exporting firms are buying soybeans, it usually means they have orders to fill; they rarely speculate aggressively. They are far more likely to know what the short-term export outlook for soybeans is than a dentist in Edinburgh, even if the dentist is a successful speculator. On a day-to-day basis it is difficult to develop a clear picture of who is buying and selling, not least because the large operators will always try to cover their tracks (by trickling orders into the pit and using locals as well as their own floor traders) to avoid driving prices against themselves. Analysts do try to follow the flow of orders, and it is certainly to the advantage of locals on the trading floor that they know better than anyone else where the buying and selling pressure is coming from.

Fortunately, some data on this are available, at least for US markets. Every month the Commodity Futures Trading Commission (CFTC) releases reports giving the extent of open commitments held by traders. These reports break down traders into three categories: hedgers, large speculators, and what are called non-reportable positions. This last category is taken to represent small speculators since it contains only traders holding positions which are smaller than the level at which the positions have to be reported to the CFTC. (These data are collected by the CFTC to help it prevent manipulation of prices by large traders.) for each group the total of long and short position is reported, and for large speculators the total of spreads (i.e. the number of longs which are held against shorts) is also reported. These data allow one to assess the extent to which recent price trends have been driven by speculative pressure or commercial demand. Hedgers, for example, a large component of whom are trading companies, will build up their long positions when they have large orders in the pipeline; conversely, if prices have been going up but there has been a large increase in speculative long and commercial short positions, one should be wary of joining in the rally. Unfortunately, comparable data are not available for UK markets; although the Bank of England does monitor markets and has a clear idea of the positions of different groups, it does not make this information public.

Chart analysis

Perhaps the most frequently used technical trading tool is a chart of price developments. The most commonly used type of chart is a daily bar chart, which summarizes each day's price movements by a vertical line connecting the highest and lowest prices recorded during the day; a tick to the left of the line is placed at the opening price, and a tick to the right is placed at the closing price. There are a number of variations on this type of chart: sometimes the opening tick is omitted, sometimes only the closing price is plotted, and at other times it is plotted for each five minutes' worth of trading rather than for each day.

Another type of chart kept by some traders is a point and figure chart, measuring each upward price movement of a predetermined magnitude with a cross and each downward price movement of the same magnitude with a zero. The chartist chooses his own magnitude: it may be as little as a tick or, for long-term charts, as much as several full points. Each column represents each consistent movement of prices, and a new column is begun when prices change direction (provided that the change is large enough). Thus, unlike the bar chart, the point and figure chart does not measure time along the horizontal axis. There is considerable division of opinion about the usefulness of this type of chart: while it has fervent adherents, to many the charts seem complicated to construct and even superfluous since they contain little information which is not present on a bar chart.

Common chart formations

The easiest way to understand how charts are used is to consider some examples. Figure 3 shows the path of the July 1982 sugar

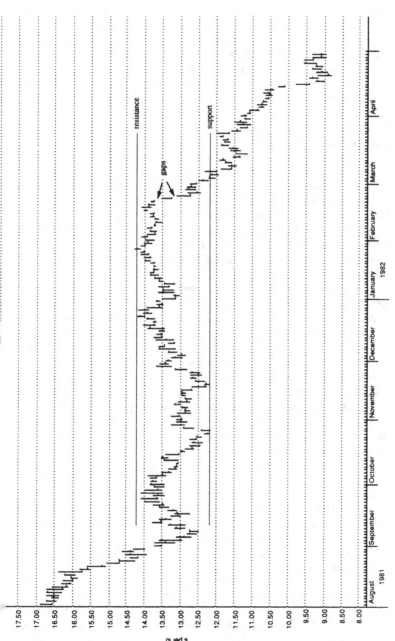

Figure 3. July 1982 sugar (no. 11) prices, New York CSCE (daily, high, low, and close)

futures contract on the New York Coffee, Sugar and Cocoa Exchange, from August 1981 to April 1982. This is an example of a bar chart, showing the highest and lowest prices recorded on each trading day. The tick to the right of each line is the closing price for each day. As the chart illustrates, sugar prices decline quite sharply over this period; they were almost 17 cents per pound at the beginning of the period, but only 9 cents at the end. The decline was not steady throughout these months, however; from September 1981 until the following February, prices fluctuated between 12.25 and 14.25 cents.

A chartist would draw two parallel lines on this chart, at the lower and upper ends of this trading range. These are the support and resistance lines; they correspond to levels at which fresh buying or selling emerged to keep the market in the range. In mid-October and again in mid-November 1981, prices bounced off the support line; in late September, in December, and in January and February of 1982 prices bounced off the resistance line. (In January the price briefly traded above the line, but not for long enough to constitute a decisive break.)

For prices to break through support or resistance, some new development must take place to provide a new impetus. The widespread use of charts by traders does mean that any movement through support or resistance will be quickly followed by new technical trading, since it is thought that the penetration of these levels means that prices will go a lot further. Obviously, support or resistance levels are usually not arbitrary; for example, a resistance level might be the price at which a government begins disposing of its stockpiles. The chart provides a visual guide to this, and if prices move through this level, it must be a sign that many traders are confident that the new supplies from the stockpile can be easily absorbed by the market.

Returning to Figure 3, it can be seen that the support line was decisively broken in late February 1982, and price quickly moved down to 9 cents. The alert chartist would have been paying close attention to the price of sugar in February as it descended rapidly towards its support line. In particular, the chart shows some gaps. They are marked on the Figure 3.

A gap is formed when the high of one day is lower than the low of the next, or, as in this case, when the low of one day is higher than the high of the next. This often happens when there is some item of news affecting the market, which occurs while the market is closed. This will cause the market to open at a much higher or lower price. It is also usually taken to be a sign of further major price movement. The chartist who had been watching sugar trading in its 2 cent range since September would be alert to the possibility that these gaps could signal the new development required to push the price out of this range. He would therefore be watching closely to see whether the support held. If it did not, the chartist would sell short on this signal.

Gaps are followed very closely by technical analysts. Many traders wait for gaps to be 'filled' on subsequent days, i.e. for trading to take place at the prices that were skipped over at the time of the major move. If a gap is filled but the market resumes its trend, it is taken to be a strong signal. Gaps which are opened, but not quickly filled can provide a new level of support or resistance at a later date. For example, if sugar price, on the July 1982 chart, had only fallen to 11 cents after breaking its support line, and had then turned higher, many chartists would be watching to see if the gaps opened in mid-February would provide some new resistance.

In Figure 3, the two lines drawn on the chart are parallel to the horizontal axis. If they were rising, they would be taken to indicate an uptrend; if falling, a downtrend. In the case of uptrends, however, often only the lower of the two lines is drawn, and in the case of a downtrend only the upper line. (Examples of trend lines are shown in Figure 6, which is discussed below.)

It can be appreciated that one of the key problems in price analysis is to determine when a change in market direction is taking place. The sugar chart above, Figure 3, shows that a breach of a support or resistance line can provide a valuable clue about price direction. There are numerous other chart patterns, however, which are taken to be significant. Perhaps the most famous is the so-called 'head and shoulders' top (and its opposite, the 'inverted head and shoulders'). This is a three-peak formation, in which the middle peak is higher than the first and third.

Figure 4 shows an example of such a formation, again drawn from the sugar market. In this example, however, it is the August 1981 contract in London which is charted. The left shoulder was formed by the break of £400 in late September, following which the price fell back to £370. The price rallied again, achieving a peak above the level of the left shoulder and forming the head. After falling, it rallied a third time to form the right shoulder. This formation suggests to the chartist that a short position should be taken, but at what point can the formation be said to be completed? The key to this is the 'neckline', which joins the bottom of the two shoulders. On Figure 4, the neckline is formed by joining the two lowest *closing* prices; an alternative is to join the two lowest recorded prices which, in this case, would produce a line sloping down to the right. The pure chartist would sell short as soon as the neckline is breached.

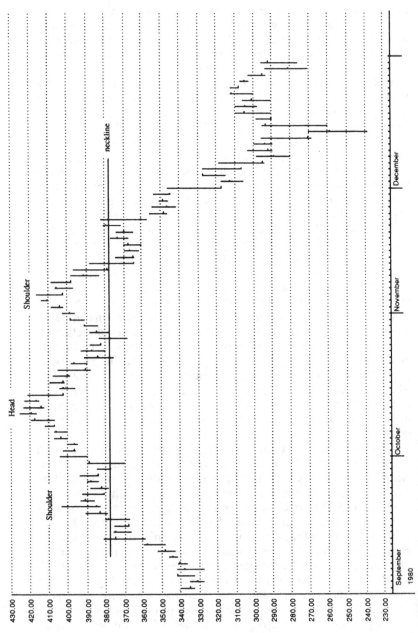

£ per tonne

Head

Shoulder

Shoulder

neckline

430.00
420.00
410.00
400.00
390.00
380.00
370.00
360.00
350.00
340.00
330.00
320.00
310.00
300.00
290.00
280.00
270.00
260.00
250.00
240.00
230.00

September
1980

October

November

December

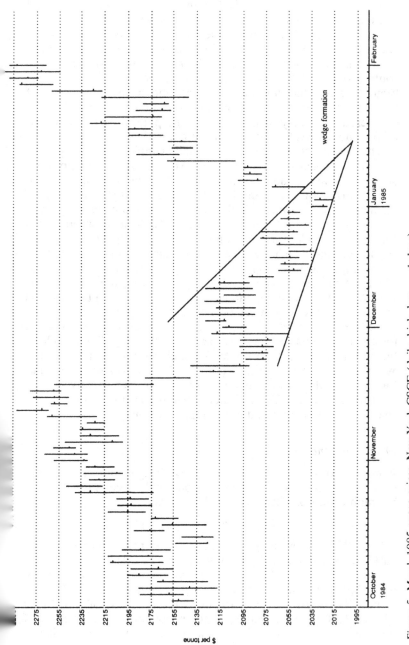

Figure 5. March 1985 cocoa prices, New York CSCE (daily, high, low, and close)

Another pattern is formed when the trend lines (or support and resistance lines) are not parallel, but converge. An example is shown in Figure 5, a chart of the March 1985 New York cocoa contract. The pattern shown here is called a falling wedge. Although the price had fallen sharply in mid-November and continued to fall throughout December, the convergence of the trend lines is a sign that the downward move was running out of momentum. Hence any fresh bullish news would be unlikely to be countered by heavy selling, and a sharp upward move would follow once prices had broken out of the wedge.

The above constitute just a small sample of the types of formations which chartists look for. Among other formations are double tops and double bottoms, formed when prices make a 'M' or 'W' formation (an example of a double top is shown in Figure 6); flags, pennants and triangles, which are variants on the wedge pattern we saw in Figure 5, island tops, formed when prices gap higher, trade for only one day at the higher level, then gap lower, and which are taken to be a strong indication that the prevailing trend will reverse itself; and key reversals, which occur when the market reaches a new high (or low), then, during the same day, turns direction and closes below (or above) the close on the previous day. The more pronounced this pattern is, the more significant it is held to be. There are probably as many chart formations and patterns as there are chartists; they all tend to have their own particular theories about which are the most significant. What is more, it is rare to see textbook examples of these chart formations. More often, patterns are rather seen creatively, and used to explain a price movement after the event. None the less, charts are extremely useful in trading, as we shall see.

Momentum indicators

A number of indicators are used to give insights into the strength of price movements. One which is commonly used is the Relative Strength Indicator (RSI). This is defined as follows:

$$RSI = 100(RS/(1 + RS))$$

Where RS is the weighted average of daily price increases in the past n days divided by the weighted average of daily price declines in the past n days. (The number of days, n, can be chosen by the user; the creator of the RSI used 14 days, but a 9-day RSI is very commonly used.) The weights are determined as follows. Begin with an RSI for a day based on the simple arithmetic average of the past n days. From that point on, each day's price change receives a weight of $1/n$, and the previous day's weighted average change receives a weight of $n - 1/n$. It follows that the more days of price increase there have been during the previous n days, and the larger these price rises have been compared to the declines, the greater will be the value of *RS*; indeed *RS* approaches infinity during periods of continuous price rises. The RSI, however, is bounded between zero and 100. The creator of the RSI suggested that values over 70 indicate that a top is near, and values under 30 indicate a bottom is near.

It should be clear that this kind of indicator would work best in a market where prices followed a regular cycle, oscillating between highs and lows, either in a trend or sideways. Certainly, if prices are going up but the RSI does not go up, there is a clear signal that upward price momentum is running out of steam and a top may be near. (This must be the case, since the RSI will only fail to go up if the price rises are of smaller and smaller magnitude.) Like the contrarian theory, however, this kind of momentum indicator does not work when prices are steadily setting new highs or lows because there is new information, and new participation in the market.

Moving averages

One way in which the direction of a trend can be distilled from the volatile day-to-day movement of prices is the use of moving averages. A moving average is simply an average where the value for any given day is the average of a number of days, centred on the given day. Thus a five-day moving average will produce as the value for any Wednesday the arithmetic average of the values for the five days Monday to Friday. One feature of moving averages is that they are never available for the current day; the latest one available will be for $n/2$ days ago, where n is the number of days in the moving average.

Moving averages remove short-term cycles in prices, and give a clearer indication of the underlying trend. One common use of them in technical trading is to compute two of different length, say, a five-day and ten-day average. Obviously the longer period average will be less volatile. When the two moving averages cross on the chart, the prevailing trend in prices has altered, and this generates a trading signal.

Clearly trading on this basis is very similar to trading a trend visually identified on a chart. Moving averages do no more than provide an objective measurement of the existence of a trend.

Technical systems

A technical trading system is simply a set of rules which are rigidly adhered to in trading. An example might be: buy when the five- and ten-day moving averages cross and hold the position until they cross again. This is a very simple kind of rule, and one might wish to add a number of conditions such as the requirement that volume and open interest are rising. Other rules might be: sell on a close below the three-day moving average. Most of these systems are not commodity specific. They are as applicable to pork bellies and soybeans as to the dollar/yen exchange rate. They rest only on the assumption that price behaviour follows regular patterns for enough of the time to make money. Of course, it is possible to build commodity-specific information into the system, incorporating the seasonality of agricultural commodities, for example, or the cyclical behaviour of interest rates. A decision rule for one commodity might be different from that in another commodity because of their different historical price behaviour. Their attraction is that they provide objective rules for entering, holding, and cutting positions and do not rest on human decisions.

With a computer, it is a comparatively straightforward, if time-consuming job, to trawl various decision rules through a mass of historic price data and see how they perform; without a computer, it is not worth attempting. The key problem with these systems is the number of false signals they give since there will always be times when prices do not move in a smooth pattern. Analysis of price trends shows that the problem lies when prices appear to break from their prevailing trend, but after a few days resume their earlier direction. This causes problems because it is most profitable to get into a market as soon as possible after prices change direction; if you wait until a new trend is clearly established, the profit potential is much reduced. Hence the two poles of trading systems are, on the one hand, an extremely sensitive and active system which makes a large number of wrong trades but a sufficient number of extremely profitable trades to end with an overall profit, and on the other hand, a less sensitive system which trades infrequently but should always turn a small profit.

Some individuals have spent many years developing their own trading systems, and they continue to attract devotees: the Elliot Wave theory, for example, was developed after its originator lost heavily in the 1929 stockmarket crash, but it is widely used in commodity markets. Another popular system is that developed by Professor W.D. Gann, which is essentially numerological in its approach. There are also astrological theories of price movements, but students of the truly arcane are referred to a 1986 Japanese publication, *The Japanese Chart of Charts* by Seiki Shimizu.

There are a large number of computer-managed commodity funds available to investors, which trade the markets using technical decision rules. Many of them show consistent real returns to their investors. Their disadvantage, from the individual speculator's point of view, is that they require their clients to be entirely passive. One of the reasons for getting involved with commodity markets is that they are an enjoyable vehicle as well as a remunerative one. The type of person who invests in a commodity fund is not likely to be the type of person who wishes to become actively and enjoyably involved in trading commodities. Of course, one can build and operate one's own technical system, but this requires considerable time and computing resources, and is likely to appeal only to full-time traders.

Using technical factors to trade

As a way of illustrating the use of technical factors in trading, let us take an example of a market and see how the chart can be used. Cotton was in a strong uptrend throughout the early months of 1987. There were good fundamental reasons for this: demand for cotton was growing, thanks to good economic conditions, and the US government had adopted an aggressive policy of export subsidies to move surplus stocks on to the world market; thus stocks were being steadily drawn down. The chart in Figure 6 shows the movements of the December New York cotton contract from 1 March to 19 October 1987.

An upward trend line is drawn in for the market during March and early April. This was a sufficient justification for taking out a long position at, say, 55 cents per pound. On 10 April the market gapped higher; it did so again on the next trading day, Monday, the 13th. This confirmed that the market was in a strong bull trend, and long positions taken out in the mid-1950s were showing handsome profits. (The New York cotton contract is 50,000 lb, so each cent move in the futures contract represents a change in contract value of $500.) In late April and early May it was clear the market was going higher, but how high? Where would it be prudent to take profits? One solution to this is to move a stop order along the trend line, so that the stop is hit when the market breaks from the trend. By late May there were two possible trend lines. One, marked A on the chart, connects the lows of 23 April and 4 May. The other, marked B, connects the lows of 6 April and 4 May. Moving the stop daily along these lines would have resulted

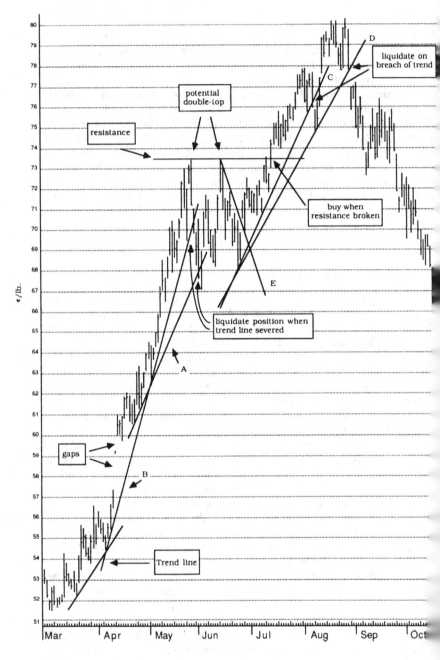

Figure 6. New York cotton: an example of chart-based trading
(December 1987 contract, 1 March–19 October, 1987)

in the long position being liquidated either on 29 May at a price of just over 70 cents per pound (trend B), or on 2 June at a price of about 68 cents per pound. Since a stop is a market order, the price at which it is filled cannot be guaranteed; hence one cannot be precise about the price at which the long position is closed out.

If we assume that the long position had been initiated at 55 cents per pound, liquidation would have brought profits of $7,500 per contract on 29 May (70 minus 55 multiplied by $500), or of $6,500 on 2 June (68 minus 55 multiplied by $500). Liquidation at the high of the market, over 73 cents per pound on 28 May and again on 15 June, would have made these profits even greater, but it is always difficult to predict precisely the top of a market.

Having fallen over 5 cents from the high on 28 May, the market rallied, but again failed to break above the previous high. Therefore, after the market closed on 15 June, one could draw a horizontal resistance line at 73.6 cents. On 16 June the market opened lower, never traded above the previous day's close, and closed at the session low, just over 71.00 cents per pound. After the close on 16 June, it therefore appeared as though a double top had been formed. This suggested that a short position would be appropriate for an aggressive trader, and the stop would have been placed either just above the resistance line or, more aggressively, along the downtrend line, marked E, formed by connecting the highs of 15 and 16 June.

As subsequent market behaviour shows, a stop placed just above the resistance line would have been hit on 15 July, causing the trade to sustain a loss. It is highly likely, however, that the kind of aggressive trader who would take a short position with the double top imperfectly formed would run a stop along the trend line; this would have been activated on 26 June, when the market gapped higher. This short position would have made virtually no profits, since the entry and stop loss prices would have been more or less the same. A more cautious trader, who would have noticed the double top forming, would have waited until the market had fallen through the level set on the first downward sweep of the top, i.e. 67.2 cents per pound, reached on 3 June. Of course, this the market failed to do.

Some evidence that the market was regaining upward momentum was provided on 26 June and 10 July, when the market gapped higher. These are not particularly bullish gaps, however, since the intervening prices had been traded a few days earlier. Nevertheless, on 15 July the market broke through the resistance line and, more significantly, closed above it. This is a strong buy signal, and a long would have been initiated either on

15 July or the next day for a less aggressive trader. Let us assume the buying price was 74.5 cents per pound. Again, the problem arises of a target for profit-taking. The two trend lines, marked C and D in Figure 1, provide some guidance; a trailing stop could be moved daily along one of these lines, allowing the position to be cut out as soon as the market fell out of the uptrends indicated by the lines. Such stops would have liquidated the long position on either 7 August (at approximately 76.2 cents per pound), or 31 August (at approximately 76.5). Profits would have been broadly similar at about 2 cents, or $1,000. Note that when the market broke the trend line D, it did so by gapping lower, a bearish signal which should have encouraged some traders to go short. In the event, these shorts would have yielded substantial profits.

The technical trader would therefore have made good profits on the cotton market over this period. Interestingly, the profits fall far short of those which could have been achieved by running the initial long position, bought at 55 cents per pound, all the way to the high at 80 cents per pound; these profits would have amounted to 25 cents, or $12,500 per contract.

What would a fundamental trader have been doing over this period? Supply–demand fundamentals suggested a long position from the late spring, when it became clear that there had been some problems with the progress of cotton planting and when both global demand for cotton and the US government's aggressive export policies were indicating a steady fall in stocks. Weekly export figures for cotton were consistently good: many of the gaps and strong days during the bull move coincided with the release of export figures or estimates for supply and demand in the USA and other important countries. Many fundamental analysts were looking for prices to reach the middle 70s, but were certainly inclined to take their profits when the market looked like forming a double top in May and June. There was a widespread expectation that once the bulk of the new crop became available from October onwards (although some Texas farmers harvest as early as July), prices would fall a little. Indeed the October contract was consistently at a premium over December for this period, reflecting the expectation for increased supplies and lower prices with the new crop. Few fundamental traders expected new crop prices to reach 80 cents per pound; most who were still long in August came out of the market early in the month when the prices moved down from 78 cents to 75 cents, which they reached on 10 August.

The above example shows many of the strengths of chart analysis. It also shows that the whole process is not entirely objective; the individual must use discretion in interpreting trends and chart formations. Moreover, not all technical indicators point in the same direction; although volume and open interest were rising steadily up to the peak in prices, the nine-day RSI peaked at 87 cents on 28 May and was only 65 cents when the market pushed through 80 cents on 27 August. This could have been interpreted as a buy signal!

Technical and fundamental analysis compared

Fundamental and technical approaches to markets rest on different propositions about the behaviour of prices: are they random, or are they not? This is a rather arid, academic debate, the result of which depends critically on the time period over which the analysis takes place. From the point of view of trading, each method of analysing markets has its strengths and weaknesses, and the cautious trader will only take a position when both techniques point to the same conclusion. There are, however, a number of observations which can be made about these two approaches and their usefulness in generating a trading decision.

Fundamental analysis often gives inadequate guidance about when to initiate a trade. There is an enormous temptation for analysts to recommend a position in a market as soon as they have completed running their models or assessing supply and demand in some other way. Yet the fact that an analyst has just discovered something does not mean it will come as a surprise to the market; the supply–demand problem which is news to the trader may be old hat to the market.

Detailed statistical forecasting of a market tends to work better when the source of instability is on the demand side. It is comparatively easy to develop models which are sensitive to changes in economic conditions and population growth; these variables can themselves be forecast with a tolerable degree of certainty, and reasonable forecasts of price can be made. Where the source of instability is weather-induced fluctuations in supply, however, it is difficult to build a model which does anything more than assess the impact on price of any given change or expected change in supply. Since markets are most sensitive to unexpected developments, and since the unexpected (clearly) cannot be forecast, fundamental analysis is vulnerable to be proved hopelessly incorrect by a new development. In this context, fundamental analysis is only useful in helping the analyst decide whether, after some time has passed, the market has fully incorporated the consequences of a new development.

A final weakness of the fundamental approach is that it can lead one to greater and greater losses. If statistical analysis leads to the conclusion that cocoa is cheap at £1,000 per tonne, it must conclude that a long position is even more strongly justified at £900 per tonne. Meanwhile a lot of money would have been lost on the long position taken out earlier. Because a technical analysis system is constantly being re-evaluated, and is basically following a trend, it will rapidly turn bearish as cocoa falls from £1,000 to £900.

Technical analysis has the great strength that it helps in determining the optimum time at which to initiate a trade, and that it rapidly corrects errors; conversely, it has the weakness that it generates a large number of false signals.

This suggests two main conclusions. The first is that technical analysis should be used to determine the timing of a trade whose justification is an anticipated imbalance of supply and demand. It should also be used to help determine where a stop is to be placed. The second is that fundamental analysis should be used to help indicate which technical signals are false ones. As we shall see in Chapter 5, stop positioning and the proper initiation of trades are crucial to successful futures trading.

Chapter five

Techniques for successful trading

Commodity prices are volatile, and futures markets provide a high degree of leverage. Thus there is clearly the potential for substantial profits. Yet both the evidence presented in Chapter I and the number of stories about the losses incurred by individuals suggest that it is difficult to make money trading futures markets. How can this apparent contradiction be resolved?

Many of the speculators who lose money on futures markets do so through failure to apply some basic guidelines to their trading. Some become addicted to trading, much as they might to gambling, and they will inevitably lose large sums of money. Others become attracted by the idea of trading, open a small account, take the first two or three recommendations from the commission house's research department, and then are surprised when they find themselves down at the end of a couple of months. Trading futures markets is no passport to easy riches; like almost any other area of human endeavour, there is a correlation between the initial investment of time, the level of understanding, and the degree of success.

This chapter lays down some basic guidelines for successful trading and looks, in turn, at futures and options markets. We do not present a recipe for certain success – and much of what we can say here will be startling for its lack of originality! Yet received wisdom is not to be dismissed lightly; most people who have lost money on futures markets have done so because they have failed to observe some of this.

Most important, trading futures and options is about risk and reward. Generally speaking, risk is directly related to profit potential. Compared to a savings account in a bank, trading futures has more risk and a potential for higher profit. But it does not follow from this that all futures trading is equally risky – or has the same trade-off between risk and reward. Risks range from the small to the frighteningly large; rewards range from huge losses to spectacular profits. Successful trading involves keeping losses as small as possible, by careful placing of stops, maximizing profits, by avoiding premature profit-taking, and finding a comfortable level of risk.

Trading straight futures positions

A straight futures position is the kind of position which most speculators are likely to have; that is, it is an outright long or short position in a market. A typical trader will have several such positions running at any given time. Because they are outright positions, their profit (and loss) potential is limited only by the fact that prices cannot fall to zero. For example, if you are long of soybeans at $6.00 per bushel, your contract value will fluctuate by $50 each time the market moves by 1 cent. If soybeans fall in value to $3.50, you will make a loss of $12,500 on each contract. The size of this loss is constrained only by the inability of soybean prices to fall to zero (and the extremely low probability that they would fall anywhere near that level). Conversely, if the price rises to $9.00 per bushel, you will make $15,000 on each contract. There are no theoretical limits on this profit, although it would be hard to see soybean prices above a certain level. The size of these profits and losses ($15,000 and $12,500 per contract) is impressive when compared to the mere $1,500 which the Chicago Board of Trade would require as initial margin for a single contract position. Yet this kind of arithmetic suggests several observations about risking $1,500, when the profit and loss potential is as it is.

First, traders should know what they are doing. They should know why they are trading, what would make them change their minds, and what they are prepared to risk and how much they expect to gain. Futures trading is not a probability game: it is not like rolling a dice with fixed and known gains and losses attached to the numbers and with probabilities attached to each outcome. Hence it is not legitimate to ask the question; what are the odds of soybeans going to $7.00 per bushel in the next two months? If soybeans are $6.00 per bushel, then you will either have a reason for believing that prices will go up or you do not. If not, do not trade the market. If you do, you should also know when you will come out of the market. As an example, consider two different, hypothetical reasons for buying soybeans. First imagine that dry weather is stressing the Brazilian soybean crop, and you believe that expectations of a shortfall will push prices to $7.00 per bushel. In this case, you will liquidate your position if news arrives of more favourable weather in Brazil and of prospects for a record crop in

Argentina. If, however, the weather remains bad in Brazil and prices reach $7.00, you will have to ask yourself whether there is any justification for a further move. Alternatively, imagine that you are a technical trader and you find technical indicators which you believe will lead prices to rally to $7.50. If this is the case, you will liquidate your position only when the target is reached or when the technical picture has changed.

Knowing why you are taking a position allows an assessment to be made of what would cause a change of mind. This means determining at what point you have been proved wrong and must take your loss. It is an excellent general rule that losses should be cut as soon as possible, limiting the financial if not the psychological consequences of a wrong decision. This can be done most easily by placing a good-'til-cancelled (GTC) stop order in the market at a predetermined level as soon as the trade is initiated. The location of the stop can be determined by the chart, which would place it at a significant support/resistance level, or it can be determined by the amount of money which can be risked on the trade. In this case, the maximum amount of variation margin which you wish to put into the market is committed in advance. Either way, a stop-loss order defines the risk which is to be run in any trade.

By the same token, knowing why you are trading defines the reward which you expect to receive since it defines an objective. No trade should be initiated unless potential rewards exceed the risked sum by a substantial amount; many traders work with the rule-of-thumb that reward should exceed risk by a factor of 3. Of course, this is no more than a rule-of-thumb, but it is useful in concentrating the mind on the relationship between risk and reward. Professional traders often assume large risks for small potential rewards, but theirs is not an example which should be followed by smaller, less experienced speculators.

A stop-loss is useful in limiting risks and losses. Clearly, one should also try to maximize profits. If there is a single 'secret' to futures trading it is to combine these two; that is, to cut losses and run profits. Adhering to this allows successful traders to show overall profits, despite participating in more losing than winning trades. Remember that the point of trading is to make money – not to get more markets right than wrong! If you lose $500 on each of nine trades, but make $10,000 on the tenth, you will show an overall profit, even though you will win no prizes for forecasting commodity price movements. Of course, it is unlikely that anyone would produce this kind of sequence of losses and gains, but most traders do make more losses than profits. They end up in profits by ensuring the losses are small and the profits large. The commonest mistake made by speculators is to do the exact opposite, by running losing positions (on the ground that 'it will come good eventually') and by taking profits when they are small (on the ground that any profits have to be seized as quickly as possible before they evaporate).

One reason why it is important to maximize profits is that commodity prices do not randomly fluctuate; they display trends which are more long-lasting than would be expected if prices were stochastic. An implication of this is that it is less than twice as difficult to benefit from a 100-point market move than two 50-point moves in two markets. It is also more profitable, since commission only has to be paid once.

One way of maximizing profits is to increase one's exposure in a market which is going the right way. Again, this should be done in such a way as to balance the risk–reward ratio appropriately, however. Increasing exposure is sometimes called 'pyramiding', and it is important to ensure that the pyramid of positions rises to a peak, rather than being built upside down. Thus it is prudent to add to a position in decreasing amounts (e.g. start with five contracts, add a further three as they move into profit, and then one more later on), but it is imprudent to add to it in increasing amounts (e.g. start with one, add three, and then five more). The former is the prudent course for two reasons: first, because it does not put at risk the entire profit from the initial position and allows the largest part of the position to make the largest profits; and second, because even strongly trending markets do fluctuate within the trend, and these fluctuations can limit the profitability of the overall exposure if the later purchases are badly timed.

Although it is important to have an objective when initiating a trade, there is no need to take profits if the market has reached the objective but appears to be heading much further. A long sugar position, initiated because of a round of heavy Russian buying, need not be closed out at the original target if heavy Chinese buying emerges as well. Initial objectives clarify the risk–reward ratio but, as new information emerges, it is sensible to reassess the objective. It should also be borne in mind that trends in markets often last far longer than people initially think. A trailing stop, moved daily in line with the market, allows profits to be locked in without closing out the position. It is another way in which the profit potential of a winning trade can be maximized.

Frequently one problem which confronts traders is that the speed with which information is disseminated and incorporated into prices leaves too little time for action. By the time news of drought in Brazil has reached the Edinburgh dentist, Chicago soybean prices may appear to be reflecting a concern with something else. This has two consequences.

The first is that profit objectives need constant reassessment, an issue discussed above. The second is that it is often hard to be in a market early enough to make the greatest profit from a move. Yet against this must be set the undoubted fact that markets do trend. Taking a position against the trend, or on what turns out to be a false breakout of the trend, is highly risky. It is, in general, not worth worrying about trying to participate in the first few cents of a market move; if wheat is going from $2.50 to $3.50 per bushel, it does not matter a great deal whether a long position is initiated at $2.50 or $2.60. If the risk is considerably reduced by waiting for $2.60, it is prudent to do so. An oft-quoted adage is that 'the trend is your friend'; there may be good reasons for taking out a contrary position, but it is riskier than simply following the trend. Following trends often seems to be at variance with another famous piece of trading advice, to buy low and sell high. Yet this advice does not take into account the risk in buying low, which is that prices will continue to fall.

The balancing of risks and rewards is not simply a question of determining entry and exit points for individual trades. It is also an important feature of managing a portfolio of trades. One approach to futures markets holds that the only way to make money is to be in all markets at all times. Most of the positions will show small profits or small losses, but a small number will show huge profits. (Recall the evidence in Chapter 1 from Bodie and Rosansky's study of returns to futures investors, which found that the bulk of the profits made in over twenty years came from a small number of markets in a small number of years.) Since most traders have limited funds, this strategy is not open to them. What most traders can do, however, is diversify their portfolios. Given the behaviour of prices, it is a simple result from probability theory that the risks from exposure in more than one market do not increase at the same rate as the potential for profit. Hence it is prudent, in terms of risk and reward, to hold positions in more than one market. It does not follow from this that the same size of position should always be held in each market, although initial exposure will be similar.

Trading spread futures positions

To take a straight futures position is to take a view on the path of prices in absolute terms. It is possible, however, to have a view on relative, rather than absolute, prices; that is, to believe that the difference between two prices will change, irrespective of the direction of absolute price change. Futures markets allow one to trade on the basis of this kind of view, using what are known as 'spreads' (or straddles). These involve taking two positions, one long and one short. For example, you might believe that wheat is going to become relatively more expensive than corn, even though you do not claim to know whether grain prices as a whole will go up or down. The way to benefit from this is to take a long wheat and a short corn position. This will be profitable if the difference between the two increases, irrespective of whether they both go up or go down. The following example illustrates this.

Imagine that wheat is trading for $2.80 per bushel, and corn at $1.90 per bushel. The difference between the two is 90 cents, but you believe the difference will rise to 110 cents. You buy one contract of wheat at $2.80, and sell one lot of corn at $1.90. Recall that each contract is for 5,000 bushels, so the contract changes in value by $50 for each 1 cent change in the price quotation. Imagine that wheat prices go to $3.30, and corn prices to $2.20, and that you close out your positions at this level. Your long wheat contract yields a profit of 50 cents, equal to $2,500. Your short corn contract yields a loss of 30 cents, equal to $1,500, leaving you with a net profit of $1,000. Alternatively, imagine that wheat prices go to $2.70 and corn prices to $1.60, and that you close out your positions at this level. Your long wheat makes a loss of 10 cents, or $500, but your short corn makes a profit of 30 cents, or $1,500, leaving you with a net profit of $1,000.

In both cases, the difference between wheat and corn prices increased from 90 cents to 110 cents (i.e. 20 cents which, at $50 per cent, is $1,000) and allowed you to make a profit. Note, however, that this profit is smaller than it would have been had you correctly forecast the change in the underlying contracts themselves: in the first case, most profit would have been made by going long of both wheat and corn; and in the second by going short of both. In other words, a successful spread trade of this kind will always result in one leg making a loss and the other leg making a profit; the plan is that the profit is greater than the loss.

Spreads therefore have a different risk–reward profile from straight futures positions; generally they involve lower risk and have lower profit potential. They are a useful component of a portfolio, however, for several reasons. First, because they are less risky, which is particularly valuable in markets which are prone to sudden moves; second, because the initial margins required by exchanges for them are lower; third, because there may be occasions on which a spread trade more closely corresponds to what a trader has an opinion about; and fourth, because there may be spread opportunities when there is nothing else promising enough to trade.

There are three kinds of spread. The first, an inter-delivery month, or intra-commodity intra-market spread, involves taking a long position in one delivery month and a short position in another (e.g. long December soybeans and short March soybeans). The second, an inter-commodity spread, involves taking a long position in one commodity and a short position in another commodity, both for the same delivery month (e.g. long March wheat and short March corn). The third is an intra-commodity, inter-market spread, which involves taking a long position in one delivery month on one exchange, and a short position in the same commodity for the same delivery month on a different exchange (e.g. long New York March coffee and short London March coffee). Each of these has rather different characteristics.

Delivery spreads

Delivery spreads are extremely common in agricultural commodities, where the inherent seasonality of production means that there are often times of the year when supply and demand considerations push one delivery month to a large premium. Two of the commonest spreads are bull spreads and bear spreads. A bull spread involves going long in a nearby month, and short in a more distant month, hoping that the nearby month will increase its premium over the deferreds. This is known as *bull spread* because it takes advantage of the tendency of nearby months to rise more sharply during bull markets. A *bear spread* involves the opposite: short in the nearby and long in the deferred; and it is used because nearby months tend to fall more sharply in declining markets. Since it is the case that nearby months absorb the brunt of the impact of major new developments, this type of spreading is a sensible, low-risk approach to markets which appear on the verge of setting new trends. As always, an outright long or short position would always prove to have been more profitable, but is riskier; the individual can choose between the two risk–reward profiles.

With storable commodities, there is a limit to the premium for distant months over the nearby contracts during any given crop year. This limit is set by the costs of physically storing the commodity from one period to the next; if a distant contract is selling at more than the full costs of storage, a trading company can buy the spot commodity, store it, and hedge it at a profit. This will continue until the premium has dropped to (or slightly below) the full carrying charge. This means that there is very little risk in buying a nearby contract and selling a deferred contract if the deferred is at a premium; the maximum risk is the full carrying charge. Conversely, there is no limit to the premium which a nearby month can enjoy over a deferred month; if there is a shortage of the material and if demand remains strong, the nearby month can go to a substantial premium over the deferred. Hence a bull spread, initiated when the deferred contract is at a premium, is a trade with a low and limited risk but a substantial profit potential.

Another delivery spread which is popular is the *old crop/new crop spread.* Every year, in markets like grains where there is a crop year, there is a body of information whose principal impact is on new crop prices. If current supply is tight and demand is strong but the weather is favourable for the crop which is still growing, the new crop price (in futures market terms the delivery contracts after the harvest) will go to a large discount to old crop prices. In this situation a long old crop/short new crop spread will yield even larger profits than a single straight futures position, because the absolute changes in price will work to put each leg of the spread into profit. Recall, however, that risk and profit potential are generally positively correlated; old crop/new crop spreads are very volatile and are therefore risky. The fact that both legs can be profitable means that both can show losses.

Spread relationships are also highly volatile in non-storable commodities such as live cattle and live hogs. Because these cannot be stored from one month to the next, each contract price reflects expected supply and demand in the contract month, rather than the cost of storing from the present into the future. Of course, spreading is very common in the livestock futures markets, but there is no such thing as a limited risk spread in cattle and hogs.

A more sophisticated delivery spread trade is a *butterfly spread,* which involves positions in three, rather than two, delivery months. A typical butterfly spread would be five short December, ten long March, and five short May, and the aim of the trade would be to profit from changes in the relationship between the December/March spread and the March/May spread. The profit potential in this type of trade is limited, and it is best left to professionals.

Inter-market and inter-commodity spreads

Spreading different commodities and different markets is altogether more complicated. The idea is straightforward, as can be seen by considering one of the simplest of such spreads, the wheat protein spread. In the USA there are three wheat futures markets; Chicago, Kansas City, and Minneapolis. Each trades a different grade of wheat: spring wheat in Minneapolis, hard red winter wheat in Kansas City, and soft red winter in Chicago. These wheats differ in their suitability for different applications and in their protein content. (It is really their protein content which determines their suitability for different uses.) Spring wheat has the highest protein content, followed by hard winter, followed by soft winter; and it is normally the case that the higher the protein content, the higher the price. The exact price relationships between these three classes of wheat, however, are determined by the supplies of and demands for them; soft red winter wheat, for example, is the preferred grade for Chinese imports of US wheat since it is better suited to making the kind of noodles which are consumed in China. Hence, when the USA has a poor crop of soft winter wheat and there is good Chinese import demand, one would expect to see Chicago wheat prices rising to a premium over Kansas. Since the demands for these three types of wheat are separate, and since the growing regions and climatic requirements for winter and spring wheats are different, the protein spreads do vary considerably from one crop year to the next, and they provide many trading opportunities. Moreover, all three contracts are the same in terms of size, so it is very easy to calculate how the spread is moving.

Spreading only becomes complicated when the contracts are different in size, or unit of price quotation, or if they are very different in total value. Consider the coffee market, where New York's contract is for 37,500 lb of arabica coffee, quoted in cents per pound. The London contract, on the other hand, is for 5 tonnes of robusta coffee, quoted in pounds sterling per tonne. To calculate the spread one would need to convert London's metric unit into New York's avoirdupois unit, and one would also need to know the exchange rate. There is also a problem with the fact that New York's contract is over three times larger than London's. In order to produce a spread trade which is equally sensitive (in terms of the total value of the spread) to movements in both London and New York prices, it would be necessary to have more than three London contracts for every one held in New York. In order to see why this is so, let us take an example without the additional complexity of the exchange rate.

Take the soybean/corn spread. Soybean meal, the principal product of the soybean, is a high-protein animal feed; corn is a high-carbohydrate animal feed. The soybean/corn spread is an important indicator of the protein/carbohydrate price ratio which, in turn, has implications for animal feeding practices. It is a volatile spread. Both contracts in Chicago are the same size, 5,000 bushels (ignoring the fact that soybeans are marketed in bushels of 60 lbs, whereas a bushel of corn weighs 56 lb); soybeans are, however, considerably more valuable than corn; a typical price relativity would be $6.00 per bushel for soybeans, and $2.00 per bushel for corn. If you believe that protein is going to become relatively more expensive, a long soybean/short corn spread would be an appropriate vehicle. Let us imagine that the trade is initiated with one long soybean contract at $6.00, and one short corn at $2.00. The problem with this is that it is not equally sensitive to a given percentage move in each of the two contracts. Imagine that corn prices do not change, but soybean prices go up by 5 per cent, to $6.30. In this case, the spread is worth 30 cents more (which is $1,500 at $50 per cent). Conversely, if soybean prices do not move, but corn prices decline by 5 per cent, to $1.90, the spread has only increased in value by 10 cents, or $500.

To produce a spread trade which is equally sensitive to price movements on both legs of the spread, each leg should be weighted by the value of the contract at the time of inception. In the case of the soybean/corn spread, above, it would be appropriate to have three corn contracts for every soybean contract, thus equalizing the financial exposure on each side of the trade.

More generally, the desired ratio of contracts in the spread can be determined by the following formula:

$$X1/X2 = P2C2/P1C1$$

where 1 and 2 denote the two commodities, X denotes the number of contracts to be held in the spread, P denotes the price of the commodities at the inception of the trade, and C denotes the contract size. In the soybean and corn case, the contract sizes are identical, but with other spread trades, such as live cattle/live hogs, the contract sizes differ. Prices would also need to be converted to a common currency in the case of markets located in different countries and trading in different currencies.

Readers with a degree of mathematical sophistication will realize that this kind of spread trade is, in effect, taking a view on the *ratio* between two prices, not on the *difference* between two prices. In general, it makes more economic sense to trade the ratio, but there is no problem with trading a price difference, if that is what one wants to do.

A special kind of inter-commodity spread can be traded within the soybean complex. Soybeans are crushed to provide soybean meal and soybean oil and there are, as a result, close price relationships between the three commodities. Two common spreads are the oil–meal spread and the crush spread. Oil–meal spreading arises because the different demand conditions in the oil and meal markets mean that it is possible for one price to move one way, while the other moves the other way. Indeed, if there is weak demand for soybean oil but strong demand for soybean meal, crushers may well increase their meal production, activity which will inevitably lead to increased oil production. This will exacerbate the weakness in oil prices. Hence there may be circumstances where a long meal/short oil spread leads to increased profits. Again, this is a higher risk spread since both positions can move into loss.

A crush spread is a low-profit potential trade which aims to take advantage of difference between the price of soybeans on the one hand, and the price of the two products of crushing, oil and meal, on the other hand. Since crushers, the companies which buy beans and produce and sell meal and oil, ought to make a profit, the product prices ought always to exceed the price of the beans. That is, there should always be a positive 'crush margin'. Of course, since soybeans have virtually no uses apart from raw material for crushing, there is a limit to the divergence which is possible between bean prices and product prices (weighting the products by their extraction factors). Seasonal factors, however, and movements in the levels of stocks of the three commodities can produce fluctuations in crush margins; indeed they are sometimes negative. These fluctuations can be traded on a spread basis. In this case, however, it is clearly nonsensical to trade equal numbers of bean, meal, and oil contracts, as they are of a completely different order of magnitude. Using standard extraction factors, 5,000 bushels of soybeans (i.e. the Chicago Board of Trade, CBOT, contract size) would produce approximately 236,220 lb of soybean meal compared to a contract size of 100 short tons, and 54,645 lb of soybean oil, compared to a contract size of 60,000 lb.

Trading spreads successfully requires the same balance of risk and reward that trading straight positions requires. The risk–reward ratio differs considerably with spreads; generally speaking, the risks are low, but there are spreads (such as old crop/new crop) and soybean oil/soybean meal which are much more volatile. With these riskier markets, it is prudent to operate a stop-loss on each leg of the spread, although this is not necessary in a conventional delivery spread. With lower risk comes a lower profit potential, and this means that the trader needs to be more concerned about the particular price at which a trade is executed. For this reason, it is advisable only to spread in actively traded contracts. It is also advisable not to have one leg of a trade in the spot month, for two reasons. The first is that most spot months do not have daily limits on price movements, which means that the adverse effect of a limit move in one month is not counterbalanced by an equal move in another month; this can work to the spread's advantage, depending on the position in the spot month, but it is an unnecessary risk to shoulder. The second is that spot months inevitably reflect the short-term, localized supply and demand conditions. Since delivery is often made against agricultural futures, it is not wise to risk a trade going awry simply because a large number of soybeans turn up in Chicago one day. Because profit potential is limited, it is foolish to put this profit at the mercy of a localized, short-term fluctuation in the delivery month.

Trading options

Options are conventionally presented as instruments with lower risk than futures, but with unlimited profit potential. In fact, as we have seen in Chapter 2, their risk–reward profile is different from that of futures positions, but not in a particularly simple way. Certainly, it is wrong to regard options simply as a low-risk version of futures trading. Successful trading of options requires that careful attention be paid to the risk–reward possibilities.

Before we look in some detail at the possibilities opened up by trading options, a caveat is in order: the range of options available for trading is increasing steadily, but the number of agricultural markets which have built up a substantial volume of options trading is quite small. Because of the way options are priced with such an important component of their price coming from their extrinsic value, it is vitally important that one trades in liquid markets. Unfortunately, market liquidity is a virtuous circle which is hard to establish; without the initial liquidity, new traders are not confident enough to enter the market, but without their entry liquidity remains low. That, however, is a problem for the exchanges, not for the traders, and until the liquidity exists, it is best to stay clear of options markets. Quite simply, without an adequate volume of trade, one would have to pay a large amount of extrinsic value to buy an option, yet one would find, on selling it, that it would only command its intrinsic value. (In other words, the bid–offer spreads are far too wide in illiquid options markets.) At the time of writing, there are no more than a handful of agricultural options markets which are liquid enough to trade and they are all in America: on the CBOT soybeans, soybean meal, soybean oil, and corn; on the CME live cattle and live hogs; and on the

Coffee, Sugar and Cocoa Exchange raw sugar. The list of active options markets will grow, but the profitability of options trades is much more heavily dependent on there being a liquid market than that of futures trades, so it is extremely important to be confident that the market is active before trading it.

One should also be careful to trade options on futures, rather than options on physical commodities. Because the underlying futures markets are liquid, it is always possible, as a last resort, to close out an option by exercising it, provided that the underlying instrument is a futures contract. This means that an option on a futures contract will never be worth less than its intrinsic value. Options on physical commodities, however, are far less reliable because of the lower level of liquidity in physical trade. That one trades options on futures does sometimes cause difficulties, however, because of the expiry date. A 'November option' will really be an option on a November future and it will, as a result, expire in October.

Trading options is simply a matter of applying to markets the principles of option price determination which were presented in Chapter 2. Recall that the option premium is a function of three things: the relationship between the strike price and the price of underlying instrument (intrinsic value), the time remaining until the expiry of the option, and the volatility of the market (these two together comprising the extrinsic value). Recall also that the option's *delta* (the sensitivity of the option premium to changes in the underlying futures price) is variable: the delta is low for out-of-the-money options, close to 0.5 for at-the-money options, and asymptotically close to 1 for in-the-money options, the deeper in-the-money they become. Deltas for out-of-the-money options are also higher, the longer there is before expiration.

Buying options

Buying an option, also known as taking or going long of an option, is straightforward, but the risk–reward ratio varies depending on the delta. Going long of an in-the-money option is very similar to taking a straight futures position with a built-in stop. The risk is confined to the premium; the profit potential is similar to that on a futures position because the delta will be close to unity. The closer the option is to expiry, the more like a futures position the option will be. Clearly, buying a call, also called a 'long call', is similar to a long futures position, whereas buying a put, or a 'long put', is similar to a short futures position.

Going long of an at-the-money option is less like a futures

position because the delta is around 0.5. Hence small changes in the futures price will produce a smaller change in the option premium, and it will take a large movement in the futures price to move the option into profit. Theoretically, the profit potential is unlimited (except in so far as prices cannot fall to zero). Going long of an out-of-the-money option is very cheap and hence low risk, but the chance of profit is small since a large price move will be needed to move the premium into profit.

Granting options

Just like any other transaction, every option has a person on each side. The person who takes the opposite side from the buyer is not called the seller, however, since selling options is what buyers do when they close out their position. The other party is called the 'grantor', or 'writer'; hence one grants, writes, or goes short of an option. To understand exactly what happens, take the example of a 550 cent November soybean call. Let us also assume that, at the time of purchase, this is an at-the-money option. The buyer of this call option buys the right to buy a November soybean futures contract at 550 cents, and for this right he pays the premium. The grantor receives the premium and, in return, takes on the obligation to sell a November delivery soybean contract for 550 cents. Hence the call buyer is bullish; he will be able to exercise or sell his option at a profit if the futures price moves about 550 cents. (Clearly, it has to move by more than the premium.) The risk is confined to the premium. The grantor's best hope is that the option will expire worthless, in which case the premium represents profit. It will expire worthless if November prices by the time the option expires are below 550 cents. Hence the call grantor is neutral-to-bearish. The grantor's loss potential is unlimited; if soybean prices rise, the grantor will face losses equal to the difference between the November price and 550 cents.

Hence a short at-the-money option position is a low-profit, unlimited risk trade. It is only appropriate when a small change in prices is envisaged. In the case of a short call (put), the maximum profit is the premium; hence if one is very bearish (bullish) of prices, there is lower risk and more profit potential in buying a put (call).

Going short of an out-of-the-money option reduces the profit potential since the premium received is lower, and will be an appropriate strategy when no major move in prices (towards and through the strike price) is foreseen. Going short of an in-the-money option is similar to taking a straight futures position. It is a slightly more profitable position when price changes are moderate, and slightly worse when they are dramatic.

The most important application for granted options in an investment portfolio is that they allow one to make money if prices do not move. The profitability of a straight futures position or a taken option position requires that prices move. An option grantor, on the other hand, receives the option premium and this will represent profit if the option expires worthless. While this happens most obviously in the event of a price move adverse to the taker, it can also happen in the case of a just out-of-the-money option if prices do not move. What is more, recall that part of the option premium will be time value, and this will erode as expiry approaches. Provided that an option has little or no intrinsic value, a grantor will tend to make money as an option moves closer to its expiry date. The value of the option premium will also decline (i.e. represent a loss to the taker and a profit to the grantor) if the volatility of a market decreases. Thus it can be sensible to grant an option shortly after prices have made a sharp move, on the grounds that option premiums reflect that move but prices will follow a less volatile path in the future.

Option grantors do not have to wait until expiry to realize their profit. They receive the premium on granting, but if they wish to remove the risk they are carrying, they can close out their option position by buying an option back. Thus an option granted at one premium can be bought back at another premium before expiry, securing a profit for the grantor (provided the second premium is cheaper in the market than the first), even if a later price move would have caused the granted option position to move into a large loss. Against this attractive feature of option granting, however, must be set the fact that risk is unlimited in the event of an unfavourable price move.

Spreading options

Just as two futures positions can be taken out, hoping to profit from moves in price differences, so option positions can be spread, to take advantage of differences in option premiums. Consider, for example, a long call and long put position, both purchased at-the-money. If prices do not move sharply in either direction, but the volatility of the market increases, both options will go up in value. Conversely, a short call and short put position will make most profit, if the volatility of prices drops, causing both premiums to decline. Thus a trader who has no view about price direction, but believes the volatility of price will change, can take a spread option position to profit from his view.

Combinations of options can also be used to produce market positions which are virtually identical to futures positions; thus a long call and short put combination is almost the same (in terms of risk and reward) as a long futures position, and a short call and long put combination is almost the same as a short futures position.

The possibilities are legion. One common type of spread trade is to buy one call and short a second call with a higher strike price. This is a somewhat less bullish trade than simply buying a call; the risk is lower since the cost of the bought call is partly offset by the premium received for the granted call. By the same token, the profit potential is lower, since higher prices will mean that the profits from the bought call will be partly offset by losses on the granted call.

As will be evident, trading options can become complicated, and more sophisticated trades, which typically have lower profit potential, are likely to be of interest to professionals, whose commission costs are negligible and who can time their entry and exit points very precisely. Within the constraints of this chapter, it is not possible to review the full range of possible trading strategies; interested readers are referred to more specialized texts.

Combined futures and options positions

Finally, it is possible to combine a futures and option position in a market. The most important way in which this can be done is as a lower-risk way of 'pyramiding' a profitable position. We have already seen that increasing one's exposure in a profitable position is one way of maximizing profits, but we also saw that it is important to do this in a way which minimizes risk. Adding a call option to a profitable long futures position (or a put to a short position) is one way in which the risk of an adverse move is minimized while the profit potential of further favourable moves is increased. Note that it is less advisable to add a futures position to an existing, profitable options position.

Other combination strategies are less advantageous; they are usually equivalent to a much simpler position and are only recommended by commission houses because they involve greater commission charges. For example, it is often recommended that a long out-of-the-money put be added to a long futures position as a way of protecting the profit on the futures position. The idea here is that if prices decline sharply, the eroding profit on the long futures is matched by the increasing profit on the put. The net loss is confined to the premium paid for the put. In fact this strategy is identical to buying an in-the-money call, in terms of market exposure; it simply results in the trader holding two positions (and hence paying two commissions) instead of one.

Another commonly recommended trade is a long futures and a short call position – sometimes presented as a well-hedged position. While some risks are reduced through this combination, it still involves the risk of a rapid and substantial price decline.

Choosing a position

The best position for an individual depends on that individual's expected probability of price distribution. That is, it depends on where an individual thinks price (or a price ratio) is going, how likely it is that price will overshoot that target and by how much, how long it will take to get there, and how volatile it is likely to be in the interim. These factors help define the acceptable level of risk and the vehicle which is best suited both to the risk and to the market objective. It is possible to become quite sophisticated about expected price distributions, but the key factors facing individual speculators are likely to be the size of price change and its timing.

Evaluating performance

Monitoring trading performance helps to identify weakness and therefore should help improve that performance in the future. After several months trading, a detailed log of executed trades will reveal to a careful eye where any problems lie: whether profits are too small, whether losses have been allowed to accumulate, whether options or futures have been better, whether bad pyramiding has led to reduced profits, and so on. Like anything else, commodity trading can be analysed and improved. Someone who is not prepared to do this would be better advised to invest money in a futures fund and not take an active role in trading.

Overall, however, the purpose of monitoring performance is to assess the level of return which has been achieved. Here the problem arises of the appropriate measure. Having a money management principle is vital to high risk investments; no one should ever put their grandmother's savings into futures markets. Most brokers will try to ensure that clients do not speculate with more than a third of their net liquid assets, and they will also limit clients' exposure in a single market to a fraction of the total invested sum. Clearly, individuals who wish to put their pension plans into the pork belly market are free to do so, but it is hardly prudent. Once the initial commitment of risk capital has been made, the return achieved from futures trading should always be measured against the total sum committed to the markets. This makes it difficult to assess each individual trade, but it is important not to measure each trade in a misleading way. It is improper, for example, to measure return from a trade against the original margin posted for the trade. Initial margin is not a cost, or a purchase price; indeed it is not a measure of anything. It is a good-faith deposit and is therefore irrelevant in terms of measuring capital or measuring return. Return should always be measured on the total capital placed at risk on the markets, not on the original and not on the maintenance margin posted for a particular trade.

One difficulty people have with this is that the value of a trading account held with a broker will fluctuate widely over the course of the year, resulting in an unstable estimate of return. This is particularly a problem for comparing trading systems when one is trawling them through past price data to find the best. The commonest way of accounting for this is the Sharpe ratio, defined as:

$$SR = (R - I)/sd$$

where R is the achieved overall rate of return, I is the rate of return which would have been obtained by putting the money into a risk-free instrument, such as a government security, and sd is the standard deviation of returns over the period. Unfortunately, despite being commonly in use, this ratio suffers from several drawbacks; notably, it is insensitive to the sequence in which losses and profits are sustained. It has the advantage, however, that it is easy to calculate, and when used in conjunction with a detailed log of executed trades can provide invaluable insights into how well an account has performed.

Some concluding comments

Speculators in commodity futures markets would do well to remember the old adage that there is 'no such thing as a free lunch'. When speculators make money, they do so through assuming risk, and unless they are astonishingly lucky, through the rigorous application of rules which manage risk and money. They do not blindly follow tips from friends or each and every recommendation from their brokerage firm. Remember that every transaction has one buyer and one seller, one person who makes a profit and one who makes a loss. It is vitally important to know what you are doing and why. It is possible to trade successfully by managing losses so they are small, and managing profits so they are large. The psychological pressures to run losses and take small profits are great enough to turn the majority of speculators into losers, irrespective of how well they forecast prices.

Chapter six

Grains

Grains – the basics

Grains have a central place in human diet all over the world. Evidence suggests that strains of wheat and barley were being cultivated as early as 6500 BC in western Asia, shortly after domestication of wild sheep and goats began in what is modern Turkey, Iraq, and Iran. Maize was being cultivated in central America by 5000 BC, and by 3000 BC grains were widely grown throughout Europe. The history of grain is almost as old as the history of settled agriculture.

From the earliest times grains were used for two purposes: as human food, and for feeding to livestock. Today they retain this dual role. The individual grains differ widely in their climatic and soil requirements and in their nutritional value, and for most of history the locally produced grain would be used for both purposes. In modern agriculture different grains are often used for these different purposes, but there is no easy distinction between foodgrains and feedgrains; as early as the eighteenth century Johnson's Dictionary defined oats as a 'grain, which in England is generally given to horses, but in Scotland supports the people'. Generally speaking, wheat and rice are the most important foodgrains, and corn (which is known as maize in Britain, but the term corn will be used here), sorghum, and barley are the most important feedgrains. The three latter grains are sometimes grouped with millet and rye, and known as coarse grains. Generally it can also be asserted that it is the grains with the lower protein content which are fed to livestock. It should not be forgotten, however, that large amounts of (low-quality) wheat are fed to livestock, especially in Europe and the USSR, and that corn and millet are human staples in many regions of the world. Another important use of grain which dates from the earliest times is the distillation of alcohol; although vital for human welfare, this is a small market in quantitative terms.

Because grains are grown very widely around the world, and

because they are so important in human diet, governments intervene heavily in grain markets, seeking to stabilize or raise the incomes of grain farmers and to ensure that consumer food prices are low, or at least stable. Given the difficulty of achieving both objectives, governments respond to the relative strength of the political forces mobilized by producers and consumers. Agricultural policies, especially in the USA and the EC, have a large and important impact on grains markets. Because of these policies, a large proportion of the world's grain is produced and consumed at prices set by governments and bearing only a tenuous relationship to the price of freely traded grains. The world market in freely traded grain is large enough, however, that it cannot be dismissed as residual; it is extremely important to many of the world's grain farmers and consumers.

The major grain futures markets are located in the USA. Although there are grain futures markets in London, they have limited significance because the EC's agricultural policy constrains the variability of European wheat prices and ensures there is only a very weak link between world market and EC grain prices. Thus the London grain markets have a low volume of trade and serve the needs of no more than the domestic grain trade. The following discussion is confined to the grains for which there are active futures markets, and for which these futures markets effectively determine world market prices. These grains are wheat and corn. There are futures contracts on oats and rice in Chicago and barley in Winnipeg, but they are only of specialized interest.

Wheat – production, consumption, and prices

In terms of consumption, wheat is the most important foodgrain and is arguably the most important food source in the world. Its principal usage is bread, but wheat flour is also used in cakes, pastries, and noodles. There are several different types of wheat, each suitable to different climates and for different end-uses. Wheat can flourish in a greater range of climates than other grains; the highest-quality wheats are grown in areas, such as Canada, where hot, dry summers mean few other crops could flourish. These wheats are spring wheats, planted in the spring and harvested in the autumn, and the hot, dry conditions are favourable to the production of a wheat with a high protein content. High protein wheats are also known as hard wheats.

Winter wheats, planted in the late autumn and harvested in the early summer, generally produce higher yields but lower protein contents, and they flourish in cooler, wetter climates such as

Europe. Flours made from low-protein or soft wheats produce breads which go stale very quickly (a feature of French bread, made from the locally produced wheat), but they are well suited to cakes, pastries, Arabic-style flat breads, and Chinese noodles (Italian pastas are made from durum wheat, a high-protein type). Of course, it is possible to blend wheats to produce a flour with the protein content desired for a particular purpose; indeed since the weather is a major determinant of protein content, most millers do blend wheats in different proportions each year when making flours of consistent quality.

Table 16 presents data on recent levels of production of and trade in wheat. The world's major wheat producers are the USSR, the USA, the EC, China, and India. Most wheat is consumed in the country of production, but the world market amounts to roughly 20 per cent of production. Imports are therefore an extremely important source of wheat for a large number of countries. Major exporters are the USA, the EC, Canada,

Table 16 Wheat market data (million tonnes)

	1983–4	*1984–5*	*1985–6*	*1986–7*
Production:				
USSR	77.5	68.6	78.1	92.3
USA	65.9	70.6	66.0	56.9
EC	64.0	82.6	71.2	72.0
China	81.4	87.8	85.8	90.3
India	42.8	45.5	44.1	46.9
World total	495.6	517.6	505.0	535.4
Exports:				
USA	38.3	36.7	23.5	27.2
EC	15.0	17.4	14.3	15.5
Canada	21.2	19.1	16.8	20.8
Australia	11.6	15.1	16.1	15.0
Argentina	9.6	8.0	6.2	4.3
World total	100.4	102.9	82.7	88.4
Imports:				
USSR	20.3	28.2	16.4	16.1
China	9.8	7.4	6.8	8.7
Japan	5.9	5.7	5.6	5.7
South Korea	2.5	3.0	3.0	4.0
Brazil	4.3	4.9	2.5	2.9
Egypt	7.3	6.6	6.6	7.1
Iran	3.6	2.6	2.1	2.5

Source: International Wheat Council.

Australia, and Argentina. Consumption of wheat tends to grow very steadily, at a rate approximately the same as world population growth. Declining per capita consumption in rich countries is offset by rising per capita consumption and growing population in developing countries. Urbanization of populations in developing countries, and the adoption of western-style foods is another important reason for the growth in wheat usage in poorer countries. Consumption does not appear to be affected a great deal by price; this is partly because most consumers are insulated from the effects of world price changes by government policies, but it also reflects the basic role of wheat in diets.

The import demand for wheat derives from three main sources. The first is countries whose domestic production capacities are so low that they have no choice but to rely on imports for the bulk of their needs such as the Gulf states and Japan. The second is production shortfalls in countries which do have large production capacities. Variable weather patterns and farmer decisions to plant other crops can leave countries with much lower than normal wheat crops, forcing them to increase their imports. Finally, there is demand from the centrally planned economies. Soviet grain imports began in the early 1970s when a political decision was made to improve the living standards of Soviet citizens and to stop the previous practice of passing grain production shortfalls on to consumers through shortages. The Soviets are now large importers of wheat, coarse grains, and soybeans, but the level of their imports can vary dramatically from one year to the next. China has also emerged as a large grain importer as a result of widespread liberalization. In the Chinese case, it does not only reflect rising consumer incomes and a political determination to improve food availability, it also reflects the increased freedom Chinese farmers have to decide on their output. On occasion, this has left the Chinese needing to import large quantities of grain. Year-to-year fluctuations in imports by the eastern bloc countries are partly determined by their own production each year, but it should not be forgotten that there is a political decision involved in importing grain.

World wheat prices are determined by the level of supply, demand, and stocks relevant to the export market. To the extent that production and consumption in any country is insulated from free market prices, and if that country neither imports nor exports, it does not influence world prices. Hence government policies, especially in the major exporters, have a large impact on prices. Indeed exporters' stocks absorb the bulk of the variation in global stock levels. Because of the USA's position as the largest wheat exporter, and because world wheat trade is denominated in dollars,

US prices are effectively world market prices, and price supports available for US farmers effectively set a floor to world prices for many years. Recently, however, attempts by the USA and the EC to dispose of surplus wheat stocks have resulted in aggressive subsidy policies by these two exporters. The EC, whose farmers are paid substantially more than world market prices to produce grain, has subsidized the export of this grain (most of which is wheat) for a long time. Partly to combat this, the USA has introduced a variety of export subsidies, and the combined effect of these policies was to exacerbate the weakness of wheat prices throughout the early 1980s.

The largest peaks in wheat prices coincide with shortfalls in production in major exporters and importers. The most dramatic peak, in the early 1970s, was principally the result of poor crops in the year after huge, unprecedented grain purchases by the USSR had caused a drawdown in stock levels. Variability in production because of changing weather patterns is a pronounced feature of the wheat market, and is particularly noticeable in the case of the two large southern hemisphere exporters, Argentina and Australia.

The 1980s, however, have been a period of steadily declining wheat prices, as Figure 7 indicates. A number of factors have been behind this decline. First, farmers in many of the exporting countries had become accustomed to the steady expansions in production and high prices of the 1970s. Certainly, US agricultural policy (in particular, the 1981 Agriculture Act) set support prices which reflected the conditions of the earlier decade. Second, production outside the USA was also given a boost by the appreciation in the value of the dollar, which began in 1981. With world market prices denominated in dollars, farmers in Argentina, Canada, and elsewhere saw their local currency returns rise. Third, the rises in US interest rates which accompanied (caused) the rise in the dollar increased the burden of debt service for many developing countries and restricted their ability to expand their domestic economies. Lower growth rates resulted in slower growth in their consumption of wheat. Finally, the export subsidies offered by the EC and USA throughout this period helped to keep prices low.

By the end of 1987, however, there were signs that production restraint in major exporters, a realignment of the dollar and improving consumption in developing countries were pulling the wheat market out of its prolonged period of weak prices. Certainly, long-term forecasts for wheat consumption, based on likely population growth in developing countries, suggest that the focus of policy-makers will be turning back to ways of expanding production by the mid-1990s.

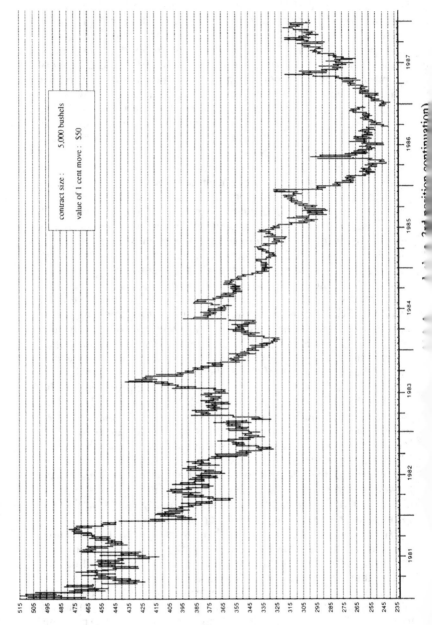

contract size : 5,000 bushels

value of 1 cent move : $50

cents/bushel

2nd position continuation)

Coarse grains – production, consumption, and prices

Feedgrains are used widely around the world. Something like 40 per cent of total world grain production is fed to animals. For the most part, locally available grain is the preferred feedgrain, with barley and low-quality wheat popular in Europe, and corn popular in the USA. Sorghum is another common feedgrain. Livestock diets affect the meat which animals produce, and help to define consumer preferences; chicken meat in the USA is yellow compared to the pale colour of European chicken, a result of the heavy use of corn in chicken feed in the USA. There is also a pronounced difference in texture and taste between grain-fed beef and that from animals which have eaten mostly grass. Grass-fed beef, however, is increasingly rare, thanks to the continuing inten- sification of livestock husbandry.

Local grain production possibilities are determined largely by considerations of soil and climate: northern Europe is too cool to grow corn successfully and barley is the most commonly produced coarse grain. Grain is valued as a source of carbohydrate in live- stock rations, and it is used alongside protein feeds in modern, intensive livestock rearing systems. Most animals can subsist on grain alone, but not at the levels of productivity needed to feed modern urban populations.

Although livestock farming is common throughout the world, the kind of farming which relies on intensively fed livestock is confined to richer countries and the areas of higher incomes and more rapid economic growth in the developing world. Hence the world feedgrain market is somewhat different from the world wheat market. The two are similar, however, in being affected by agricultural policies in the major nations. The EC heavily protects its farmers, but is only a small net exporter of feedgrains; some corn is imported, partly offsetting the exports of barley and feed wheat.

Table 17 presents summary data on the world coarse grain market. Two important features of the market are revealed by these data. First, world trade as a percentage of production is smaller than in the wheat market; this simply reflects the fact that most feedgrains are consumed in the country of production. Indeed, a sizeable proportion is consumed on the farm where it is grown, with many dairy, beef, and hog farmers growing some of their feed requirements. Second, world trade is much more heavily concentrated – with the USA in a dominant position and the two largest exporters, the USA and Argentina, accounting for almost three-quarters of world exports. There is also considerably more concentration on the import side, arising from the fact that only countries prosperous enough to have relatively advanced animal-feeding industries import feedgrains in large quantities. Thus among the major markets are Europe, the OPEC nations, Japan, and the rapidly growing economies of the Pacific Rim. As in the wheat market, however, imports by the USSR are a large and variable factor. Not only is the total Soviet import requirement not known in advance, but its breakdown between wheat and feedgrains is also uncertain.

A further important feature of demand is that it is more sensitive than wheat to the economic cycle in the industrialized countries. This is because of the role of feedgrains in meat production, which itself is linked into trends in consumer incomes. Therefore, any change in world economic performance will have a greater impact on feedgrains than on wheat.

As in the wheat market, world feedgrain prices are effectively

Table 17 The world coarse grain market (million tonnes)

	1983-4	1984-5	1985-6	1986-7
All coarse grains				
Production:				
USSR	105.0	90.5	100.0	106.2
USA	137.1	237.7	274.9	252.9
China	92.0	98.4	84.5	89.9
EC	74.5	90.5	89.0	81.9
World	691.3	821.1	856.8	848.6
of which:				
corn	347.5	460.2	489.6	480.1
barley	164.8	175.5	179.6	186.2
Exports:				
World	91.9	102.1	85.1	85.8
of which:				
corn	60.8	67.4	55.0	55.3
Corn exports:				
USA	47.6	49.2	33.5	34.0
Argentina	6.3	6.9	7.0	5.6
China	3.8	5.0	5.7	4.6
Corn imports				
USSR	7.0	20.8	9.5	8.6
Japan	13.8	14.3	14.9	14.9
South Korea	3.1	3.2	3.7	4.1

Source: International Wheat Council.

determined in the USA. Price regulation in the EC keeps London futures trading on feedgrains illiquid. Because corn is the dominant feedgrain produced in and exported from the USA, and because of the dominance of the USA in coarse grain exports, it is the corn market, and more particularly the Chicago Board of Trade (CBOT) corn futures market, which sets the key market price for freely traded feedgrains. Of course, the premiums and discounts for different grains vary, but the corn price is by far the most important. Table 18 presents summary data on US corn production, consumption, and trade.

Table 18 The US corn market (million 56 lb bushels)

	1983–4	*1984–5*	*1985–6*	*1986–7*
Beginning stocks	3,523	1,006	1,648	4,040
Production	4,175	7,674	8,877	8,250
Domestic consumption	4,793	5,170	5,255	5,906
Exports	1,902	1,865	1,241	1,504

Source: USDA.

As the table shows, the fact that the USA dominates world corn exports does not mean that exports dominate US production; rather it is domestic consumption which accounts for the bulk of corn utilization. Animal feeding accounts for slightly less than two-thirds of US corn use, with corn being fed to dairy and beef cattle, hogs, and poultry. One rapidly growing use of corn in recent years has been as a feedstock for the production of high-fructose corn syrup (HFCS); HFCS is a liquid sugar substitute production of which has been effectively encouraged by high, government-guaranteed prices for sugar in the USA.

The data in the table overstate the volatility of US production, which was unusually low in 1983. In that year, a combination of drought and a new policy initiative, designed to reduce stocks by giving farmers corn from government stocks in return for their taking land out of production, led to sharply lower than normal production.

As Figure 8 shows, corn prices rose sharply in 1983 in response to this large reduction in the US crop. From then, prices fell steadily and reached 14-year lows after the 1986 harvest. However, these low prices both discouraged production in 1987 and encouraged consumption, both in the USA and elsewhere. Prices therefore began to recover from these low levels early in 1987.

131

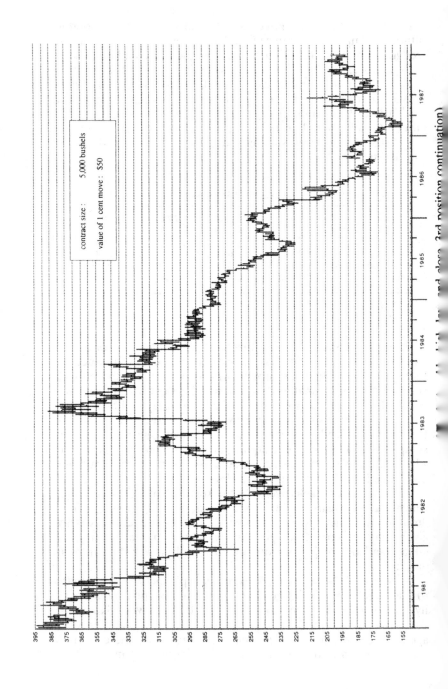

contract size : 5,000 bushels

value of 1 cent move : $50

Trading the grains markets

Trading the grains markets is a matter of forming a view on one or other of the factors which influence the supply–demand balance. Variations in supplies have the most important impact on the market since it is these which determine exportable supplies and import requirements in those countries which use imports to supplement domestic production. Production of an annual crop, like wheat or corn, is the product of harvested area and yield. Accordingly, it is most important to follow the progress of farmer plantings (the major determinant of harvested area) and the weather (the major determinant of year-to-year fluctuations in yields).

Farmer plantings are influenced by the price of all the possible crops which can be grown on the available land, and by government policies. The USA, for example, has a set-aside programme, under which farmers who wish to benefit from government-guaranteed prices must idle a proportion of their land (the proportion varies from year to year). It also has a conservation reserve programme, under which farmers are paid to leave land uncultivated. Most wheat farmers, in most countries, have a range of alternative uses for their land, ranging from sheep husbandry in Australia to barley growing in Europe. In the case of US corn farmers, the major alternatives are soybeans and hogs. The agriculture ministries in the main grain-producing states provide regular information about plantings, and these can be used to form an early view about next year's production. Recall that winter wheat is sown in the autumn and harvested in the early summer, whereas spring wheat is planted in the spring and harvested in the autumn. Since wheat is produced in both northern and southern hemispheres, there are few months of the year in which a wheat farmer somewhere is not planting. In the case of the corn market, the dominance of the USA and Argentina makes the job of following plantings rather easier.

Weather patterns exert a powerful influence on grain prices. Again, because there are winter and spring wheats, there are two critical periods for the wheat crop. Winter wheat germinates in the autumn, but is dormant over the winter proper. Mostly winter wheat is grown in regions where the winter is either mild or where a thick blanket of snow can be expected to insulate the crop from the worst of the cold. However, if it is very cold, and if there is inadequate snow cover, the crop is vulnerable to 'winterkill'; i.e. the plant is killed in the ground by the cold. Very often when winterkill occurs, the land can be reseeded with spring wheat, and all the farmer loses is whatever he would have used his land for over the summer. However, in some parts of the world, and particularly in some parts of the USSR where winter wheat is grown, the summer is not really long enough for spring wheat to mature. In these circumstances winterkill can be very serious, and an early indicator of reduced production.

Spring wheat, like corn and all other spring-sown grains, is vulnerable to excessive heat and insufficient moisture during the summer months. Because of the dominance of US corn in world exportable supplies of feedgrains, and because corn cultivation is concentrated in a rather small geographical area of the USA, corn prices are more sensitive than wheat prices to adverse weather developments. After all, by the time the North American spring wheat crop is under threat from bad weather, the winter wheat crop has already been harvested.

Weather developments are of importance not only to exporters, but also to importers. The market pays closer attention to exporters, simply because export production is much more concentrated than import demand. One importer whose weather patterns are closely followed, however, is the USSR; after all, Soviet import requirements are heavily influenced by the size of their own harvest. The Soviets guard very secretively the details of their grain plantings, yields, and production and the information they publish officially is patchy. Under the terms of successive USA–USSR long-term grain supply agreements, however, which have attempted to minimize the disruptive impact of Soviet purchases on market prices, agricultural officials from the two countries meet regularly and exchange information. The quality of the information passed to the Americans is a direct function of the state of US–Soviet relations. In recent years developments in satellite technology have enabled the USA to improve their information on Soviet weather patterns and crop developments. From all this, it has also become possible in recent years to develop a reasonably good indication of total Soviet import requirements. Two other features of Soviet demand, however, remain uncertain.

The first is the amount they purchase from the USA rather than from other countries. President Carter put an embargo on US grain exports to the Soviet Union (above the minimum called for in the long-term supply agreement) after the USSR invaded Afghanistan, and although the newly elected President Reagan lifted the embargo in 1981, one index of the state of relations between the two superpowers has been the level of grain trade between them. The Washington summit meeting between Reagan and Gorbachev in December 1987, for example, was preceded by a heavy round of Soviet purchasing of wheat, soybeans, and soybean meal in the USA. Similar considerations affect Chinese imports of US grain; following tension over US relations with Taiwan and a dispute about China's exports of textiles to the USA, Chinese imports of US grain fell sharply in the 1982–3 crop year. It is sometimes asserted that the origin of the grain bought by the Chinese and Soviets is immaterial for world prices, provided the quantities are not reduced. If the USSR buys 3 million tonnes of wheat from the EC rather than from the USA, world consumption has still gone up by 3 million tonnes and prices should respond the same. In fact it does matter, at least in the short run. Heavy Soviet purchasing of Argentine wheat will have two effects: it will affect the overall level of wheat prices, but it will also affect the relationship between Argentine and US wheat prices. In the years following the Carter embargo, Argentine wheat sold at a large premium to US wheat. In other words, it is imprudent to go long of wheat, expecting heavy Soviet purchases, when relations between Washington and Moscow are cool.

The second key element of uncertainty is the breakdown of Soviet demand into its components of wheat, feedgrains, and vegetable proteins. All Soviet importing is linked to their need for animal feedstuffs; they produce more than enough grain to meet their bread needs. They need imported grains and proteins to maintain and expand their livestock production. The Soviets do import bread wheat, however, since it is often more efficient to feed some of their own wheat to animals and make bread with imported wheat. With a poor internal transportation network and grain and livestock production centres located at a considerable distance from many population centres, while some of these centres (notably Leningrad) are close to ports, the economics of the whole sector are complex. It rarely makes sense, for example, to ship grain from a producing region to Leningrad when imported grain is being shipped from the Baltic ports back to the producing region to be fed to the livestock there. The mix of imports also depends on the quality of the Soviets' harvest; if they have a large but low-quality harvest, they are likely to import more wheat and less feedgrain than if they have a small but high-quality harvest. A final influence on the decision is relative prices on the world market.

Export subsidies on wheat available from the USA and the EC became an important feature of the world market in the early 1980s. The EC has subsidized its exports for many years, but the USA only began to retaliate when its own share of the market appeared to be under threat. The main effect of these subsidies was to depress export prices, but there is some evidence that, in the USA, they were helpful in reducing the stocks which the government had accumulated under its price-supporting activities in previous years. Of importance to the futures market, however, was the fact that the daily and weekly decisions made by governments about the size and targets of these subsidies had a major influence on day-to-day price movements.

Traditionally the focus of the grains markets is on supply disruptions, and these certainly cause the largest movements in prices. Demand side developments should not be ignored, however. There are two kinds of development which deserve close attention.

In the wheat market developing countries account for a large and growing share of world consumption. The rate of growth of this consumption is influenced by the health of their economies, via two mechanisms. The first is through their ability to finance imports of wheat. The second is through higher consumer incomes leading to higher demand. Bad economic conditions in developing countries or constraints on their foreign currency earnings (such as heavy debt service burdens) restrict their purchases of wheat. There is no similar kind of pressure in developed nations, where demand for wheat is not sensitive to consumer incomes.

In the feedgrain market rising consumer incomes do influence demand since they lead to increased demand for meat. Unlike wheat, however, this is only significant in countries where consumers are rich enough to have large demands for meat. Given the importance of domestic feed demand for corn in the USA, demand prospects are a source of price variability in the corn market. Farmers' expansion of meat production will lead to increases in corn consumption, and Chapter 8 gives some indications about the conditions under which farmers do expand their meat production.

Often, the earliest indications of changes in the level of demand on the world market come from the two major international spot markets, in the Gulf of Mexico and Rotterdam. The gulf prices are, effectively, US export prices since the largest proportion of US grain exports go through gulf ports. Rotterdam is an important entrepôt centre for grain (and indeed for many other agricultural commodities) and new demands from importers are often registered first of all in these markets. Gulf prices, however, must be interpreted with caution since they are usually quoted relative to the nearest Chicago futures prices. Thus a typical quotation for export corn would be '10 cents over March', which means the price is 10 cents higher than the March contract on the Chicago Board of Trade (CBOT).

One further issue in the wheat market is deciding which market to trade. Wheat futures contracts are traded on the Minneapolis Grain Exchange, the Kansas City Board of Trade, and the CBOT. The Chicago contract is by far the most actively traded, and is therefore the one which attracts the widest interest. The three markets trade different kinds of wheat, however, and prices are not the same; Minneapolis trades hard spring wheat, Kansas hard red winter, and Chicago soft red winter. Hard spring is top-quality bread grain, used for blending with lower-protein wheats to produce bread flour. Hard red winter is a standard grade of bread wheat, whereas soft red winter is a low-protein wheat, normally used for cakes and pastries in the USA, for flat breads in the Middle East, and for noodles in China. Hard winter wheats are the most important class of US wheat both in terms of production and exports, but exports of hard spring and soft winter comprise a higher percentage of production. Export markets also differ in the type of wheat they prefer; the USSR normally buys hard wheat, whereas the Chinese and the Arab nations normally buy soft wheat. In other words, each class of wheat has its own supply-demand balance, with different producing regions and different demands. While there is a high degree of substitutability among the three, and while higher protein wheat normally sells at a premium, the price ratios are not fixed.

This has two consequences for trading. First of all, it is necessary to choose the market. In view of the low level of liquidity on the Minneapolis market, the choice is effectively confined to Kansas and Chicago. Although there are options on wheat futures on Kansas, only the Chicago options are liquid enough to be attractive; hence any option trading on wheat really has to be done on the Chicago market. Choosing a market for futures trading is simply a matter of interpreting one's analysis of the market; the impact of changes in plantings and weather will vary depending on the area of the USA which is affected; Soviet buying will normally boost Kansas relative to Chicago, whereas Chinese buying will boost Chicago relative to Kansas.

The second consequence is that it opens up possibilities for spread trading. The protein spread is wide and variable and is therefore a higher-risk, higher profit-potential trade than an inter-delivery spread trade, but is lower risk than taking an outright futures position. This is a particularly valuable trade when Chicago is trading at an unusually high premium to Kansas, since the market is more likely to revert to a normal pattern than to continue to price Chicago so highly. Thus a long Kansas, short Chicago position can be a low-risk trade with a high-profit potential.

Clearly, there are many other spread trading possibilities within the grains markets. Old crop/new crop spreads are a special kind of inter-delivery spread, with higher risk and higher profit potential. The price difference between the last delivery month in one crop year and the first delivery month in the next is not determined by the carrying charges alone since there is information about supply and demand which has a greater impact on the prices for new crop months. For example, when supplies are tight but there is an expectation for a good harvest, the old crop will rise to a substantial premium to the new crop. The wheat crop year runs from July to June, and the corn crop year runs from October to September; the first active contracts in the new crop are July wheat and December corn. Because there is such interest in these old crop/new crop spreads, it becomes possible to trade distant contracts much earlier in the case of grains than other commodities; thus it is possible to take an outright position in a new crop month very early without fear of trading in an illiquid market.

The crop spread provides a lower-risk way of trading the 'weather market' in grains during the critical growing periods for the crops. For example, bad weather in the summer will send corn prices higher, and will be particularly bullish for new crop prices. The risk with an outright long position is that a sudden change in the weather will send the market sharply lower, and the risk of going short in a weather rally is that bad weather will drive the market sharply higher. An old crop/new crop spread, run as a bull or bear spread depending on one's view, is a way of limiting the risk somewhat.

Another popular spread is to trade wheat against corn. Except in truly remarkable circumstances, wheat sells at a premium to corn, but the premium fluctuates in size considerably. A good rule-of-thumb is that the wheat premium should be at least 12 per cent, for the following reason. Wheat can be used to feed livestock, and it has a nutritional value about 5 per cent higher than that of corn. Also a bushel of wheat, at 60 lb, is 7 per cent heavier than a bushel of corn, which weighs 56 lb. Thus, if per bushel wheat prices are less than 12 per cent higher than per bushel corn prices, it will be profitable for feedgrain users to switch from corn into wheat. Thus a long wheat/short corn spread is a low-risk trade when the wheat premium is less than 12 per cent. More generally, the different price dynamics of the wheat and corn markets can be used to decide which way to trade this spread; good US demand for feed-grains at a time when world market demand for wheat is weak will argue for a short wheat/long corn position. This spread is also a good vehicle for taking a view on the breakdown of Soviet grain imports between the two grains.

Another common use of the wheat–corn spread is to take advantage of the different seasonal price patterns of the two grains. They both tend to be at their lowest prices during and immediately after their harvests, but harvest in each case is at different times of year. July is the first wheat new crop future; December that for corn. A long December wheat/short December corn spread can be initiated in June and July, when wheat prices are at their seasonal lows and liquidated in November, as corn prices move to their seasonal lows. The trade can be run the other way, long December corn/short December wheat from March until June, taking advantage of the weakness in wheat prices as the harvest of winter-sown wheat approaches.

Finally, corn can be spread against soybeans or soybean meal, trades which are discussed in Chapter 7.

Chapter seven

Oilseeds, oilmeals, and oils

Oilseeds and their products – the basics

Vegetable oilseeds are cultivated to satisfy two different sorts of demand, that for vegetable oils and that for protein meals. Typically the processing of oilseeds yields both meal and oil, although the proportions of each vary from crop to crop. With very few exceptions, there is no market for oilseeds except for processing into meal and oil; therefore, their value is determined by the value of the meal and oil they contain.

Vegetable oils are consumed directly by humans in the form of cooking oil, margarine, mayonnaise, and a range of other food products. Smaller quantities are used in the production of soaps and detergents, and there are some uses for vegetable oils in the production of paints, lubricants, and plastics. It is the food markets which are by far the most important, however. The modern vegetable oil industry dates from the 1870s, when the process of hydrogenation, or hardening, was discovered, which allowed margarine to be produced much more cheaply than had been possible beforehand.

Vegetable oils account for about three-quarters of the total non-mineral oil market; the balance is comprised of products such as butter oil and various marine oils. Over forty plants are used as sources of vegetable oil, and they are classified into three main groups. The soft, or edible oils such as soybean, cottonseed, rape-seed, sunflower, olive, and corn; the hard oils such as palm, palm-kernel, babassu, and coconut; and the industrial oils such as linseed, castor, and tung. Palm-kernel, coconut, and babassu, which are suitable both for edible and inedible usage, are also known as lauric oils. Technological advances in processing are making the oils increasingly interchangeable, especially in margarine production, but they do have different chemical compositions and each enjoys specialized markets. There are also strong consumer preferences in certain markets.

Soybean oil, or soy oil, is by far the most important vegetable oil, accounting for over 30 per cent of total production. Palm sunflowerseed, and rapeseed each have an approximately 15 per cent share, and cottonseed and coconut each account for about 7 per cent. The conditions under which these oils are produced vary enormously. At one extreme is palm-oil, a tropical tree crop, grown mostly on plantations. The oil is the main reason for cultivating the tree. At the other extreme is cottonseed oil; cottonseeds, which produce both meal and oil, are a by-product of cotton fibre production. Therefore production of cottonseed oil is affected much more heavily by the price of cotton than by the price of vegetable oil.

Oilmeals are valued as sources of protein for animals, particularly simple-stomached animals. Cattle, being ruminants and therefore able to synthesize amino acids from carbohydrate feeds, are typically fed very little protein. It is pork and poultry production which comprise the largest markets for protein meals; hence demand for protein meals is concentrated in countries where there is a modern livestock-farming sector.

Just as there are a large number of vegetable oils, so there are a large number of vegetable oilmeals; of the major crops in this sector, only oil palm does not produce significant quantities of meal in addition to oil. It is important to note that oilseeds, such as rapeseed or soybeans,[1] produce both oil and meal on processing; processors therefore do not have the choice of producing meal *or* oil. Equally important, however, are the varying proportions of meal and oil which come from different oilseeds. At one extreme is the soybean, 100 lb of which produces 79 lb of meal and 18 lb of oil. At the other extreme is the oil palm fruit, which directly produces no meal, although palm-kernels, extracted from the fruit bunch during primary processing, are themselves processed into palm-kernel oil and palm-kernel meal. Most oilseeds have a position between these extremes: rapeseed produces about 35 per cent oil and 60 per cent meal, and sesame seed about 47 per cent oil and 49 per cent meal.

The importance of soybean meal, or soymeal, in the meal market is even greater than that of soybean oil in the oil market. It accounts for approximately 60 per cent of world oilmeal production and the second most important meal, cottonseed, has only a 15 per cent share. The individual shares held by other meals are small.

Clearly, soybeans dominate the entire oilseed sector. This dominance has been diminishing, however: the rapid growth in production of, first, oil palm in South-east Asia, and second, rapeseed in Canada, the EC, and India have caused some erosion in the market share of both soybean oil and soybean meal. Despite this dominance, soybeans are different from other oilseeds in two main respects.

First, they produce rather more meal and rather less oil per unit than other oilseeds. This means their price is more closely correlated with meal prices than other oilseeds, which are more heavily influenced by oil prices. Hence the vegetable oil market is prone to instability; output of its single most important component is determined principally by conditions in the market for vegetable proteins.

Second, most other oilseeds are processed in the producing country, with only the products entering international trade. With the soybean complex, on the other hand, some of the most important trade routes involve beans. The EC, for example, imports beans from the USA and consumes the meal internally but exports much of the oil.

Because of the central role of soybeans in the entire complex, and because the most actively traded futures contracts in the complex are soybean and product contracts, the rest of this chapter concentrates on the soybean and its products. Other contracts are discussed where relevant.

Soybeans – production and prices

Soybeans were being cultivated in China as early as 2000 BC. They were introduced to the US in the early nineteenth century, but widespread cultivation did not begin there until the 1920s. They are planted in the late spring (normally in May and early June in the Midwest) and are harvested in the autumn (normally in October). Soybeans are found three to a pod on a bushy plant, containing up to 80 pods.

World production of soybeans expanded rapidly in the 1950s and 1960s, growing from 17 million tonnes in 1950 to 48 million tonnes in 1971. This was principally the result of expansion in the USA, where output grew from 8 million tonnes in 1950 to 32 million tonnes in 1971, and was caused by two factors. First, US government policies designed to limit the growth of corn and wheat production meant that plentiful land was available for soybeans. The climate and soils of the Midwest are ideal for the cultivation of soybeans, so land withdrawn from grain was easily devoted to soybeans. Second, the expansion and intensification of meat production, and especially pork and poultry production, in those years led to a dramatic expansion in the market for protein

Table 19 World soybean production (thousands of metric tons)

	1983	1984	1985	1986
Argentina	7,000	6,750	7,300	7,300
Brazil	15,400	18,280	13,400	17,300
China	9,765	9,690	10,500	11,000
USA	44,518	50,644	57,113	52,800
World	83,150	93,010	96,290	98,300

Source: USDA.

meals and animal feeds. This took place first in the USA, but higher consumer incomes and the adoption of modern livestock farming practices in western Europe and Japan quickly led to increases in these markets for protein meals.

As Table 19 shows, world production in recent years has almost breached the 100 million tonne level, with the USA still accounting for over half of total output. China's output is almost wholly consumed domestically and is of rather less significance to world markets. Brazilian production has expanded sharply since the early 1970s, but the country exports few soybeans; the bulk are processed domestically and either consumed or exported as soybean meal.

The dominant position of the US in production and its role as the major world market source of beans, together with the location of the major market in Chicago, mean that US conditions assume a great importance. Table 20 presents some summary data on the US supply–demand balance.

In terms of farmers' decisions on soybean output, the main alternatives are corn, which is similar in its requirements, and in the USA at least, hog production. Many farmers in the Midwest run mixed operations, raising corn, soybeans, and hogs, and although they cannot easily move acreage from crops to livestock, they can switch their attention and efforts, with important

Table 20 The US soybean market (million 60 lb bushels)

	1983–4	1984–5	1985–6	1986–7
Beginning stocks	344	176	316	536
Production	1,635	1,861	2,098	1,940
Crushings	983	1,030	1,053	1,179
Exports	743	598	740	757

Source: USDA.

consequences for production. Clearly, it is the prices of these outputs which have the greatest impact on farmers' decisions, so we need to look at how the prices of soybeans are determined.

To all intents and purposes, there is no market for soybeans except for crushing into meal and oil. The value of beans therefore, is determined by the market value of the meal and the oil which the beans contain. Generally speaking, since crushers must cover their costs, the total value of the meal and oil they sell must be slightly higher than the value of the beans they buy. More specifically,

$$Pb = PmXm + PoXo - CM$$

where P is price of beans; b, m, and o denote beans, meal, and oil respectively, X denotes the extraction factors, or percentage yield of meal or oil from the bean; and CM is the 'crush margin', i.e. the return earned by crushers from their activities. It appears as a negative value, above, but that is simply because it is on the right-hand side of the equation; in so far as crushers make money, it will be positive. This equation can be generalized for any oilseed. Note the following features of the relationship.

First, the lower the oil extraction factor, the tighter will be the correlation between meal and bean prices. In the case of soybeans, where the meal extraction factor is just below 0.8, there is a very close correlation between bean and meal prices. Similarly, a very large swing in soybean oil prices will produce only a small change in soybean prices. Rapeseed, on the other hand, which yields more oil and less meal, will behave rather differently.

Second, the proportions of the value of beans which is accounted for by meal and oil can vary. The extraction factors are fixed, but the product prices are not; hence it is possible for meal prices to fall, oil prices to rise, and soybean prices to remain unchanged.

Third, although the crush margin must in the long run be positive (or else everyone would leave the crushing business), it is not fixed. Indeed it will fluctuate as there are short-term fluctuations in supply and demand for the three commodities. It can be, and often is, negative for short periods of time. One great attraction of the Chicago soybean complex futures markets is that they allow crushers to hedge themselves, covering not only their bean purchases, but also their meal and oil sales by offsetting futures market transactions.

Finally, note that this is not a behavioural relationship; it does not make any implicit claim about the flow of causation. It simply describes the relationships among these three prices.

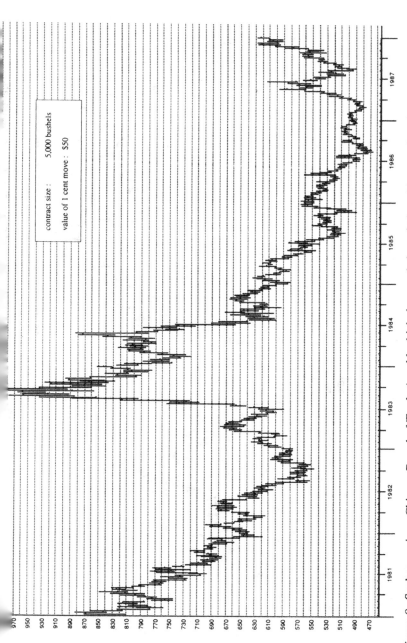

Figure 9. Soybean prices, Chicago Board of Trade (weekly, high, low, and close, 3rd position continuation)

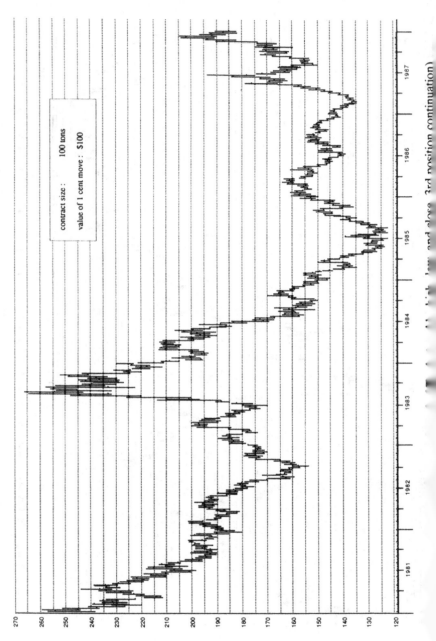

contract size : 100 tons

value of 1 cent move : $100

dollars/ton

(N, high, low and close 3rd position continuation)

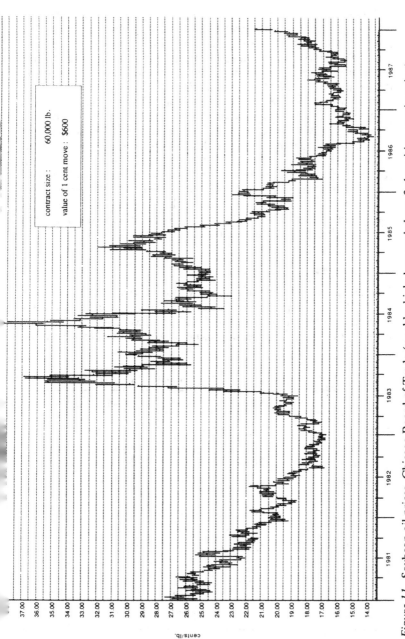

Figure 11. Soybean oil prices, Chicago Board of Trade (weekly, high, low, and close, 3rd position continuation)

Figures 9–11 illustrate these price relationships for the soy complex. They also illustrate the variable flows of causation. Soybean and soybean meal prices are closely correlated; but note that the sharp price peak in soybeans in 1984 came at a time when soybean meal prices were declining. Causation runs both ways in the complex; in 1983 a combination of factors led to a sharp reduction in the US soybean harvest. This supply restriction pushed up the prices of the complex as a whole. In 1984, however, a shortfall in Malaysian palm-oil production, coupled with strong demand for vegetable oil (and low levels of soybean oil stocks because of the poor 1983 bean harvest), led to a dramatic rise in soybean oil prices. This, in turn, pulled up soybean prices, despite the weakness in soybean meal. Note that, in 1984, oil prices peaked at higher levels than in 1983, but the peak in bean prices was greater in 1983; this is because of the relatively small amount of oil which can be extracted from the soybean.

Soybean meal

Soybean meal has some uses in baby foods and as a meat extender, but well over 90 per cent of the market consists in animal feed. The industry standard form of soymeal contains 44 per cent protein, but there is increasing usage of 49 per cent protein meal.

Table 21 Soybean meal market data (thousands of metric tons)

	1983–4	*1984–5*	*1985–6*	*1986–7*
Production				
Brazil	9,702	10,170	9,660	11,190
EC–12	10,330	9,820	10,230	10,900
USA	20,646	22,250	22,630	25,180
World total	55,510	58,160	60,300	65,430
Exports:				
Brazil	7,706	8,440	7,380	8,370
USA	4,860	4,460	5,450	6,660
World total	21,400	22,290	22,550	25,540
Consumption:				
EC–12	17,680	18,060	18,150	19,310
USA	15,980	17,670	17,340	18,490
World total	56,100	59,280	61,430	65,740

Source: USDA.

148

It is popular among farmers, partly because it is readily available, partly because of its favourable amino acid balance, and partly because its use does not impart any taint to the flesh or eggs of the animals which eat it. Soymeal also does not cause any digestive disorders when fed in large quantities, which is not true of some other meals (see Table 21).

The geographical location of soymeal production differs from that of soybeans principally because of the large crushing industries within the EC and Japan, both of which crush imported beans. There is also a large volume of exports of meal; it should be noted that Brazil exports more meal than the USA, despite having a much lower level of bean production.

Consumption of meal is concentrated in the EC and the USA, with Japan and the USSR the next major consumers. Clearly, consumption is concentrated in countries with modern livestock-rearing practices. Within the USA the largest market is poultry feed, which accounts for about 60 per cent of soymeal consumption. Hog feed accounts for a further 25 per cent or so, with cattle feed taking roughly 10 per cent and the small balance going to sheep and pet foods. However, the EC is an unusual market, in that the price provisions of the Common Agricultural Policy (CAP) make the protein–carbohydrate price ratio within the EC significantly different from that on world markets. This acts as an incentive for EC farmers to use rather more protein and rather less domestically produced carbohydrate (principally grains) than they would otherwise. For example, a typical hog in the UK would be fed a diet with a soymeal inclusion rate of over 20 per cent, whereas for a typical hog in the USA the figure would be around 11 per cent.This gives the EC a greater importance in the soybean market than the numbers of animals there might suggest.

Recently the EC has threatened to revoke the agreement under which US soybeans are imported free of duty; this is part of a package under which the EC has offered to reduce its subsidised exports of wheat and restructure the CAP. Discussions about this are taking place in the Uruguay Round of talks under the General Agreement on Tariffs and Trade (GATT); the results of these talks are potentially of great significance for the overall structure of soybean prices.

Soybean meal prices reflect the supply of soybeans and the demand for protein feeds which, in turn, is determined by the overall level of feed demand and the price of soymeal relative to grain. When farmers are expanding their meat production, demand for soymeal will improve. They will also boost their use of protein when it is cheap relative to grain and also when they are anxious to ensure their animals put on weight rapidly. Utilization of soymeal in cattle feeding in the USA is particularly sensitive to this; ordinarily cattle are fed little protein, but their rations will be boosted if farmers wish to move them quickly to market.

Soybean oil

Clearly, the geographical distribution of soybean oil production is the same as that of soymeal production. Much of the world's soybean oil is consumed in the country of production, but there is a large world market for vegetable oils, and some oils, such as palm, are produced primarily for this export market. The price of soybean oil is determined by the level of supply and demand for vegetable oils as a whole, although the premiums and discounts for different oils certainly do vary when there is a shortage or a glut of some particular oils.

Table 22 presents summary data on the world vegetable oil market. Total vegetable oil production is determined by a variety of factors. Given the structure of the soybean market, output of soy oil is in the long run principally determined by the demand for soy meal, since the oil is a by-product of meal production at normal price ratios. In the short term output of soy oil is determined by the soybean harvest; that is, by farmers and the weather in the major producing countries, the USA and Brazil. Output of cottonseed oil is principally determined by the availability of cottonseed; i.e. it is determined by what is happening in the cotton market. Output of other oils is more closely related to oil prices, but they are not all annual crops. Palm-oil, the output of which has been growing rapidly since the mid-1970s, is produced from the fruit of the oil palm. These trees do not yield for several years after planting, but once they have reached maturity go on producing fruit for twenty years or more. The long time lag between planting and production means there is little which farmers can do to change oil output in response to short term fluctuations in prices. Farmers can and do alter the application of fertilizers, but the impact of this is often on later seasons rather than on current output.

Demand for vegetable oils is somewhat more straightforward. The largest element in demand is for cooking oil, salad oil, and margarine. Per capita demand for these products has reached saturation point in most developed countries, leaving population growth as the major force for expansion in those countries. Demand for oil, however, is growing extremely rapidly in developing countries, especially in those where economic performance has

Table 22 Vegetable oil market data (thousands of tonnes)

	1984	1985	1986	1987
Production:				
Soybean oil				
USA	4,793	5,249	5,415	5,734
Brazil	2,235	2,560	2,306	2,546
World total	13,422	13,958	14,345	14,424
Palm-oil				
Malaysia	3,716	4,133	4,544	4,546
World total	6,347	6,854	7,494	7,480
Rapeseed oil				
World total	5,192	6,035	6,387	7,280
Sunflowerseed oil				
World total	5,871	6,548	7,246	7,266
World total				
(8 major oils)	40,132	44,643	46,637	47,536
Consumption:				
Soybean oil				
USA	4,498	4,556	4,581	4,843
EC	1,461	1,397	1,535	1,559
World total	14,054	13,979	13,903	14,791
Rapeseed oil				
China	1,509	1,426	1,612	2,015
India	913	1,020	1,237	1,232
World total	5,248	5,831	6,412	7,355
Palm oil				
EC	559	591	946	964
India	577	743	972	970
World total	5,968	6,536	7,472	7,866
Sunflowerseed oil				
USSR	1,970	1,847	1,959	2,050
World total	6,013	6,541	7,170	7,273
World total				
(8 major oils)	40,620	43,671	45,929	48,233

Note: The eight major oils are those listed, plus cottonseed, palm-kernel, coconut, and groundnut.

Source: Landell Mills Commodities Studies.

been tolerably good. In many of these countries rapid population growth is adding to the demand pressures. Thus India is one of the largest import markets for vegetable oils, despite having large domestic production capacity. Imports are also large into countries such as Egypt, Iran, and Pakistan; i.e. populous middle-income countries with expanding economies. Imports into many of these countries are designed to supplement local production, so there is often considerable variability in imports from one year to the next as local production is affected by the weather. In other countries, especially those in North Africa and the Middle East, demand for imports is constrained more by availability of foreign exchange than by anything else.

Trading the oilseed complex

There are a great number of ways in which it is possible to trade oilseeds, oilmeals, and oils. There are active markets in soybeans in Chicago, Tokyo, and Hong Kong, and in soybean meal and soybean oil in Chicago; there is an active rapeseed market in Winnipeg, Canada, and there is an important crude palm-oil market in Kuala Lumpur. There is also a London soybean meal futures market. Contracts in rapeseed oil (in Winnipeg) and soybean oil (in London) have fallen into disuse, but they may be revived one day. There are also active options markets in soybeans, meal, and oil in Chicago. Because of the variety of contracts, it is possible to devise trading strategies which closely fit one's reason for trading, and the choice of trading beans, meal, oil, or some combination rests on one's perception of what is moving the markets. Recall the fundamental price relationships; that soybean and soybean meal prices are closely correlated; that soybean oil and crude palm-oil prices are closely correlated, but can move independently of the prices of beans and meal; and that rapeseed prices are correlated with soybean prices, but the closeness of this correlation is affected by the fact that rapeseed contains more oil and is thus more heavily influenced by oil prices.

Given these price relationships, it is more straightforward to trade one of the two soybean products. Let us consider the demand side influences on these products; these are simpler and somewhat easier to disentangle than the supply side influences.

The demand for soybean meal is a function of the demand for feed as a whole and the price of protein relative to other feedstuffs. Within the USA this second consideration does have some weight, with farmers often increasing their use of soybean meal when it is cheap relative to corn. Overall, however, it is the total feed demand, and particularly the feed demand from protein-using meat sectors, which is most important. This is determined by the profitability of meat production. Accordingly, trends in consumer demand for meat, and particularly demand for pork and poultry products in the USA, Japan, and western Europe, have the most direct impact on the soybean meal market. Generally speaking, there is a positive correlation between economic growth and demand for meat, but the inherent lags in meat production, which are discussed in greater length in Chapter 8, mean that there can be a lag between a surge in consumer demand on the one hand, and an increase in farmer demand for feedstuffs on the other hand.

Purchases by the Soviet Union can be large, but are unpredictable in size and frequency. Over the longer term there is little doubt that Soviet protein import requirements will rise as meat consumption rises, but there will continue to be wide fluctuations around this trend. Soviet purchasing can also vary between beans and meal, depending on their domestic production of oil-bearing crops and the availability of their crushing capacity.

To the extent that one holds a bullish view of soybean meal consumption, one ought to trade soybean meal rather than soybeans. One caveat, however, is the following: because soybean meal is consumed in the meat industry, a bullish view of soybean meal is often the result of a bullish view of the pork and poultry markets. It is therefore possible (and indeed perfectly sensible) to be holding long positions in soybean meal, hogs, and corn for the same underlying reason; that consumer demand for pork is expanding strongly. This is of concern only in terms of portfolio balance; if one has only a small portfolio, it may not be prudent to become over-exposed in what can effectively be the same trade.

Soybean oil prices are determined as part of the whole vegetable oil complex. Although the premiums and discounts for different types of vegetable oil do vary, all the major oils follow the same trend. Generally speaking, good economic performance and growing consumer incomes in the populous developing countries of the world will lead to increases in demand for vegetable oils. If this coincides with any production difficulties in any of these countries, there can be a sudden large increase in demand for oils from the world market. The Indian drought in summer 1987 led to a sharp increase in India's imports of palm, rapeseed, and soy oils; rapid economic growth in China is leading to increases in Chinese oil imports.

Palm-oil is perhaps soy oil's most important competitor. For this reason, the level of palm-oil supply is an important influence on soy oil prices. Monthly statistics on production and stocks in Malaysia are provided by the Malaysian authorities, and they often give advance notice of future price changes in soy oil. Palm-oil production can vary in the short term because of the weather, even though it is a tree crop, and the concentration of so large a share of world palm production in a small area of South-east Asia does expose the crop to adverse weather patterns. Developments in the palm-oil market in Kuala Lumpur, and in the cash vegetable oil markets in Rotterdam, often provide valuable clues about future price directions in the Chicago soy oil market. Located in Chicago, soy oil futures tend to put exaggerated weight on US developments and are insufficiently sensitive to what is going on halfway around the globe; astute traders can take advantage of this. The Kuala Lumpur palm-oil futures market is a valuable guide to what is happening to the vegetable oil market in South and South-east Asia, an area of crucial importance for the world vegetable oil supply–demand balance.

Trading on the basis of a supply side view is somewhat more complicated. Clearly, the supply of soybean meal and of soybean oil is determined by the supply of soybeans. Therefore, disruptions to the supply of oilseeds affect beans, meal, and oil, but the effect on oil prices is likely to be less, because of the availability of a wider range of alternative vegetable oils. However, if reduced production of soybeans occurs at the same time as reduced production of palm-oil, the effects on vegetable oil prices can only be described as dramatic.

The two main determinants of soybean (and rapeseed) production are planted area and yield; therefore, plantings and weather developments in the major producing countries should be carefully followed. Soybeans are planted in the spring, usually after the alternative crops have been sown, and are sensitive to hot, dry conditions during the summer. The major producers are the USA, Brazil, and, of lesser importance, Argentina; because the crop is produced in both hemispheres, there are four periods of the year when the supply side developments need to be followed carefully (i.e. the planting and growing seasons in both hemispheres). Developments in the USA need to be followed with particular care, partly because of the size of the US crop and partly because the US is effectively the only supplier of whole soybeans; Brazil and Argentina export very few unprocessed soybeans, preferring to export the meal.

The major opportunities to trade soybeans come regularly throughout the year. In the spring US farmers make their planting decisions. The two most important influences on these are, first, the corn–soybean price ratio, and second, government policy. The US Department of Agriculture has a wide range of policies which affect farmers' output decisions, including price supports, land set-asides, and land conservation programmes. As information about plantings becomes available, it becomes possible to take a view on the supply–demand balance for the coming season and to trade accordingly.

The rather high degree of concentration of US and, indeed,

world soybean production in the American Midwest makes the market extremely sensitive to the weather in the key growing period of the summer. An example of this sensitivity is provided by the behaviour of the November 1987 futures contract during the summer of that year. (November is the first delivery month of the new crop year.) In March the contract traded between $4.70 and $4.80 per bushel. Low farmer plantings in the spring started the market on an upward move, and in early May a wave of hot, dry weather led to concern that the newly seeded crop would be unable to establish itself. This pushed prices to a high of just over $6.10 per bushel in mid-May. As temperatures cooled prices fell back, but did not fall through $5.40. In June a second wave of hot, dry weather led to concern over yields and prices were pushed up to a high of $6.24 per bushel on 16 June. There is a farmers' adage, however, which holds that dry weather is good for planting, since it encourages the crop to build a strong root system; so when the rains came at the end of June, they were early enough to save the crop and prices fell all the way back down, reaching a bottom of $4.92 per bushel on 12 August. Therefore, between March and August the market moved by over $1.20 per bushel up and then down not because the crop was affected by drought, but because there were fears that it would be.

Trading soybeans during this period (when it is a 'weather market') can be highly profitable; each cent move on the Chicago soybean contract is worth $50, so a $1.20 move is worth $6,000. Weather markets have some particular characteristics, however. Because weather forecasts are unreliable (and are more unreliable the further into the future they cover) they are risky markets. Moreover, they are riskier to trade on Fridays than Mondays; the market is closed on Saturday and Sunday, so Friday's trading must reflect the weather forecasts for two days, whereas trading on the other days of the week does not have to deal with as much uncertainty. Just as coffee prices rise before the frost season, and then fall *if there is no frost*, so in a 'weather market' soybean prices will rise on Fridays and will fall on Mondays *if there is no adverse weather over the weekend*. A high-risk high-profit trade is to short soybeans on the close on Friday, and take the position out on Monday. On two occasions during the 1987 'weather market' soybeans moved down the daily 30 cent limit on Mondays: i.e. on 18 May and 22 June. A slightly less risky way of running this trade is to buy a put option on Friday.

As the summer draws to a close, the size of the crop becomes widely known. As newly harvested soybeans move on to markets cash and futures prices typically reach their seasonal lows, with the futures reacting to the pressure of heavy hedging sales. At this time, the market turns its attention to an assessment of likely demand over the coming year. Attention quickly turns, however, to the southern hemisphere crops, which enter their weather-sensitive stage during the northern hemisphere winter months. The size of the Brazilian crop is not known with any certainty until late March, by which time the market is turning its attention back to prospects for next season's plantings in the USA.

At each of these stages, a view can be taken on the supply-demand balance and a position initiated on the basis of the view. One further feature of the soybean market should be noted, however. Soybeans have often been called the 'gold' of the agricultural commodities, meaning that it is the most important vehicle used by speculators. Often a widespread perception about general price trends (inflationary or deflationary) will lead to increased speculative trading in soybeans, which are often seen as a key indicator of general price movements. In the very short term (i.e. hour to hour) there is often a very close correlation between the direction of movement in gold and soybean prices, for this reason. Of course, they can and do diverge in the longer term.

Apart from outright positions in beans, meal, or oil, the soy complex is rich in spread trading possibilities. One popular spread is the old crop/new crop spread, using the July and November soybean contracts. When current year stocks are tight but there is an expectation for a good harvest from the new crop, a long July/short November spread will work well. Conversely, when current supplies are adequate but there is the expectation of a poor harvest, a short July/long November spread will work well. In either case, the position is less risky than trading the new crop month outright. This makes a spread an attractive way of trading the highly volatile 'weather markets'.

There are also two common spread trades taking advantage of the linkages among bean, oil, and meal prices. The first is an oil-meal spread. Imagine that demand for soybean meal is very strong, but demand for vegetable oils is poor. To satisfy the demand for meal, crushers will increase their processing pace, leading to a large build-up in the supply of soy oil; with weak oil demand, it is a recipe for low oil prices. Provided that there are adequate supplies of soybeans, an increase in soy meal demand need not push up prices of beans, but it will, under these circumstances, mean that meal prices must go up relative to those of oil. Hence a long meal/short oil spread will yield considerable profits. This type of trade is a way of taking position on the proportion of the soybean's value, which comes from its oil and from its meal.

A second type of trade is to take a view on the crush margin. The gross processing margin measures the cost of soybeans in relation to the revenue from selling meal and oil. The crush margin can be simply calculated from quoted prices by recalling that one 60 lb bushel of soybeans will yield 48 lb of meal and 11 lb of oil, and that soy meal prices are quoted in dollars per short ton. The product value will be the oil price multiplied by 11, plus the meal price divided by 2,000, multiplied by 48. (There are 2000 lb in a short ton.) Thus the crush margin will be this, minus the price of a bushel of soybeans.

For example, at the close of trading on 8 January 1988, May 88 futures were quoted as follows: beans $6.40 per bushel, oil $0.226 per lb, and meal $183.20 per ton. Therefore, the product value is:

$$(0.226 \times 11) + (183.2/2000 \times 48) = 2.486 + 4.367 = \$6.88$$

The crush margin therefore is:

$$6.88 - 6.40 = 48 \text{ (i.e. \$0.48/bushel)}$$

From week to week, the crush margin does vary considerably. If this level of 48 cents is a profitable level, a processor might hedge by 'putting on the crush', buying soybean futures and selling oil and meal futures. This will assure the processor of a gross processing margin of 48 cents; the soybean futures position will be closed out when the beans are bought in the cash market, and the meal and oil positions will be covered when cash market sales are made. The speculative opportunity comes when crush margins decline to a level where they no longer provide an adequate return to the processor. This can happen for a variety of reasons connected with the short-term supply and demand pressures in the market. In this situation the crush margin will have to rise; hence one can take out the opposite position to the normal hedge. This is called the 'reverse crush' and consists of selling soybeans and buying meal and oil, on the ground that the product return must rise relative to the beans to ensure the profitability of crushing.

The reverse crush is a low-risk trade, the exchange margin requirement for which is very low. By the same token, it is a low-profit trade. Because of its popularity floor traders in Chicago offer it as a package: in the above example, they would offer the crush at 49 cents and bid it at 47. The reverse crush is commonly taken with a 1:1:1 ratio of contracts, but an exact correspondence between futures exposure and the normal yield of soybeans would require ten bean, nine oil, and twelve meal contracts. The normal 1:1:1 ratio is accurate enough for most purposes, however.

There are, of course, many other spreading possibilities.

Chicago soybeans can be spread against Winnipeg rapeseed, but this trade will be affected by the exchange rate between the US and Canadian currencies. Chicago soy oil can be spread against Kuala Lumpur palm-oil, but this again involves substantial exchange rate risk.

A popular inter-commodity spread is the soybean–corn, or soy meal–corn spread. The protein–carbohydrate price ratio is important in determining both farmers' plantings and their animal feeding practices. Another reason for its popularity derives from the popularity of soybeans among the speculative community. During bull markets in grains and oilseeds as a whole, soybeans often go up in price by more than grains; indeed soybean prices are generally more volatile than grain prices. Soybean–corn spreads provide one way of profiting from these movements.

Chapter eight

Livestock and meat

Livestock and meat – an introduction

Livestock are husbanded the world over, principally for their meat, but also yielding milk and eggs as a source of protein for human diets. These protein sources are central to human diets, especially in rich countries, giving animal husbandry an important role in the world's agriculture. In the USA livestock production accounts for one-third of total farm income. In fact this importance is all the greater because of the large quantity of the world's grain which is used as animal feed; hence many of the world's arable farmers are producing to satisfy consumer demands for animal protein. There is, however, enormous variation in the types of meat which are favoured in different countries and the agricultural systems which are used in their production; this limits international trade in meat and is one reason why meat markets tend to follow domestic developments rather more closely than international factors. The international trade which does take place tends to be of particular types of meat on concentrated trade routes. There is really no definable 'world market' for meat.

Livestock and meat products are among the most interesting commodities which can be traded on futures markets, although they have a short history by the standards of futures trading in grains. The introduction in 1962 of a contract on pork bellies by the Chicago Mercantile Exchange (CME) ushered in a range of other contracts, both in Chicago and in other centres around the world. Currently meat complex futures contracts are traded in Chicago, London, Amsterdam, Sydney, and São Paulo.

The factor which inhibited the earlier development of meat complex futures was the difficulty in devising a contract. Meat products are not easily defined as commodities, given the heterogeneity of the animals from which they are made; yet the liquidity and the range of industry interest which are essential for a successful

159

futures contract can only be secured if a contract can be devised which is relevant to the needs of those involved in the underlying physical trade. This ceased to be a problem when intensification of agriculture in the postwar period (especially in North America) led to considerable advances in livestock breeding and feeding practices. One consequence of this was increasing uniformity in the age and weight of animals at slaughter and, in the USA at least, it became possible to view a range of animals and meat products as commodities.

The CME's pork belly contract was the first meat complex contract. Bellies are unsliced bacon and not only was it possible to treat them as a commodity, but they can also be stored in refrigerated warehouses. They are also subject to extreme price volatility, for reasons which will be explained. Therefore, it was comparatively straightforward to incorporate pork bellies into the then existing framework of storable, agricultural commodities once it was possible to define quality standards for bellies which were relevant to a large volume of cash market transactions.

A number of other contracts on meat or animal carcasses have been developed, following the CME's lead. Boneless beef was traded for many years in Chicago and New York, and one of many meat contracts which have been attempted in London was a pigmeat contract, denominated in lots of 50 carcasses meeting set quality requirements.

A much more significant innovation, however, came with the introduction of live cattle futures on the CME in 1965, followed by live hogs in 1966. Live cattle and live hogs are slaughter-ready animals; hence the price of these animals in the spot market is the price paid by abattoirs for animals for immediate slaughter.[1] Again, these animals could be defined as commodities because agricultural production techniques had reached the point in the early 1960s where standardized quality classifications could be drawn up for slaughter-ready animals, in the knowledge that the quality of the carcass could be assessed while the animal is still alive. What is distinctive about contracts for live animals, however, is that they cannot be stored.

The optimum slaughter weight of an animal is defined by the cost of feeding it (i.e. the price of grain and the interest rate), the rate of weight gain (i.e. the rate at which the animal converts feed into meat), and the price of meat. The rate of weight gain is partly determined by the animal's age; as they get older they become less efficient at converting feed into meat. This seriously constrains a farmer's choice about when to send animals to market; doing it early, while the animal is still putting on weight efficiently, is to forgo some weight gain, whereas doing it late, when the animal is no longer gaining weight efficiently, is to waste the money spent on feed. In practice, almost all animals are sent to market at approximately the same age, with little more than a few weeks' variation around the average age.

Clearly, live cattle and hogs cannot be stored in the way that, say, grains can be; once the animal has been slaughtered, its meat can be frozen and stored, but fresh meat (which commands a price premium over frozen meat)[2] obviously cannot be stored for long. Moreover, contracts on meat, rather than on animals, do not provide hedging opportunities for farmers. The absence of stocks which can be built up or drawn down in response to price movements and the limited ability of farmers to adjust the timing of supply of animals to market mean that cash prices are volatile. It was also thought that the absence of stocks would make it difficult to establish a futures market since traders would not be able to set price differences between contract months on the basis of carrying charges. In the event, trading in meat complex futures has been extremely successful in the USA; the CME live cattle and live hog futures contracts are among the most actively traded agricultural futures in the world. Elsewhere meat futures have not met with the same success. Because of the dominance of Chicago in meat complex futures, the following discussion concentrates on these markets. At the end of this chapter, however, information is presented on the smaller markets elsewhere.

As we saw in Chapter 1, some of the most interesting questions about the performance of futures markets in reducing cash market volatility and forecasting cash prices have been raised in connection with livestock futures. The evidence indicates that futures trading has reduced cash market volatility, but livestock futures are themselves highly volatile; this increases their attractiveness to both hedgers and speculators. Let us examine the reasons for this volatility.

Price volatility is the result of the cyclical pattern of supply and demand. Demand for meat is income elastic, the result of consumers' willingness to buy meat (a relatively expensive item) when their incomes are high and growing. The cyclical pattern of supply, however, is both more interesting and more important in determining the path of prices, and it derives from the limited flexibility which farmers have in adjusting their meat production. Each animal can be raised for slaughter (i.e. for meat now) or it can be retained for breeding (i.e. for the meat available later from its offspring). In the case of beef cattle, the time lag between a decision to expand beef production and the beef actually being produced can be as long as two years. What is more, once the decision has been made, there is little flexibility in the timing of production.

A classic cattle cycle begins when favourable economic conditions cause consumers to increase beef consumption, thus driving up beef prices. Farmers respond to this by expanding their herds, but a consequence of this is that near-term supplies of beef are reduced, as animals are held back for breeding. This drives beef prices even higher. By the time the additional beef supplies reach the market, consumer taste for beef is waning, so that the additional supplies push prices down. Reacting to lower prices, farmers liquidate their breeding herds, thus both increasing the short-term pressure on prices through the increment to supply and setting the market up for its next cycle as the smaller breeding herd means beef supplies will be reduced in the future.

Clearly, no cycle follows this exact pattern, although there was an astonishing degree of regularity in cattle cycles throughout the 1950s, 1960s and 1970s. Fundamentally, however, the cycles are the results of the inherent lags in cattle production, which are the result of the biological constraints on cattle reproduction and growth. When prices for beef and for the major inputs in beef production, feedstuffs, and interest rates are free to fluctuate, cycles are exaggerated; but cattle cycles occur even in economies where government regulation limits the ability of prices to move.

Within the hog market[3] exactly the same pattern is seen, although the cycles have a much shorter periodicity. This arises because pigs have shorter reproductive cycles, multiple births, and reach optimum slaughter weights faster. The hog cycle has also attracted the interest of economists: one of the first studies of the time-path of prices in a competitive market, which resulted in the famous 'cobweb theorem',[4] was based on the hog market.

Successful trading of meat complex futures rests on the ability to identify and forecast the path of these cycles. In order to indicate how this can be done, we need to look more carefully at the individual markets.

The cattle cycle and the determination of cattle prices

There are two cattle contracts on the CME, feeder cattle and live cattle. Feeder cattle are young animals, sold by breeding herd operators to feedlots. Typically a feeder will be 5–6 months old and will weigh 600–650 lb when it is sold. On a feedlot it is fed intensively for approximately six months, up to a weight of 1,000–1,100 lb, when it is sold for slaughter. Live cattle are these slaughter-ready animals. The live cattle contract is more actively traded by both hedgers and speculators, but the price of feeder cattle is watched closely by careful traders because of the clues it gives about the evolution of the cattle cycle. Before considering the supply side influences, however, let us look at the demand side factors which influence the markets.

Consumer demand

Traditional analysis of cattle markets downplayed consumer demand. The rationale for this was that fluctuations in supply were far more important in determining short-term market movements. Moreover, beef was for a long time the favoured meat of the US consumer, and it was assumed that this loyalty gave beef a privileged position in meat markets. More recently, however, it has become necessary to pay close attention to the evolution of consumer demand for three main reasons.

First, price competition with other meats has increased. The rapid intensification of pork and, especially, poultry production has brought sharp real price falls in these meats. Beef production, on the other hand, has been much less susceptible to advances through improvements in breeding and feeding practices.

Second, the poultry industry, which is much more vertically integrated than beef production, has adopted sophisticated marketing strategies to increase the popularity of poultry products; there has been a particularly marked success in boosting consumption of poultry in restaurants and fast-food outlets. Even fast-food hamburger chains, which are a major market for beef, now offer chicken products to their customers.

Third, red meat in general has suffered a loss of popularity as a result of the general swing in US diets away from foods containing large amounts of animal fats and towards lighter, low-fat foods. This has been part of a change towards what are seen as healthier life-styles.

Taken together, these factors have had two principal effects. The first is to reduce the severity of the fluctuations in beef prices since consumers will no longer continue to buy beef when supply shortages push its price up; and the second is to increase the sensitivity of beef prices to developments elsewhere in the meat complex. In years past, traders would routinely go long of cattle without bothering to check the prospects for pork and poultry production; now such a course would be imprudent, to say the least.

Overall, then, there are three main demand side factors which need to be assessed when trading the cattle market. The first is the level of economic growth and its implications for consumer income. Generally rising consumer income is bullish for beef prices, and falling income is bearish. To the extent that economic growth benefits the lower-paid section of the workforce, it is especially bullish for beef: poorer people in the USA have a higher income elasticity of demand for meat in general, and they have been less affected by the general trend away from beef and towards poultry.

The second is the changing pattern of consumer tastes. The meat industry spends very heavily on advertising, and there are short-term cycles in consumer preferences which are important. In part, these are seasonal: poultry consumption is high at Thanksgiving, whereas beef consumption tends to rise around the time of the Memorial Day (late May/early June) and Labour Day (early September) holidays. In general, however, a period of strong beef demand is often followed by a period of weaker demand. Advertising campaigns are frequently the reason for rises and falls in the popularity of the different meats.

The third is the likely level of competition with other meats. It is very unusual to see beef prices rise sharply when prices for pork and poultry are falling sharply, although the three meats certainly do not have stable price relationships.

Supply

To assess supply of beef is to assess what farmers and feedlot operators are doing. This involves consideration of the longer-term trends in herd rebuilding and liquidation, on the one hand, and the shorter-term movements of cattle to slaughter as feedlot managers exercise what flexibility they do have in the placing, feeding, and marketing of animals, on the other hand.

Decisions made by farmers about long-term expansion of their herds rest on their estimates of the future profitability of beef production, which will be a function of current and expected beef prices, feed prices, interest rates, and the other costs involved in farming. A number of attempts have been made to quantify this relationship, but none has been particularly successful. A less rigorous, but very useful, approach is to concentrate on the following three comparatively straightforward pieces of information.

The first significant indicator is the steer–corn price ratio. The price ratio is calculated as the number of bushels of corn which can be purchased with the revenue from 100lbs of slaughter-ready steer. (This is easy to calculate since the prices for slaughter-

164

ready cattle are normally quoted in dollars per hundredweight; the US Department of Agriculture (USDA) calculates the ratio for Omaha, Nebraska, every week, and it is this ratio that is followed by analysts.) Since corn is the major element in the cost of feeding cattle, this ratio gives a rough-and-ready index of the profitability of being a cattle farmer. Broadly speaking, values of this ratio over 30 are considered to be a signal for farmers to begin herd expansion since they indicate that there are profits in beef production. Therefore, this is a bullish sign for live cattle prices since animals will be held back from the market for breeding. The ratio is volatile, however, so it is important not to attach too much weight to individual weekly calculations. Here the fact that it is a ratio cannot be stressed too much: there are many examples of trades being initiated because feed prices are changing, whereas farmers respond to the profitability of beef production, not the absolute level of their costs. Grain price rises which are not followed by beef price rises may well affect farmer behaviour, but it is important not to look at feed costs in isolation.

Second, it is important to watch what happens to heifers in the cattle herd. Since male calves are routinely sent to slaughter anyway, the decision is about whether to slaughter or breed female calves. A sharp drop in the number of heifers sent for slaughter will indicate that herd expansion is beginning. The sex breakdown of slaughtered animals can be followed on a regular basis, but one of the most reliable indicators of what is happening to female cattle is provided by the twice-yearly livestock census. This, then, is the third important piece of information to which close attention should be paid. The census provides a comprehensive breakdown of the cattle population by age, sex, and weight, and it is possible to get a good idea of the number of heifers being kept for breeding from the data it contains. An increase in heifer retentions is another bullish signal for live cattle prices.

Taken together, these three pieces of information are vitally important in determining the longer-term movements in cattle prices on their cyclical path. In the shorter term, however, it is possible to follow closely the behaviour of month-to-month fluctuations in supply through the regular 'cattle on feed' reports.

Every month the USDA provides figures on the activities of feedlots in the seven largest cattle-feeding states. Every quarter the coverage is expanded to the thirteen largest states. In these statistical reports there are three important figures: the number of cattle placed during the month; the inventory of animals on the feedlots; and the number sold from feedlots for slaughter. These figures, therefore, provide valuable information about the flow of animals through the system. High placements one month will lead to high levels of marketings between five and seven months later; if the fifth and sixth months pass with light marketings, then it is highly likely that there will be heavy supply in the seventh. Combining figures on the weight of slaughter animals with these monthly feed-lot figures can lead to valuable insights into the short-term movements in cattle supply. Although cattle from feedlots are not the only supply of beef in the USA, they are the most important for the live cattle futures contract since the quality specifications for delivery are strict. The other element of beef supply, known as 'non-fed slaughter', can affect wholesale beef prices and thus exerts an indirect influence on the futures markets. Imports of beef are permitted but controlled by quotas, which are linked to the condition of the US market. As a result, they do not have a marked impact on price patterns.

One final indicator of the future course of live cattle prices is the price of feeder cattle. An old adage in the cattle market is that 'feeders are the leaders', an expression of the widely held belief that price movements in feeder cattle are a leading indicator of price movements in live cattle. The underlying rationale for this view is that, if the industry foresees strong prices for live cattle, then feedlot operators will compete for the available supply of feeder cattle, driving up supplies. Moreover, if herd rebuilding is under way, then the impact of farmers holding back animals for breeding will be felt first in the form of lower feeder cattle supply.

All the factors combine to make the cattle market fluctuate cyclically within quite narrow bands. As Figure 12 shows, Chicago live cattle prices are rarely below 50 cents per pound and rarely above 70 cents per pound. Within these bands, however, there are opportunities to trade.

The hog cycle and the determination of hog prices

The Chicago Mercantile Exchange has contracts on live hogs and pork bellies. Live hogs are, like live cattle, slaughter-ready animals; each hog produces hams, loins, and bellies. Bellies, two of which are cut from each animal and which come from the lower central part of the anatomy, are sliced into bacon. There used to be a futures contract on hams, but it was withdrawn after failing to generate a sufficient volume of trade. Clearly, these two contracts are closely related, because supply of fresh bellies is determined by the slaughter of hogs and because the demand for bellies is one determinant of the demand for hogs. For the most part, the two markets do move in the same direction, although the pace and size

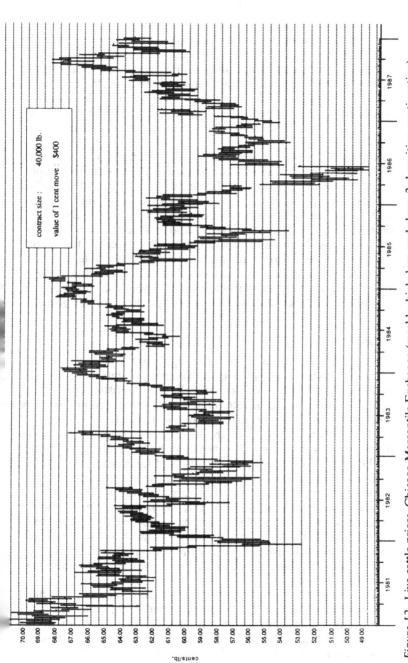

contract size : 40,000 lb.

value of 1 cent move : $400

Figure 12. Live cattle prices, Chicago Mercantile Exchange (weekly, high, low, and close, 3rd position continuation)

of movements certainly are not always the same.

Cyclical patterns dominate the pork markets, and many of the factors which affect cattle are relevant to hogs and pork bellies. Certainly, the general trend in consumer diets has affected pork adversely. It is increasingly important to pay close attention to the demand for pork and for meat as a whole, and to the supply of competitive meats, when assessing the movements in hog prices. Hence the factors discussed in the section on cattle, above, are also relevant here.

Demand pressures, however, are less important in the pork belly market, which can still be analysed in the traditional, supply-oriented way. This is because the demand for bacon, which bellies are used to produce, is highly inelastic; people who consume bacon with their breakfast appear not to be very sensitive to changes in the price at which bacon is sold. While the total demand for bacon has been affected by consumer preferences for lighter, less fatty meats, there is no bacon substitute available for those who still enjoy meat for their breakfast. This contrasts strongly with the demand for meat at other meals, where consumers appear willing to switch between beef, pork, and poultry on price grounds.

Supply

Since pork bellies can be frozen, the supply to the market, the most important factor affecting price movements, is determined by the fresh supply and the level of stocks. Regular statistics on the flow of bellies into and out of refrigerated warehouses are provided by the USDA, and they need to be followed closely. Obviously the level of fresh supply is set by the level of hog slaughter; this takes us to the cyclical nature of hog production. As in the case of cattle, the key problem is to identify the stages of the hog cycle.

The hog cycle is, in essence, the same as the cattle cycle, in that it springs from the choice faced by farmers over whether to breed or slaughter female pigs. However, because hogs have shorter pregnancies than cattle ($3\frac{3}{4}$ months compared to 9) and have multiple births (cattle have single births), and because they reach slaughter weights faster (5-6 months compared to 12), the hog cycle is shorter than the cattle cycle; there are also some other important differences.

First, hogs need more complex diets than cattle;[5] the two main components of diets are soybean meal and corn; hence the hog–corn ratio is a less satisfactory indicator of the profitability of hog production than its counterpart in cattle. One needs to pay attention to the relative cost of soybean meal, too.

168

Second, the structure of hog production is different from that of cattle. Whereas cattle production is concentrated in large feedlots, hogs are produced by a much larger number of smaller farmers, who raise hogs alongside their other activities. Typically they also engage in the entire process, from breeding to fattening. As a result, there is only a small market in feeder pigs; most are fattened on the farms where they are born. Hog production is attractive for corn farmers since, if they raise hogs, they can market their corn either as grain or pork. Hog-raising also helps them to spread their labour requirements around the year, and allows them to diversify their risks.

This more diffuse production structure implies that it is much more difficult to collect regular and comprehensive data. The key data source is the quarterly *Hogs and Pigs Report*, which surveys hog farmers in the major producing states. It produces data on the size of the pig herd, the average number of pigs per litter, and the age and sex composition of the herd. It also surveys farrowing intentions; this is the number of farmers who intend to breed their sows over the coming period. This is therefore an indicator of future hog herd expansion, but it must be interpreted carefully since intentions do not always correspond to later behaviour.

The data contained within the report, coupled with the hog–corn and hog–soybean meal price data, provide the best indicators of the evolution of the hog cycle. In the short term, one needs to follow the daily and weekly slaughter figures and the average weight of the hogs which are slaughtered, but these numbers must be complemented by sensitivity to the behaviour of farmers; since many hog farmers also grow corn and/or soybeans, there are periods when daily hog marketings fall because the farmers are attending to their crops. During the spring sowing and autumn harvesting periods there can be unusual short-term movements in hog prices as the flow of hogs to market is affected by farmers' other activities.

Like the cattle market, the live hog market fluctuates within a band, rarely below 35 cents per pound and rarely above 60 cents per pound, as is shown in Figure 13. It is quite volatile within this band, however.

Trading the livestock markets

Farmers, feedlot operators, and meat-packing companies are active users of the livestock futures markets to hedge their cash market positions. The cyclical fluctuations in the markets, however, also give a great opportunity to speculators. Another

169

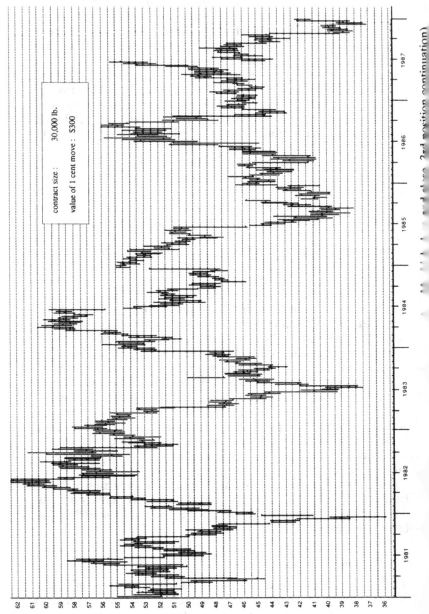

cents/lb.

contract size : 30,000 lb.

value of 1 cent move : $300

advantage of these markets to speculators is that, because they are moved by domestic American factors, they are not affected by fluctuations in exchange rates.

Taking a position on the livestock markets involves making a judgement about the supply and demand factors, described above. Because of the uncertainties inherent in the data, however, the influence of technical factors is perhaps greater than in some other markets; accordingly, it is important to watch the chart pattern closely. The cyclical variations of cattle and hogs, however, mean that it is rather low in risk to short cattle and hogs at the upper range of the cycles, with a stop above the long-term. Similarly, a long position can be prudently initiated at the cyclical low.

A second type of trading possibility arises because of the lack of storability of the animal contracts. This prevents the establishment of 'normal' carrying charges and thus increases the chances for developing spread trades. The price for each contract month reflects the expected balance of supply and demand for that month, and the spreads between months can vary considerably. The cattle on feed figures provide regular opportunities for this, as each figure gives an indication of slaughter six months hence, but the initial response of the market tends to be similar across all actively traded months. Spreading feeder cattle against live cattle is a way of trading the markets at turning-points in the cattle cycle; feeder cattle rise in price earlier than live cattle as the rebuilding begins since feedlots have to compete for the lower supply of young animals. The reverse is true when herd liquidation begins.

It is also possible to spread live cattle against live hogs, taking advantage of the different periodicities of the hog and cattle cycles. For example, a sharp fall in grain prices, if accompanied by a steady meat market, will encourage both hog and cattle farmers to expand their herds. The increased supply of hogs will hit the market much earlier than the cattle, however, opening up the possibility of developing a long cattle/short hog spread. Finally, a popular spread is pork bellies against hogs. The seasonal variations in bacon and ham demand make it possible to spread these markets at several times of the year. For example, the demand for hams at Christmas often means that hogs gain on bellies in November and December; conversely, demand for bacon traditionally picks up in January and February and allows bellies to gain on hogs (see Figure 14).

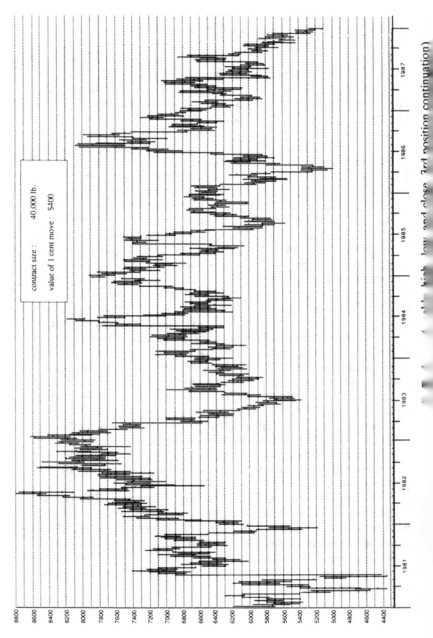

(weekly high, low and close, 3rd position continuation)

Other livestock markets

Outside the USA, a number of attempts have been made to establish livestock and meat futures markets, but nowhere has there been very much success. London has developed a range of contracts, but none has proved able to generate sufficient trading volume to ensure its continued vitality. There is a live porker contract in Amsterdam, and a live cattle contract on the São Paulo exchange. Since these markets respond entirely to domestic market developments, they do not attract a great deal of international interest.

The Sydney Futures Exchange has a history of trading livestock futures; it has experimented with a lamb contract and traded live cattle for many years. Because Australia is a substantial exporter of beef to the USA, Australian cattle prices are sensitive to changes in US demand; in fact the Australian cattle cycle is closely synchronized with that in the USA, except when exceptional weather conditions disrupt it. The Sydney market, however, has experienced difficulties in maintaining liquidity. The contract specification has been altered several times in an attempt to improve its attractiveness, but it remains very thinly traded.

Chapter nine

Coffee, sugar, and cocoa

Because coffee, sugar, and cocoa are traded together on New York's Coffee, Sugar and Cocoa Exchange (CSCE) and London's Fox, there is a tendency to think of them as closely interrelated. In fact the linkages between them are few and remote, especially when compared to the linkages within the grains, oilseeds, and livestock complex. As their supply and demand conditions are different, each of the three needs to be analysed separately.

Coffee

Coffee – the basics

Coffee is one of the world's most popular beverages. Although some quantities are used as a flavouring in the baking and confectionery industries, these are too small to be of interest. It is believed that it originated in the Kaffa province of Ethiopia, and it was being used by Arabs to make drinks as early as AD 1300.

Coffee beans are extracted from the fruit, known as cherries, of the coffee tree. The trees (which would more accurately be called bushes) take at least three years from planting before they produce a good crop, but then can be harvested every season for many years; there are examples of trees yielding fruit for up to fifty years. The two main species, arabica and robusta, differ in their climatic requirements, but both flourish only in tropical areas. Arabica coffee, grown mostly in Latin America, is milder and generally commands a price premium over robusta, grown mostly in Africa and South-east Asia, which is stronger and mainly used in blends and instant coffee.

The distinction between arabica and robusta is crucial for the futures markets, since London and Paris trade robusta and New York arabica, but for the purpose of fully understanding the market we need to draw a further distinction between 'milds' and other arabicas. Milds are produced by removing the flesh of the cherry after washing, a process which leaves only a thin parchment envelope around the beans; after drying, the parchment is removed. This is an expensive process, but it produces a higher and more consistent quality of coffee which normally sells at a premium. The main producers of milds are Colombia, and Central American countries, Kenya, and Tanzania. Other arabicas are produced by simply drying the beans in the sun, after which the outer skin and parchment are easily removed. This produces coffee which is less even in quality and somewhat rougher in taste. Brazil is the major producer of this type of arabica, but Brazil's production is not all of arabica, also producing 'conillon', a robusta-type coffee.

Supply

Table 23 presents data on recent production patterns. Brazil has been the world's major producer for a century, but its share of the world market has been steadily eroded by newer producers. African producers expanded rapidly in the 1960s, and the 1970s saw growth in Asian production. What is most important about Brazilian production, however, is its variability; it can vary by as much as 40 per cent from one year to the next. The cause of this variability is weather and, in particular, frost. Frosts, which can occur from May until September but are most likely in July, do not have a large effect on the current crop, but may reduce output for up to three successive seasons. A new source of concern is

Table 23 Coffee production (thousand 60 kg bags)

	1983–4	*1984–5*	*1985–6*	*1986–7*
By country:				
Brazil	30,000	27,000	33,000	11,200
Colombia	13,000	11,000	12,500	11,900
Ivory Coast	1,420	4,900	5,000	5,170
Indonesia	5,500	5,400	5,450	5,350
World total	90,049	90,070	86,360	89,830
By type of coffee:				
Colombian milds	15,020	15,030	15,140	13,480
Other arabicas	26,900	24,810	21,200	25,540
Robustas	23,000	26,000	25,390	24,830
Other milds	25,120	24,230	24,630	25,980

Source: USDA; Landell Mills Commodities Studies.

drought, which hit Brazil in the summer of 1985–6 and led to a sharply reduced 1986 crop. Unlike frost, the impact of this drought was immediate, yet posed no threat to subsequent crops; Brazil's 1987 harvest was one of the largest on record.

Disruptions to Brazilian production have an even greater impact on supplies to the world market, since the country is the second largest consumer in the world, and tends to cut back exports rather than domestic consumption when there is a shortfall. A second effect is that through prices: the high prices consequent on a poor Brazilian crop encourage new plantings by coffee farmers elsewhere, but because of the lags inherent in the crop, this only results in increased production in later years, when Brazilian output has recovered. There is a long-term trend for overproduction of coffee, whose consequences have always been mitigated by a remarkably fortuitous frost or drought in Brazil, resulting in surplus stocks being run down just when they are becoming onerous.

Consumption and prices

Consumption of coffee is highly inelastic with respect to normal price fluctuations, although it does react against the very high prices which occur periodically. Trends in incomes and consumers' tastes appear to be much more important. In the USA, which is the largest importing country, per capita consumption has declined steadily, mainly as a result of consumer preference switching to soft drinks and other beverages, particularly among younger people. Several European countries – notably France, West Germany, and Scandinavia – now consume more coffee per head than does the USA. The UK continues to lag behind other European countries in terms of quantity imported. The Japanese market, on the other hand, is growing strongly. Imports into the USSR and eastern Europe are very low and growing only slowly. Data on recent import patterns are shown in Table 24.

Consumption is large in the producing countries, especially in

Table 24 Coffee imports by ICO members (million bags)

	1983	*1984*	*1985*	*1986*
USA	19.71	20.14	20.24	19.34
EC	24.53	23.33	24.09	26.50
Scandinavia	3.48	3.54	3.12	3.31
Japan	3.85	4.01	4.30	4.51

Source: Landell Mills Commodities Studies.

176

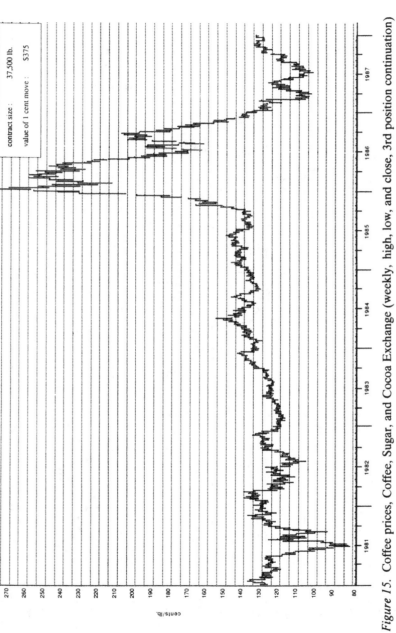

Figure 15. Coffee prices, Coffee, Sugar, and Cocoa Exchange (weekly, high, low, and close, 3rd position continuation)

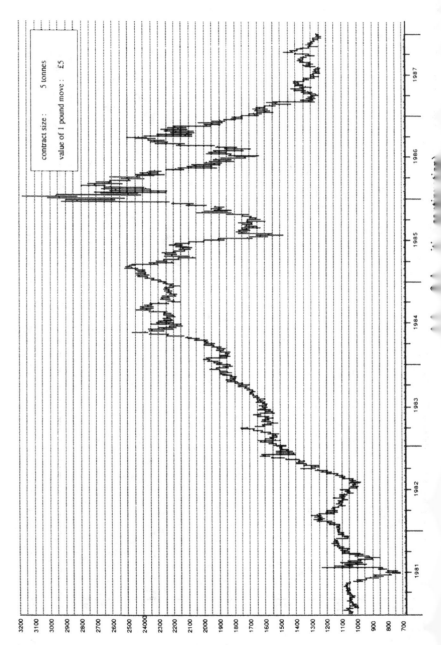

contract size :   5 tonnes

value of 1 pound move :   £5

pounds/tonne

3200 3100 3000 2900 2800 2700 2600 2500 2400 2300 2200 2100 2000 1900 1800 1700 1600 1500 1400 1300 1200 1100 1000 900 800 700

1981   1982   1983   1984   1985   1986   1987

Brazil. It is also less sensitive to the world market price since most producers sell coffee on to their domestic markets at regulated prices. For this reason, most analysts concentrate on following consumption trends in the major importing countries.

An important feature of consumption is its composition in terms of ground coffee on the one hand, and soluble, or instant, coffee on the other hand. For the most part, soluble coffees contain much more robusta and much less arabica than ground coffees, and there appears to be a general trend in consumption towards ground coffee as consumers get richer.

The price of coffee displays a strong cyclical pattern; there have been eight major price peaks since 1852, each of which has been caused by a disruption to the Brazilian supply. Each of these peaks causes a subsequent expansion of supply, which hits the market several years later, exacerbating the downward pressure on the market. Figures 15 and 16 show the price path in recent years in both the London and New York contracts; the 1985 price peak in both markets was caused by the Brazilian drought that summer.

Market intervention

Over the years there have been a number of attempts to limit the fluctuations of coffee prices. In the 1920s and 1930s, Brazil periodically destroyed her stocks in order to boost prices. In 1980 a group of Latin American producing countries formed a trading operation, Pancafé, which attempted to drive up prices by buying futures contracts. The most important regulation of the market, however, comes from the International Coffee Agreement (ICA) which, in various guises, has been operational since 1962. It has enjoyed a longer and more successful life than any other commodity agreement, principally because of the support which successive US governments have been prepared to give it. (This support stems from the strategic interests of the USA in Latin America, the major coffee-growing region; the coffee agreement represents substantial economic aid to coffee producers, and since it is paid by coffee consumers rather than by taxpayers through official budgets, it is less susceptible to political horse-trading.)

The fourth current agreement seeks to stabilize prices within a range through export quotas allocated to producing members. Consuming country members agree only to import coffee which is exported under the quota. When prices fall, quotas are cut; when they rise, quotas are increased. A large rise in prices causes the quotas to be suspended. This mechanism, which effectively regulates the flow of coffee into the export market, has been reasonably successful, but it has not resulted in a market devoid of instability and continued volatility arises from the following factors.

First, even suspension of quotas has not been able to offset the effects of serious disruption to the Brazilian crop. Because of the Brazilian drought in 1985 and the price increases it caused, quotas were formally suspended in February 1986 (having been effectively non-binding since December 1985) and were not re-introduced until October 1987. Therefore, for almost two years prices fluctuated freely, between a high of over 270 cents per pound and a low of just over 100 cents per pound.

Second, the price which the quota system defends is the ICA composite indicator price, an average of a large number of spot market quotations. It is quite possible for the ICA price to go one way and the trading futures markets to go another.

Third, and closely related to the second point, is the fact that the agreement is a political as well as an economic agreement. This manifests itself in its allocation of quota shares to countries, with little regard to the type of coffee which they produce. Given the great variety in types and qualities of coffee beans, and the fact that one country can produce a range of these, it is possible for the quota system seriously to distort the availability of certain types of coffee. This has long been a concern of importing countries, and in February 1987 they blocked the re-imposition of quotas in an attempt to change the formulae used for distributing quotas among producers.

The ICA quota and price system divides coffee into four categories: Colombian Milds (produced in Kenya and Tanzania as well as Colombia), Other Milds, Brazilian, and Other Arabicas and Robustas. The principal impact of any mismatch between these quotas and the actual availability of certain types of coffee is felt on the spot market, but there are implications for futures since the coffees traded in London and New York are of different qualities. A shortage of good-quality coffee and an excess of lower-grade coffee could leave the ICA indicator price unchanged, but it would increase the premium for New York over London.

Fourth, although virtually all producers are members of the ICA, not all consumers are; there is therefore a market in non-quota coffee. When the quota regime is very restrictive, producers expand their exports to non-quota markets, and some of this coffee finds its way into the ICA member consumers (it is known as 'tourist' coffee). Moreover, instant coffee is not covered by the quota system, although its importance in international trade is growing.

Clearly, all these features of the Agreement limit the effectiveness of the quota system. Yet it should be remembered that the ICA's aim is not to remove price instability, only to contain it within a range. What is more, despite the weaknesses of the Agreement, it is important to pay close attention to the ICA indicator price and to be aware of the implications of changes in this price for quotas. They do exert an important influence on futures market prices.

Trading the coffee markets

Since the most dramatic coffee price movements are caused by frosts and droughts in Brazil, the trading opportunities with the greatest profit potential occur at the times when the Brazilian crop is at its most sensitive to weather conditions. A large number of speculators take out long positions in April, May, and June, simply gambling that there will be a frost in July or August. It is worth bearing in mind that this trade can be profitable even if there is not a frost; it is only necessary for near-frost temperatures to strike the coffee belt for there to be a rally large enough to allow a well-timed trade to make money. Of course, the disadvantage of the 'frost trade' is that it is a pure gamble; the more cautious trader may prefer to let the market settle down after any frost and then take out a short position when it appears the market has reached a peak.

A considerably less risky opportunity is to trade the arabica–robusta differential. A shortage of good-quality coffee will increase the premium which New York enjoys over London, and therefore will make a long New York/short London spread trade profitable. Obviously the reverse spread works when there is a shortage of robusta. It should be remembered, however, that exchange rate fluctuations can affect this spread trade: if sterling strengthens against the dollar, then if nothing changes in the supply and demand for coffee, either London will go down or New York will go up, or both, simply as a result of the change in the exchange rate. In the past when there were controls on access to foreign currency, UK traders were able to use the coffee market as a way of taking a position on the sterling/dollar exchange rate.

Cocoa

Cocoa – the basics

The first recorded use of cocoa was that of a beverage in the Aztec civilization. It was brought to Europe in the sixteenth century, where it continued to be used as a beverage until 1828. In that year, van Houten found that cocoa butter could be pressed out of ground cocoa beans. Mixing this butter with ground beans and sugar produced a malleable sweet mass, chocolate. In 1876, in Switzerland, it was discovered that milk solids could be added to a mixture of ground cocoa beans, cocoa butter, and sugar; this produced milk chocolate and led to a rapid expansion in the market for cocoa. Chocolate manufacture now accounts for the great bulk of cocoa utilization.

Cocoa beans are found in the pods of the cacao tree, whose climatic requirements are such that it only grows in regions close to the equator. The beans, which can be stored for up to a year in tropical areas and up to three years in temperate areas, are fermented, dried, and then ground into liquor. This liquor is processed into powder and butter; the butter is mixed with liquor for chocolate and the powder is used in beverages and as a flavouring. New varieties of cocoa tree begin to yield only two years after planting, compared to the four years with a traditional tree. Peak yields are reached after eight to ten years, and continue until the tree is at least 20 years old. Yields are, however, affected by diseases, weather conditions, and cultivation practices.

Pods are harvested from the tree twice every year. In Brazil the two crops (known as the main and temporão crops) are approximately equal in size and quality, but in other countries the mid-crop yields fewer and lower-quality beans than the main crop.

Supply

West Africa is traditionally the major supplier of cocoa to the world market. Ghana alone supplied about 40 per cent of world production as recently as 1971. New plantings in Brazil, Malaysia, and the Ivory Coast, however, and economic difficulties in Ghana and Nigeria, have changed production patterns considerably.

One of the most serious problems in the analysis of the cocoa market is the quality of the production data. In many countries cocoa is grown by smallholders, and there are few, if any, satisfactory data on tree plantings, ages, or yields. Therefore, estimation of crop sizes requires rather more heroic assumptions than are needed to get a satisfactory statistical picture of other crops. Production estimates made by different authorities vary widely as a result.

Table 25 shows recent trends in the cocoa market. The rapid growth in Malaysian production is one obvious feature of the data; another is the high degree of variability in world production. The

182

Table 25 Cocoa supply, demand, and stocks (thousand tonnes)

	1983-4	1984-5	1985-6	1986-7
Production:				
Ivory Coast	389	523	570	575
Ghana	160	176	215	225
Brazil	294	421	381	395
Malaysia	80	92	130	150
World total	1,482	1,823	1,903	1,941
Consumption:				
West Germany	191	205	199	205
Netherlands	163	165	174	190
Other western European	283	289	304	329
USSR	141	165	177	177
USA	208	195	187	219
World total	1,663	1,770	1,811	1,888
End-period Stocks	397	451	543	596

Source: Gill and Duffus; ICCO; Landell Mills Commodities Studies.

most important cause of this variability is the weather; more particularly, drought in West Africa and Brazil is the principal weather risk.

Consumption and prices

Consumption of cocoa is heavily concentrated in high-income countries. It is rather stable, and responds to price changes only with a considerable lag. These changes in consumption, in market economies at any rate, have more to do with manufacturers' behaviour than consumers'. Most confectionery companies make both chocolate and non-chocolate products and when cocoa is cheap they attempt to boost the proportion of chocolate in their total output. Western Europe is the largest market, and buys most of its cocoa in West Africa. Brazilian cocoa, which produces a slightly more bitter chocolate, is mostly exported to the USA. Eastern Europe is of increasing importance, and per capita consumption levels there are only half those in western Europe, but imports are volatile since they are subject to political and foreign exchange constraints. The level of eastern bloc buying is one of the principal uncertainties on the consumption side of the market.

Because of the traditional trade routes, the New York futures contract tends to reflect availability of Brazilian cocoa, although all cocoas are deliverable. Similarly, the London and Paris markets reflect West African cocoas. The differences between these are not of great significance to the futures traders, however; it is not like coffee, where there is a crucial difference between arabica and robusta.

Prices are very closely correlated with the stock–consumption ratio. Because of the periodic disruptions to supply, this ratio can fluctuate widely, causing periods of rapid price rises. These high prices encourage more careful husbandry and new plantings, which lead to increases in the level of supply, a build-up in stocks and lower prices. An example of this is provided by the market since the early 1970s. A series of weather-related supply problems in both Brazil and West Africa, coupled with good demand, led to a steady decline in the stock–consumption ratio, starting in 1973. Particularly bad weather in 1977 and the worst cocoa crop for eight years pushed inventories to their lowest level since the 1950s and the stock–consumption ratio to a record low. Spot prices for cocoa in London rose from £827 per tonne in March 1976 to £3,382 per tonne in September 1977. This dramatic price rise, however, had two consequences. (See Figure 17.)

First, it helped to encourage an increase in cocoa plantings, especially in Brazil, Malaysia, and the Ivory Coast. As Table 25 shows, these countries now account for a large proportion of world output. By the mid-1980s this production was beginning to weigh on the market. Given that the cocoa tree continues to yield for over twenty years, serious oversupply is likely to be a feature of the market for several years (in the absence of weather problems) until consumption grows sufficiently to absorb the increased output.

Second, consumers began to investigate substitutes for cocoa in chocolate manufacture. This culminated in the development of cocoa butter substitutes made from vegetable oils which are now being used in some countries, where regulations about what can be legally described as chocolate permit.

Therefore, forecasting cocoa prices simply requires a good forecast of the stock–consumption ratio. Although forecasting consumption is comparatively straightforward, the difficulties in assessing, let alone projecting, production make an accurate forecast of stocks extremely hard to obtain.

Market intervention

As in the coffee market, there have been a number of unilateral and multilateral attempts to restrict the volatility of cocoa prices.

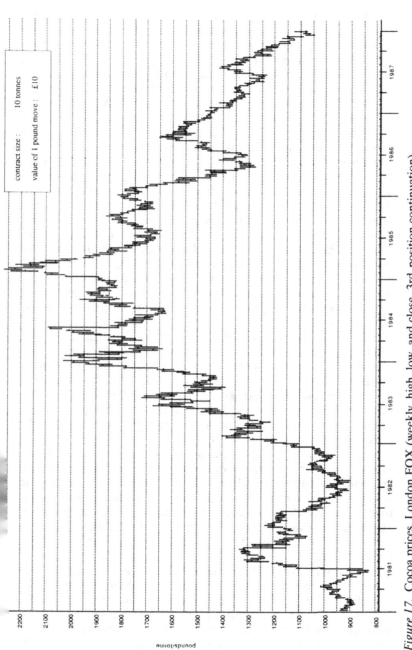

pounds/tonne

contract size :   10 tonnes

value of 1 pound move :   £10

Figure 17. Cocoa prices, London FOX (weekly, high, low, and close, 3rd position continuation)

The most important of these have been the various International Cocoa Agreements (ICCAs, distinguishing them from the International Coffee Agreements, ICAs). For the most part, these have been less than successful, principally because of the refusal of the USA to join. Successive US administrations' hostility to market intervention has never been outweighed by the strategic considerations which have made them willing to support coffee agreements.

The first ICCA was signed in 1973, and the second was signed in 1976, extended in 1979 and expired in 1980. Both of these Agreements envisaged the use of export quotas and a buffer-stock scheme to regulate the flow of cocoa to the market, but since prices were consistently above the levels at which these provisions would have been called upon, they were never used. The third ICCA came into force in 1981, but the Ivory Coast, the largest producer, did not join. Like its predecessors, it had provisions for the use of export quotas and a buffer stock, but unlike its predecessors, it had to use them. Indeed the buffer-stock manager had accumulated 60,000 within two weeks of the agreements coming into force. The buffer stock later rose to 100,000 tonnes, exhausting the ICCA's reserves, and since prices never rose to the level at which it could be sold, the stock was still intact when the Agreement expired.

The fourth ICCA was agreed in 1986, although it did not commence operations until 1987; Ivory Coast did join on this occasion. Again, the Agreement uses a buffer stock to support prices, and took over responsibility for the 100,000 tonnes of previously accumulated stocks. In the face of falling prices in early 1987, it quickly accumulated further substantial tonnages of cocoa.

One further important point about the fourth ICCA is that the price it seeks to defend, which is, like the coffee indicator price, an average over various market quotations, is denominated in SDRs/tonne (the SDR, or special drawing right, is a basket of major international currencies which was originally developed by the International Monetary Fund); the reason that this artificial unit is used in the ICCA is to minimize the impact on its operations of exchange rate fluctuations. Trading the cocoa market when the buffer-stock manager is active does require monitoring of the SDR exchange rate.

There are a number of reasons why the ICCA has not been very successful in restricting price volatility; the absence of the USA and the selection of the target prices are the most important. During the first and second ICCAs prices were set too low; during the current Agreement they have been set too high and the buffer stock has accumulated large tonnages of cocoa with no appreciable impact on the market price. Underlying the failure, however, is that there is no reason to believe that a buffer-stock capability of a size which the major consuming countries are prepared to support can have a serious impact on prices. In part, this is because as long as there is a buffer stock willing to absorb the costs of stock-holding, and using highly visible criteria for its decisions to accumulate or liquidate, private operators have a diminished incentive to carry stocks themselves. Thus buffer stocks largely displace private stockholding; to affect market prices they would need to represent additional storage, and this means that the costs of effective buffer-stock schemes are huge.

Trading the cocoa market

Since it is the stock–consumption ratio which determines cocoa prices, trading the market requires taking a view on this ratio. And since consumption is relatively stable, it is supply shifts which are the most important influence. As in most of the other agricultural markets, however, the biggest supply shifts are caused by weather fluctuations. Assessing the impact of weather developments, or other influences on supply, is made somewhat difficult by the poor quality of the data on production, but against this it should be remembered that the cocoa market does trend strongly. Because the level of production is so uncertain, it is not possible for the market quickly to digest the true meaning of, say, dry weather in Ghana and move its attention to other factors. As a result, the market will continue to move for several days in response to what appears to be the same piece of news.

It is not entirely true, however, that the demand side of the market can be ignored. Although consumption moves sluggishly in response to prices, it does move, and the timing of its moves can signal changes in the major trend in prices. A bear market can be turned round by increased consumption; a bull market can be broken by consumers' (and chocolate manufacturers') resistance to higher prices. Consumption trends therefore repay close study, especially when a supply-driven market movement appears to be running out of steam.

Unlike the coffee market, there are no real opportunities for trading New York against London and Paris. The two contracts do not differ simply by the sterling/dollar exchange rate, since New York primarily reflects Brazilian cocoa and London and Paris reflect West African, but the exchange rate is by far the most important factor. In the days of exchange controls it was possible to use cocoa to speculate on the exchange rate, but since foreign exchange futures contracts now exist, this is not a sensible practice. It is worth taking into account an exchange rate view when deciding which market to trade, however: if one is bearish of cocoa and bullish of sterling, it is better to take a short position in London where the currency movement will reinforce the movement in cocoa.

Sugar

Sugar – the basics

Sugar, or sucrose, to give it its chemical name, is an important source of energy in human diets. It is consumed directly in the household, and indirectly in soft drinks, confectionery, and bakery products. In industrial countries these uses of sugar account for as much as two-thirds of consumption. Apart from its nutritional value as a carbohydrate, sugar is also valued for its sweet taste and for its textural properties as a bulking agent in bakery products.

Sugar is produced from two different sources, sugar-beet and sugar-cane, but the end-product is chemically identical. Cane, which is a tropical plant, is believed to have originated in India over 2,500 years ago, and is now cultivated as far north as southern Spain and as far south as northern Argentina. It accounts for slightly more than 60 per cent of world sugar production. The technology for extracting sucrose from beets, a temperate-zone crop, was discovered in Germany in the mid-eighteenth century, but beet cultivation did not become widespread until Britain's naval blockade of continental Europe during the Napoleonic Wars reduced imports of cane sugar. Beet sugar now accounts for slightly less than 40 per cent of world output. A small number of countries, such as the USA, China, Japan, and Spain, produce both beet and cane, but climatic conditions normally dictate that a country produces only one.

Although the end-product of beet and cane cultivation is the same, there are important differences between the two crops in terms of production and processing. Beets are an annual crop, planted in the spring and harvested in the late autumn/early winter. Typically they are planted in rotation with grain crops. In modern factories beets are processed directly into the white sugar which is so familiar to consumers. Cane is often planted on land for which there are few other uses, and is not an annual crop; first production from new plantings is not for eighteen months or two years, and the same plant will usually yield further crops, called 'ratoons', for three or four years. Indeed, if yields are high and prices are too low to encourage farmers to plant new cane, up to eight ratoons may be taken. After harvesting, cane is processed into raw sugar, and then subsequently refined – often in a different location – into white sugar. Traditional methods of producing sugar from cane are still widely used in India; the end-products, gur and khandsari, are classified as non-centrifugal sugars (since they do not use centrifuges to separate sucrose from impurities) and are normally excluded from statistical analysis of the sugar market.

Production

Production of sugar is very widely distributed around the world, and one consequence of this is that poor production in one country is often offset by good production elsewhere. Certainly, sugar production is not as sensitive as cocoa or coffee production to weather patterns and consequent disruptions in one growing region. The EC, a beet producer, is the largest producer in the world, although its share of world output has rarely exceeded 15 per cent. The position of the EC as the leading producer is a

Table 26 Sugar production and consumption (million tonnes, raw value)

	1984	*1985*	*1986*	*1987*
Production:				
EC	13.30	13.86	14.13	13.38
Cuba	7.78	7.89	7.47	7.49
Brazil	9.26	8.46	8.00	9.03
India	6.63	7.02	7.59	9.16
USA	5.34	5.42	5.68	6.33
Eastern Europe	14.48	13.98	14.26	13.62
World total	99.20	98.55	100.26	102.53
Consumption:				
USA	7.74	7.29	7.09	7.30
EC	10.64	10.73	10.79	10.83
South America	10.67	10.60	11.49	11.26
Asia	28.31	30.20	30.88	33.15
Eastern Europe	19.35	18.66	19.40	20.49
World total	96.48	97.69	100.41	104.25
End-year stocks	51.99	51.67	50.96	48.25

Source: Landell Mills Commodities Studies.

Note: These data refer to centrifugal sugar only.

relatively recent phenomenon and largely the result of a policy of encouraging production after the 1974–5 price peak; data on recent production patterns are presented in Table 26. The Soviet Union, which is the second largest producer in the world, is included in the east Europe figures in the table. The major exporters are the EC, Cuba, Brazil, Thailand, Australia, and the Philippines. As a beet producer, the EC exports white sugar, and because of the growing importance of the EC the share of white sugar in world exports has been growing.

Consumption

Because sugar is consumed so widely, its growth path tends to be very stable, with the shortfalls in production being made up by stocks. Demand is inelastic with respect to the world market price for two main reasons. First, the high proportion of sugar which is consumed in processed goods means that even a large change in sugar prices will have only a small impact on the retail price of confectionery. Second, the effective regulation of sugar prices by government policies limits the exposure of consumers to the fluctuating world price. One important consequence of government interference in price-setting, however, is that it has established a protective umbrella under which the production of substitutes can flourish. In the USA the industry making high-fructose corn syrup (HFCS), a sugar substitute made from wet-milling corn, has expanded to the point where HFCS now accounts for a greater share of the total US sweetener market than sucrose.

This development in the USA, which has been followed albeit less dramatically in other countries, draws our attention to the relationship between income and sugar consumption. One reason for the rapid erosion in sucrose's share of the total sweetener market is the growing popularity of non-caloric sweeteners. The latest of these, aspartame, which is marketed as NutraSweet, has proved very successful, and further new products are to be launched in the near future. In the past non-caloric sweeteners, such as saccharin, were confined to a small market because of their inferior taste, but the latest generation of sweeteners do not have this drawback. They are, therefore, able to make a strong appeal to consumers anxious to reduce their calorie intake. Sucrose therefore suffers on two counts: first, because demand for caloric sweeteners as a whole is growing very slowly in rich countries; and second, because HFCS is capturing a large share of the caloric sweetener market.

In short, the income elasticity of demand for sugar is declining in rich countries. A corollary of this is that income elasticities are higher, the poorer a country is – and an important consequence of this is that the growth in sugar consumption is increasingly concentrated in poorer countries. This trend is further aided by the more rapid population growth in developing countries.

Another important feature of the utilization of sugar has nothing to do with human food consumption. Following the oil price rises in the 1970s, Brazil embarked on a major programme to use its agricultural potential to produce energy. As a result, about 65 per cent of Brazilian cane production is not used for sugar but is used in the fermentation of ethanol. This is used as an automobile fuel. Brazil's sugar exports are simply the residual once domestic sugar and ethanol needs have been satisfied, which means that both components of domestic demand are important for the evolution of world sugar prices.

The major importers are the USSR, China, Japan, and Canada. The USA used to be an extremely important importer but its growing production of both sugar and HFCS and its sluggish market for sucrose are causing a sharp contraction in its imports. Much of the Soviet import requirement is covered by a long-term agreement with Cuba (at prices which constitute a massive grant of aid to the Cubans), and the EC also imports some sugar from associated developing countries at preferential prices. The most rapid growth in imports in recent years has come from the OPEC countries.

Prices

Given the comparative stability of both production and consumption of sugar, one might think that sugar prices would also be stable. This is not the case, however, because a number of factors combine to make the sugar market rather unusual. Because it is produced in almost every country in the world, and is an important source of farmer revenue in many countries, and because it is also an important basic foodstuff, governments take an extremely active role in their internal sugar markets, seeking to give good returns to their producers and stable prices to their consumers. Indeed so much sugar is produced, consumed, and traded at prices fixed by governments or long-term trading arrangements that there is only a tiny 'free' market in sugar. Estimates suggest that less than half of the sugar which is traded internationally is traded at the free market price. Since less than one-third of sugar production is exported, even small fluctuations in world output and consumption can produce large changes in the amount of sugar which is traded freely. This is a clear recipe for extreme price instability.

What is more, because farmers and consumers are largely insulated from the free market price, there is only a limited influence of prices on production and consumption. Even a large rise in sugar prices on world exchanges will have only a tiny impact on consumer prices in most countries, and a government-imposed floor on prices in many nations limit the capacity of consumption to respond to lower prices. Similarly, if farmers are receiving guaranteed prices, they will not cut back production when world prices fall. Even when cane farmers do respond to high prices by increased plantings, it will be at least eighteen months before the extra output reaches the market.

Of course, there are many countries where farmers are exposed to world price fluctuations, to a greater or lesser extent. Certainly, farmers generally benefit from higher world market prices rather more readily than they suffer from lower; this is just the way government policies operate in many countries. The ability of cane farmers to take ratoons at low costs also allows production to be maintained, even when prices are too low to recover the full costs of production. In the past a typical pattern for sugar prices would be a short-lived, but extreme price peak, caused by a supply disruption in a major producer, and consequent heavy demand on free stocks. This would be followed by a prolonged period of price weakness as the new plantings generated by the price peak led to increased production. The long tail of ratoon production from a cane planting is clearly important in the supply response to high prices.

There is some evidence that this pattern is changing. First, the growing importance of EC beet sugar in world exports increases the speed with which sugar production can respond to price changes; beet sugar reaches the market more quickly after planting than cane and does not have cane's long tail. Second, the fact that Brazil can switch cane between sugar and ethanol also increases the ability of sugar availability to respond quickly. Finally, the decreased share of sugar in the total sweetener market, and the fact that production of other sweeteners can be expanded quickly if prices encourage it, also has implications for the price of sugar.

These longer-term trends in price behaviour notwithstanding, the key determinant of prices is the stock–consumption ratio. Whenever this ratio drops, or is expected to drop, to a critical level, it implies severe pressure on free market sugar prices.

The most spectacular bull run on the sugar market was in 1973–4, when a series of production problems occurred against a background of steady growth in consumption. Prices began rising in the summer of 1973, and when the 1974 EC beet crop appeared to be under threat prices reached the extraordinary peak, in November 1974, of 66 cents per pound. At that time, there was a widespread expectation that the stock–consumption ratio would be about 20 per cent at the end of the 1974 crop year, or below 40 per cent by the end of calendar year 1974. With the cool perspective of history, it is easy to see that this bull move was wildly overdone, and that a lot of the upward pressure was aggressive covering by nervous holders of short positions, who had sold into the early stages of the rally. Many of these short positions were held on the strong argument that the fundamentals of the sugar market did not justify such high prices for sugar: indeed this view was correct, as the subsequent slump in prices demonstrated, but the huge losses on short positions illustrate the difficulties in trading on a purely fundamental basis. None the less, this kind of move illustrates the sensitivity of sugar prices once the stock–consumption ratio drops below 50 per cent (at the end of the calendar year).

The 1980 bull market was even more interesting, even though it was less spectacular: the peak in the market was 45 cents per pound. Again, it was the prospect of the stock–consumption ratio falling well below 50 per cent that excited the market. The end-1978 stock–consumption ratio was 52 per cent; in 1979 it was 47 per cent, and in 1980 44 per cent. From that point it began to increase, to 46 per cent in 1981 and 53 per cent in 1982. Again, the price peaked in the final quarter of 1980. What is most interesting about this price peak, however, is that it was largely fuelled by expectations that the fall in the level of stocks would be even more substantial and would take the stock–consumption ratio to 40 per cent or lower. In the event, production especially in Europe was not as bad as had seemed likely; certainly, the price at 45 cents per pound was not justified by the final ratio of 44 per cent. The important point, however, is that the market is extremely sensitive to rapid upward movements once the ratio drops below 50 per cent.

From 1981 to 1987 there was a prolonged bear market, which surprised many by its length. Price behaviour in a prolonged bear market cannot be explained by the activities and expectations of futures traders; it has to be explained by supply and demand developments. Moreover, it is just as important, from the point of view of successful trading, to know why markets go down as to know why they go up. (See Figure 18.)

Four popular explanations of the bear market are the growth in the importance of non-sucrose sweeteners, the aggressive export subsidies of the EC, the generous price supports for production of sugar in the USA, which are reducing that country's import

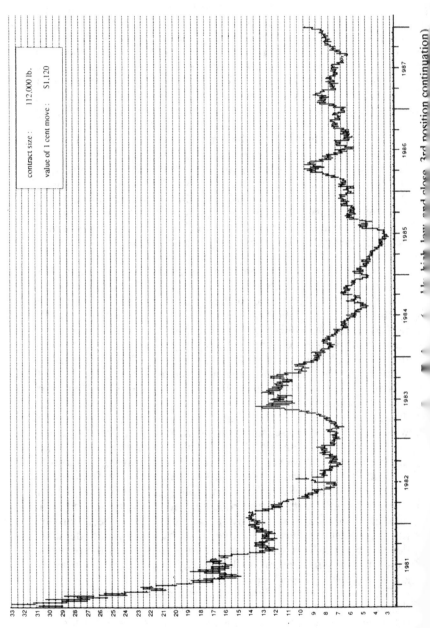

contract size : 112,000 lb.

value of 1 cent move : $1,120

cents/lb.

(weekly high, low and close. 3-rd position continuation)

requirements and, finally, the impact of the overvalued dollar from 1981 to 1985. Certainly, each of these factors played a role. A far more important reason, however, was the economic performance of Latin America and Africa over the 1980s. Comparing the two periods, 1975–80 and 1980–85, one finds that per capita consumer expenditure in Africa rose at an average annual rate of 0.56 per cent in the earlier period but declined at 1.73 per cent in the later. For Latin America the figures were growth of 1.6 per cent and decline of 0.4 per cent, and for the Middle East +2.7 per cent and −1.58 per cent. In all these regions high real interest rates (and hence heavy repayments on debts) and poor growth in export earnings led to slow economic growth and a squeeze on consumer incomes. This seriously affected consumption of sugar in these regions – Mexico and Brazil, in particular, whose difficulties have been behind 'debt crisis' headlines, and have seen actual declines in sugar consumption. Taking Latin America as a whole, total sugar consumption declined from 15.7 million tonnes in 1980 to 15.5 million in 1983, and was 16 million in 1984, despite rapid population growth. African consumption has also lagged behind the region's population growth.

These consumption patterns are important because developing countries' share of world sugar consumption is rising steadily; it was about 33 per cent in 1960, 40 per cent in 1970, and 50 per cent in 1980. This is the result of more rapid population growth in developing countries and the fact that poorer countries are at the point on their income–consumption curve where consumption grows rapidly when income increases. Conversely, consumers in developed countries are more likely to be concerned to reduce their sugar consumption, reflecting the general trend in diets towards low-fat, low-carbohydrate foods.

In other words, the 1980s bear market in sugar was principally the result of the uneven pattern of world growth. Although the USA and Europe enjoyed rapid growth from 1982 onwards, this was very unevenly transmitted to developing countries. Only in East Asia was economic performance good enough to generate increases in sugar consumption. An important lesson to take from this is that for many agricultural commodities, consumption in developing countries is extremely important. It is, however, often ignored, or treated too lightly by analysts; markets frequently appear happier when they can focus on demand developments in the countries where data are better. Markets traditionally are only interested in developing countries as producers of commodities; but as the recent example of sugar shows, demand in poorer countries is far too important to be ignored.

Market intervention

Apart from the panoply of measures used by governments to regulate their domestic sugar prices, there have been five attempts to contain the volatility of world sugar prices. The International Sugar Agreements of 1953, 1958, 1968, and 1977 specified price bands for free market sugar. The floor and ceiling prices were defended by export quotas, which were cut back or expanded as needed. None of these Agreements was effective, however, and negotiations to renew the 1977 Agreement on its expiry in 1984 collapsed. Since then, the International Sugar Organization has continued to exist, gathering statistics on sugar and acting as a forum for government contacts, but it has no remit to influence sugar prices.

Trading the sugar market

There are a number of sugar futures markets around the world, most of which trade raw sugar and reflect the free market price. There are two raw contracts in New York, the 'world' contract, number 11, and the 'domestic' contract, number 14; the latter has a price floor set by US government policy and is therefore only actively traded when world sugar prices are higher than the floor prices established by the government. Actively traded markets in sugar are located in New York, Honk Kong, Tokyo, Paris, and London, and there is a newly established market in Manila. There are also some other, less active markets in Japan. The Paris market trades white sugar, and both the London and New York markets have recently introduced whites contracts, to complement their contracts on raws. This reflects the growing importance of white sugar in physical sugar trade.

There are, therefore, two principal types of trade on the sugar market: taking a view on sugar prices as a whole, and taking a view on the raws–whites differential. There is also a liquid raws options market in New York, which allows trades to be constructed against the volatility of the market as well as its level.

Taking a view on sugar prices is to take a view of the actual and expected stock–consumption ratio; this needs to be done with care. Since so many countries are important, in terms of production, consumption, exports, and imports of sugar, and since the free market is so small, an attempt to calculate the world stock–consumption ratio is fraught with difficulties. Small percentage errors in estimates for a small number of countries can sum to a large fluctuation in the pressure on the free market. There are also serious problems with the quality of the available information on sugar stocks. While it is important to maintain a view on the overall statistical picture, it is equally important to remember that the sugar market is peculiarly sensitive to supply and demand prospects when the stock–consumption ratio is near a critical level. Accordingly, one needs to be watching for developments which signal a move in stock levels.

As in other commodity markets, the level of purchases by the Soviet Union and China is one key indicator. As always, however, these are difficult to foresee, but advance warning of Soviet purchasing sometimes comes from the Cubans. The Cubans have a long-term supply agreement with the USSR, under which they export sugar at prices which are normally well above those on the free market. When the Cubans have problems with their crop, they often buy sugar on the world market and sell it to the Soviets, taking advantage of the difference between world market prices and their preferential prices. Evidence of Cuban buying is widely seen as a bullish signal for the market.

As we have seen in the previous section, consumption in developing countries is of growing importance to the market. Economic performance in these countries, therefore, should be closely monitored for signs of expansion or contraction.

Seasonal factors are also important in the sugar market: prices are often strong in September and October, and often weak in December and January. Counter-seasonal trades should only be instituted if there are very strong reasons for so doing.

Another feature of sugar is that it is comparatively expensive to store. As a result, the normal contango is a wide one. One early signal of a bear market is a narrowing of this contango.

Finally, cash market developments are often an important leading indicator of futures prices. This is particularly important when the market in the Pacific basin begins to diverge from that in the western hemisphere. London, New York, and Paris respond first to developments in the west, but the impact of Chinese purchasing is often felt in the Pacific region, especially if the purchases are sourced in Thailand and Australia. Cash markets (and of course the Pacific region futures markets) signal imbalances in supply and demand rather sooner than the western futures markets.

One interesting feature of sugar prices is their relation to molasses prices. Molasses is the residue of sugar production from which no further sucrose can be economically extracted. It is a viscous fluid, used as an animal feed and as a feedstock for fermentation. (In East Asia most sake, i.e. rice wine, and monosodium glutamate, is made from molasses.) It is extremely difficult to store molasses, which makes its cash price rather unstable. Because it is a by-product of sugar production, changes in sugar production levels will bring about changes in molasses production, and hence molasses prices (as long as there is no offsetting change in molasses demand). Since sugar can be stored, the price of the non-storable molasses will be more sensitive to production levels (again, provided there are no unusual movements in demand). It is sometimes said therefore that a bull market in sugar which is caused by a production shortfall will be signalled first of all in the molasses market. This was the case with both the 1980 and 1987 sugar bull markets. It certainly cannot be dismissed as a wild theory. A number of sugar analysts pay close attention to developments in the molasses market, looking for early warning of sugar price movements.

The other trading possibility is to spread white sugar against raw. The premium for white sugar, after adjustment for the losses in refining, fluctuates between less than 1 cent per pound and over 2 cents; this is quite a large movement. Trading the whites–raws differential is difficult, however. In part, this is because the whites contracts are considerably less liquid than the raws. A further consideration is that the short-term fluctuations in white sugar exports are largely determined by the EC's weekly export tenders. Therefore, taking spread positions is something best left to professionals. It should be remembered, however, that the choice about whether to trade whites or raws should be determined by the nature of the underlying reason for trading. Growth in demand for sugar from those importers (principally the OPEC nations and India) who tend to buy refined sugar will tend to boost the price of whites rather more than that of raws; similarly, a shortfall in EC production will squeeze availability of white sugar. Conversely, supply–demand developments in exporters and importers of raw sugar will have a greater impact on that market.

Formerly, exchange rate considerations had an important impact on sugar trading since the London contract was denominated in sterling. An additional complication was that the London contract was a c.i.f. contract, whereas New York was f.o.b. Caribbean. This meant that the London prices differed from New York prices by the amount of the cost of shipping sugar across the Atlantic. More recently, however, the London contract specification has been changed, and it is now a dollar f.o.b. contract. It differs from New York only in the unit of quotation: London is quoted in dollars per tonne, New York in cents per pound.

Chapter ten

Other commodities

The preceding chapters have been concerned with the major groups of agricultural commodities which are traded on futures markets. There are, however, a number of other commodities for which futures markets exist but which do not fit easily into a broader grouping. For some of these, such as potatoes, this is because the markets are purely of domestic interest, but for others, such as cotton, the futures markets are of significance to the international agricultural economy.

Cotton

Cotton – the basics

Cotton fibre is produced in the seed pods, or bolls, of the cotton plant, which is a hardy annual bush. These seeds swell and burst, giving the characteristic white, fluffy appearance of a cotton field. Each boll contains approximately 30 seeds, to each of which is attached a tuft of cotton fibre, or lint as it is known at this stage. After harvesting, the lint is separated from the seed by a process known as ginning. The cottonseeds then become part of the oilseed market, and are crushed for cottonseed meal and cottonseed oil. These are, however, strict by-products of cotton fibre production.

Cotton fibre is extremely heterogeneous, and is normally classified on the basis of the length of the fibres. Coarse staple cotton has a fibre length of less than 1 in; medium staple between 1 in and $1\frac{1}{8}$ in; long staple between $1\frac{1}{8}$ and $1\frac{3}{8}$ in; and extra long staple above $1\frac{3}{8}$ in. Staple length is the key determinant of the suitability of cotton for different applications and long staple cottons command a price premium. The finest-quality Egyptian cotton will have a staple length as high as $2\frac{1}{2}$ in.

Cotton used to dominate world fibre production, but throughout the 1950s and 1960s it lost market share steadily to the new generation of synthetic fibres, particularly nylon and polyester. More recently, however, this erosion has been stabilized, thanks to improvements in the 'easy care' properties of cotton, a swing of fashion trends towards natural fibres, and a recognition that cotton is considerably more comfortable than synthetic fibres to wear next to the skin. This last factor is due to the ability of cotton to absorb moisture and gives cotton an advantage over synthetics in several applications. The major uses for cotton are in clothing and household textiles such as sheets and towels.

Production, consumption, and trade

Cotton is a hardy plant which grows very widely throughout the world. Apart from Europe, where small quantities are grown in Spain, Italy, and Greece, cotton is produced in every region of the world. The three most important producers are the USA, USSR, and China, and it is rare for these three to account for less than half of world production. The remainder of the world's crop is accounted for by a large number of producers, with India being the only other country whose production approaches the level of the 'big three'.

Production in many of the developing countries and in the USSR and China is affected very little by fluctuations in world prices, whereas production in the USA is very heavily affected. It used to be said that the USA accounted for almost all of the fluctuations in world output and stock levels, and although this is no longer the case, it is true that US producers are the most exposed to world market prices.

Farmer planting decisions are influenced by the price of cotton relative to their alternatives. In the USA the major alternative is soybeans, but in much of China land is switched between cotton and grains.

Cotton is deemed to be 'consumed' in the textile mills which turn it into yarn and fabric. The textile industry is highly competitive, and there has been a major switch in processing capacity from the industrialized to the developing countries. Textiles is one of the most sensitive industries to changes in exchange rates since it is so competitive and comparatively open to trade. Despite the success of developing countries in expanding their textile industries, Europe, the USA, and Japan are still major consumers of cotton. Overall, final demand for textiles is linked to the general business cycle, and much cotton which is 'consumed' in developing countries is exported as textile goods to the USA, Europe, and Japan.

The USA and the Soviet Union are the two largest exporters of raw cotton. Most Soviet exports go to eastern Europe, but some of their cotton also reaches the UK, Italy, and West Germany. The USA exports cotton all over the world, but its major markets are in East Asia. Other important exporters are Pakistan, Egypt, Turkey, and Sudan. A statistical summary of the cotton market is provided in Table 27.

Apart from revealing the extent of the dominance over the market exerted by the three main countries, the data in Table 27 also show the fluctuations to which the market is prone. Production in and exports from the USA have varied dramatically in recent seasons, as has consumption in China. Given the New York location of the cotton futures market and the role of the USA as the major swing producers, it is important to pay close attention to the US supply–demand balance.

The USA operates a price-support scheme for cotton under which farmers can take out a loan from the government, using their crop as collateral. The crop is valued at the support price. If market prices are below the support price, the farmer can keep the loan and forfeits the cotton to the government. The agency which

Table 27 The world cotton market: summary data (thousand bales)

	1983–4	1984–5	1985–6	1986–7
Production:				
USA	7,771	12,982	13,432	9,731
USSR	12,282	11,528	12,396	12,100
China	21,300	28,720	19,046	16,264
India	5,878	7,925	8,355	7,418
World total	67,479	87,797	79,394	70,501
Exports:				
USA	6,786	6,215	1,960	6,684
USSR	3,202	2,920	3,170	3,000
World total	19,198	20,397	20,514	25,376
Consumption:				
USA	5,926	5,540	6,399	7,410
USSR	9,083	9,322	9,600	9,800
China	16,300	16,200	19,796	19,709
India	6,614	7,117	7,150	7,847
End-season stocks	24,983	42,793	45,912	32,292

Note: A bale of cotton weighs 480 lb.

Source: USDA; International Cotton Advisory Council.

Table 28 The US cotton market (thousand bales)

	1983–4	1984–5	1985–6	1986–7
Beginning stocks	7,561	2,906	4,088	9,041
CCC stocks	4,766	590	1,809	6,829
Production	7,771	12,982	13,432	9,731
Mill consumption	5,928	5,540	6,399	7,400
Exports	6,786	6,215	1,960	6,660

Source: USDA.

operates this scheme is the Commodity Credit Corporation (CCC). As with grains, US prices effectively set world market prices, and US prices are clearly underwritten by the support price. When prices are low, the CCC stocks rise; but periodically the US government takes extraordinary action to reduce its stock levels.

Table 28 presents summary data on the US market, and Figure 19 shows the path of cotton prices on the New York Cotton Exchange. To understand the pattern revealed by these data, we need to go back to 1980 when unusually heavy Chinese imports combined with a general supply–demand tightness to push cotton prices sharply higher. New York futures prices peaked at 97 cents per pound in September 1980. These high prices encouraged plantings, and prices fell, touching 60 cents per pound in November 1981. Good demand in 1982–3 allowed prices to recover, but in 1983 the US Department of Agriculture (USDA) introduced its Payment-in-Kind (PIK) programme, under which farmers withdrew land from production but received their normal yield from government stocks; PIK was designed as a one-off programme to reduce overhanging stocks of a number of commodities, and it was because of this programme that production was only 7,771 bales in 1983–4. Similarly, stocks were reduced from over 7 million bales to under 3 million, with a dramatic fall in CCC stocks. This pushed prices higher, but increased production the next year pushed them right back down again, reaching 60 cents per pound in December 1985. Despite this fall, US cotton exports fell (largely because of a large rise in exports of cheap Chinese cotton); this led to a further large build-up in stock levels.

Having tried the route of lowering US production, the next policy initiative developed by the USDA was to subsidize exports; accordingly, for the 1986–7 season, a programme was developed whereby commercial exporters qualified to receive cotton from government stocks to bridge the gap between US and world prices. As a result, exports increased, and carryover stocks were cut back.

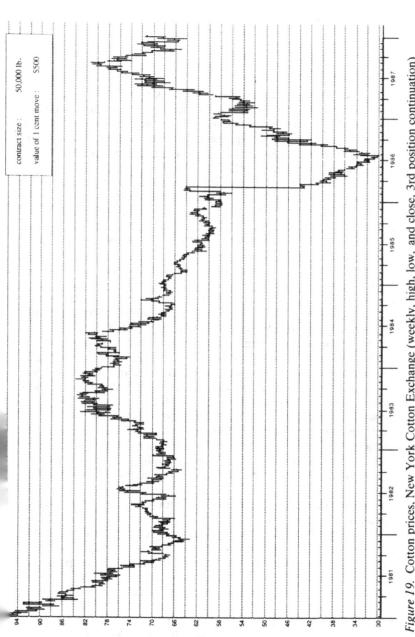

Figure 19. Cotton prices, New York Cotton Exchange (weekly, high, low, and close, 3rd position continuation)

Partly in response to these export improvements, cotton prices increased, with New York futures reaching 80 cents per pound in August 1987.

Trading the cotton market

The cotton market is rather volatile, and is therefore a rather risky one to trade. Although there are options on cotton futures on the New York Cotton Exchange (NYCE), they are traded rather illiquidly and should be approached with caution. The futures contract is a large one, and its daily price fluctuations are large; hence a large amount of capital needs to be committed to trade the market with a reasonable stop. By the same token, it is an exciting market to trade, capable of yielding large returns.

The two most important influences on the market are production and trade levels in the USA and China. Obviously it is hardest to develop a clear understanding of what is happening in China. Government policy towards the rural sector in China is changing, and the increased freedom being given to farmers is leading to large fluctuations in output of many crops as farmers exercise their choice. Of course, policies and prices are not the only determinants of production; the weather plays a crucial role. The net supply position of the Chinese, however, and particularly whether they export or import, is very important for world price movements.

Developments in the USA are rather easier to follow. Policies do change, but the changes are announced well in advance and it is normally possible to assess the likely impact of policy changes before their implementation. Planting of cotton takes place between March and May, and many farmers will have to make a decision about planting cotton or soybeans. Over the summer months cotton prices can move sharply higher if there are fears of bad weather damaging yields. Prices normally peak in August, and are weak during the harvest, which is concentrated between late August and early December. From December the market is paying increasing attention to the level of domestic and international demand.

Intercrop spreads in cotton are very volatile, and are not for the faint-hearted. The cotton crop year runs from August to July, implying that the October contract is the first new crop month. The development of mechanical harvesting, however, which takes place somewhat later in the year, has reduced the amount of cotton available for delivery in October, and December is now regarded as the first new crop month. An old crop/new crop spread therefore should be done with July and December.

One important indicator of the strength of demand for cotton is the cash market. The widely accepted world indicator prices are the two price indices computed by the Liverpool-based Cotton Outlook. The A and B indices, which are based on the prices paid in the Liverpool market for a variety of origins of cotton of longer and shorter staple lengths, provide the best available indicator of the state of world cash market supply and demand. They should be followed closely.

Natural Rubber

Natural rubber is produced from the liquid collected, or tapped, from the rubber tree (*Hevea brasiliensis*), which originated in the Amazon Basin, and that region enjoyed a period of prosperity in the nineteenth century because of the income provided by early tapping of its rubber. In 1877, however, its seeds were transplanted to South-east Asia, where it flourished, and the South American producers soon found themselves unable to compete with the new Asian production. The tree is very demanding in its temperature and rainfall requirements, and can only be grown in a small number of regions in the world.

During the Second World War when supplies of rubber to the USA and western Europe from South-east Asia were disrupted, considerable efforts were made to increase production of synthetic rubbers. These petrochemical-based rubbers were being produced in small quantities in the 1930s, but expanded rapidly during the war. This growth was given a further impetus by the rapid expansion of the automobile industry in the 1950s. Automotive applications account for approximately three-quarters of total rubber demand, and tyre production is by far the most important of these. As the automobile industry expanded production of natural rubber was unable to increase to meet this growing demand; moreover, the low prices at which synthetic rubbers could be produced were a strong disincentive to natural rubber production.

Natural and synthetic rubber are not perfect substitutes; the only synthetic rubber which exactly matches the structure and properties of natural rubber is polyisoprene. This is extremely expensive to produce and is only manufactured in large quantities in the Soviet Union where dependence on imported rubber is considered undesirable. The most important synthetic rubber produced elsewhere is styrene-butadiene rubber, which has different properties from those of natural rubber, but competes with it on price grounds in applications where technical performance is not of paramount importance.

Table 29 World rubber production and consumption (thousand tonnes)

	1983	1984	1985	1986
Natural rubber:				
Production				
Malaysia	1,564	1,529	1,470	1,542
Indonesia	997	1,115	1,116	1,110
World total	4,025	4,260	4,335	4,425
Consumption				
USA	665	751	764	745
Japan	504	525	540	535
World total	3,985	4,240	4,355	4,395
Synthetic rubber:				
Production				
USA	1,987	2,219	2,026	2,145
Japan	1,003	1,161	1,158	1,150
World total	8,300	9,100	9,045	9,175
Consumption				
USA	1,883	2,061	1,999	2,075
World total	8,335	8,985	9,045	9,175

Source: International Rubber Study Group.

Production and consumption patterns for natural rubber are rather different from those of synthetics. Natural rubber production is concentrated in Asia, with Malaysia and Indonesia accounting for well over half of total production. These two countries are even more important in world exports. Production of synthetic rubber, on the other hand, is concentrated in industrialized countries. Total production of synthetic rubber is also considerably greater than that of natural rubber. Table 29 illustrates these production patterns.

Rubber consumption patterns vary not so much by geographical area as by application. Natural rubber is rather more dependent on the tyre industry than synthetic rubber, and this dependence is growing. Tyre demand for natural rubber accounts for about three-quarters of total demand for natural rubber in industrialized countries, up from two-thirds in the early 1970s. This is because natural rubber accounts for a high proportion of the rubber used in the production of radial and heavy tyres. The general trend to radialization is increasing the output of radial tyres relative to cross-ply tyres.

Prices of natural and synthetic rubbers do move broadly in line with each other because there are numerous applications where substitution is possible. None the less, it appears that most rubber users are more concerned with technical performance than with price, which makes them reluctant to substitute unless price differentials are large.

Generally speaking, the main source of instability in the rubber market is the demand side. Although natural rubber production is affected by variations in weather and by farmers' activities (such as fertilizer application), the impact of these fluctuations is much less than that of variations in the level of demand. Demand for rubber is principally determined by the economic cycle in industrialized countries, although rapid expansion in automobile (and tyre) production in countries such as South Korea is increasing their influence over rubber demand.

Since the early 1980s the volatility of natural rubber prices has been limited by the activities of the International Natural Rubber Agreement (INRA). The Agreement, which came into force in 1981 and has since been renewed, established a buffer stock, designed to accumulate rubber in years of surplus and dispose of rubber during years of shortage. The buffer stock's first purchases were made in November 1981, and 360,000 tonnes of rubber were accumulated in order to shore up rubber prices. The job of supporting prices was made somewhat more difficult by widespread destocking in commercial interests; with an internationally funded buffer stock willing to assume the risks of stockholding and buying and selling on the basis of public decision rules, private operators have little incentive to carry stocks themselves. None the less, INRA was successful to an unusual degree among commodity agreements and, in response to growing demand for rubber, was able to begin sales from its stockpile in 1987.

The success of the international agreement over this period limited the usefulness of futures markets for producers and consumers. The London futures market, which was reasonably liquid until the early 1980s, is now inactive, and repeated attempts to establish a contract in New York have not been successful. There are many reasons for this, including the reluctance of the major tyre companies to use hedging facilities and poor contract design, but a major factor has been the comparative stability of the market because of the operations of the INRA buffer stock. Certain futures markets have survived, however; futures contracts on selected grades of rubber are traded on the Kuala Lumpur Commodity Exchange and on several exchanges in Japan. Rubber futures on these exchanges owe their continued existence to the active physical trade in their localities and, in the case of Japan, to the support of the main Japanese importers. Overall trading volumes, however, are not high enough to present attractive speculative opportunities to the international community, and international hedging business is limited by the currency and transportation cost risks involved in trading markets in East Asia.

Potatoes

Surprising as it may seem, potatoes have been an unusually interesting commodity for students of futures markets. Like many other agricultural commodities, they have the combination of inelastic demand and weather-disrupted supply which makes for price instability. On top of this, because they are bulky and low valued, and therefore expensive to transport, one country's production shortfall is less easily made up by imports (or surplus relieved by exports) than is the case with other commodities. This tends to exacerbate the instability of prices. What is most interesting about potatoes, however, is that stocks cannot be economically held from one season to the next. In the absence of expensive controlled storage facilities potatoes deteriorate too rapidly to be able to be stored from one harvest through the next harvest and still be of high enough quality to compete with the new crop. In and of itself, this may seem an unremarkable fact, but it does place a great burden on potato merchants (and all other stockholders).

Merchants have to meet the regular, day-to-day demands of potato eaters. At harvest time, therefore, they have to put into storage enough potatoes to meet demands throughout the year, up to the next harvest, in just the same way that grain stockholders do. Because consumers will prefer new potatoes as soon as they are ready, every merchant would like to end each season with no potatoes in store; as soon as the new crop is available, the old crop is virtually worthless. This, of course, is different from grains. But it is impossible to know exactly when the new crop will be available; the weather can advance or delay the harvest by a long time. The value of potato inventories will fluctuate dramatically as the new harvest approaches; each delay will push up prices, to ration the declining supplies over the remaining period; each advance will push prices down as merchants try to run down their stocks. Recall that one of the most important functions of futures markets is to set prices for storage. It follows that futures prices for potatoes will be prone to great volatility. It was exactly these price fluctuations which led the US Congress to prohibit futures trading in onions, which share with potatoes this feature of being unstorable from one season to the next. Blaming on speculation what is an essential feature of market clearing, the legislators banned the markets.

Such action has not been deemed necessary with potatoes, but potato futures markets have faced their own difficulties. Various contracts have been traded in New York and Chicago, but they have all foundered on problems of contract specification. The potato futures contract on the New York Mercantile Exchange ceased to trade in May 1987. In early 1988 there were three futures markets; London, Amsterdam, and Lille. Of these, only the London market, which opened in 1980, is large enough to warrant detailed attention. (The reader may derive a certain wry pleasure from the observation that the only commodity for which London boasts the most important futures market is potatoes.) The following discussion, therefore, focuses on the British potato market.

The summary data presented in Table 30 reveal some of the important features of the potato market: the stability of consumption, the limited role of international trade, and the fluctuations in production (which are largely caused by the weather). In fact the potato market is changing in many ways; imports of processed products are growing and a number of attempts are being made to improve the quality of British production.

By far the largest part of production consists of main crop, or ware potatoes, which are planted in March or early April and harvested between late October and early December. There are also two other components of the crop, the 'earlies' and 'second earlies'. Early potatoes are planted as soon as possible in the New Year, and often as early as January in Cornwall and Pembroke. (New potatoes are also imported before the domestic crop becomes available.) The second early crop is planted and harvested somewhat later.

Reflecting this pattern of seasonality, the London market trades contracts on November, February, March, April, May, and far November. The November price is the new crop price,

Table 30 The British potato market (thousand tonnes)

	1982–3	*1983–4*	*1984–5*	*1985–6*
Production	6,539	5,525	6,985	6,596
Imports	769	942	800	804
Exports	114	127	16?	158
Consumption	5,738	5,789	5,840	6,079

Source: Potato Marketing Board.

corresponding as it does to the harvesting period for the ware crop. February and March represent the mid-point of the storage life of the potatoes harvested in the previous November, and the April and May contracts reflect the arrival of the early crops. (See Figure 20).

The main price movements come in response to supply developments and, in particular, to the weather. A general pattern is for price stability from November to March, although very cold weather over the winter can raise fears of damage to potatoes in store. Unseasonally warm weather over the winter can also affect the quality of stored potatoes. From March onwards prices can be very volatile as the storage of ware crop potatoes is run down and the early crop comes to market. Weather developments in the spring affect the maturing early crop and the plantings of the main crop and hence have an effect on prices; later, over the summer, the main crop becomes vulnerable to adverse temperatures and rainfall; finally, as the harvest of the main crop approaches heavy rain can hinder the ability of farmers to lift their crops and thus affect the movement of the new crop to market. Successful trading of the potato market is therefore a matter of monitoring weather patterns and taking a view on their impact on the potato crop.

However, one caveat should be applied: the role of imports should not be ignored. Although the English Channel and the North Sea act as a disincentive to imports because of the high freight costs, Dutch farmers do regard the UK as a natural export outlet, and the Amsterdam futures exchange closely follows the London market. Imports make only a small contribution to total supplies, but they can increase their market share during times of high prices.

Frozen concentrated orange-juice

A futures contract in frozen concentrated orange-juice (FCOJ) has been traded on the New York Cotton Exchange since 1966. This represents perhaps the most rapid evolution in commodity market history, since the technology for concentrating orange-juice was not developed until after the Second World War; FCOJ is the major source of orange-juice in the US market; and orange-juice is, in turn, by far the most important fruit juice consumed in the USA. Consumption levels in other countries are nowhere near those in the USA, and the FCOJ futures market is therefore primarily of significance to the US economy.

Consumer demand for FCOJ is somewhat more elastic (with respect to both income and price) than many other agricultural

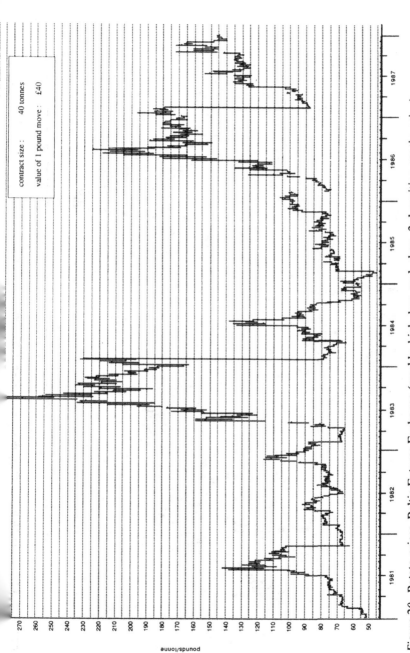

Figure 20. Potato prices, Baltic Futures Exchange (weekly, high, low, and close, 3rd position continuation)

contract size : 40 tonnes

value of 1 pound move : £40

pounds/tonne

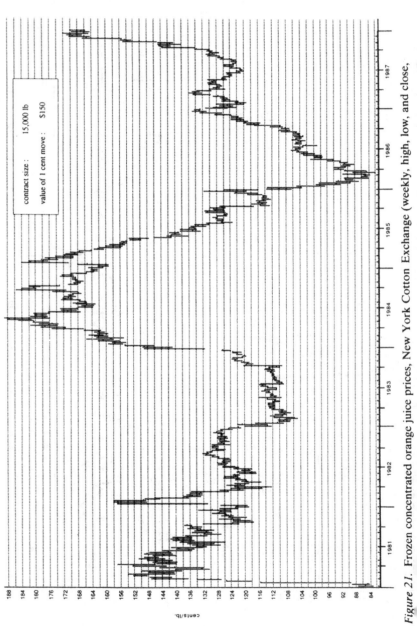

Figure 21. Frozen concentrated orange juice prices, New York Cotton Exchange (weekly, high, low, and close,

commodities but, like other commodities, there is considerable weather-related uncertainty on the supply side. It is this uncertainty which generates the volatility in prices. Almost all of the oranges which are used in the US for FCOJ are grown in Florida, and Florida's production is year round: early and mid-season oranges are harvested from October until March, and the later maturing Valencia crop is harvested from March until the late summer. Most FCOJ is a blend of both types of orange, implying that production over the whole year is important for the supply of FCOJ.

The only other significant source of FCOJ for the US market is imports from Brazil. Brazilian production began in the mid-1960s, and exports to the USA have been growing rapidly. These imports are essentially residual, however; when the US has a large crop, imports tend to be reduced. When the US has a small crop, and needs large imports, the price at which these imports are available will obviously influence US FCOJ prices.

The size of the Florida crop is therefore the key factor in the market, and the most important influence on year-to-year variations in production is the weather and, more particularly, whether there is a freeze in the winter and how severe it is. From December until mid-February, orange groves are at risk from freezing temperatures. The duration and severity of the freeze determine the extent of the damage; a freeze can reduce the juice content of oranges, render oranges unusable and, in extreme circumstances, damage the wood of the trees. In the first two cases, only production in the current year is affected, but in the third case production can be affected for up to five years while the tree recovers.

Among the US speculative community FCOJ is a favourite during the winter months. Volume of trade from October until March is usually much higher than in the rest of the year, and the fear of a freeze can lead to sharp, but short-lived, rallies in prices. In the event that a freeze scare turns into a real freeze, prices move sharply higher and hold these higher levels. An indication of these price movements is provided by Figure 21. Therefore, trading the FCOJ market is primarily a matter of monitoring Florida temperatures and acting accordingly.

Chapter eleven

The future of futures

Commodities have been traded on futures markets since the Dojima Rice Exchange was established in 1730, but this history, although long, has not been one of continuous innovation. In 1865 the development of a commodity exchange in Chicago ushered in a period of expansion in both the commodities traded on futures markets and the geographical location of the exchanges. For the first sixty years of this century, however, there was little that was new or innovative in futures markets. The 1960s saw the development of futures markets in non-storable commodities, a significant step, but it was the 1970s and the development of futures contracts on currency exchange rates, interest rates, and other financial instruments which provided a time of innovation comparable to that of the late nineteenth century.

If there has been a key theme of the 1980s, it has been geographical expansion, with new futures exchanges trading financial instruments in a number of new locations. The London International Financial Futures Exchange is perhaps the most notable example of this. Agricultural commodities, which for so long dominated futures trading, have ceded their predominance to financial instruments, and they have shared little in the new period of expansion. New contracts have been devised and new commodities traded, but the pace of growth in the agricultural sector has been slow. It is also the case that there are fewer and fewer 'new' commodities which can be introduced to futures trading; unless the cash market for the underlying commodity is both large and volatile, there is little chance of a futures market prospering.

Looking forward to the 1990s, what are the key issues which futures markets will face, and how will agricultural commodities be affected? This chapter examines these questions, and divides them into two groups: those concerning the exchanges themselves, and those concerning the relationship between futures trading and the economy as a whole.

The organization of trading

Exchanges themselves are naturally concerned to increase their own business, but are beginning to run up against the problem of the limited number of contracts which they can introduce. One approach to this problem which became popular in the early 1980s was to develop links between exchanges in different countries. The idea behind this was to allow the same contract to be traded in more than one location, thus increasing business and allowing an increase in the period of time for which trading was possible. A number of links have been formalized, with perhaps the most notable being that between the Chicago Mercantile Exchange (CME) and the Singapore International Monetary Exchange (SIMEX), under which a number of the CME's financial instrument contracts can be traded through SIMEX. The Chicago Board of Trade (CBOT) is negotiating a link with the London International Financial Futures Exchange (Liffe), under which US, UK and Japanese government bonds will be traded under the same contract terms in both markets.

It is fair to say, however, that links between exchanges have not been very successful. Apart from the regulatory problems of linking markets which operate under very different legal authorities, links require exchanges to collaborate when their normal behaviour is fiercely competitive. The CBOT, for example, introduced an evening trading session when it became concerned about losing some business to Japan. One alternative to a link with Liffe is an early morning trading session; and the CBOT's planning committee has certainly considered the idea of starting trading in Chicago at 2.00 a.m. in order to attract the business which is normally done in London. The idea of three eight-hour trading shifts providing round-the-clock trading in Chicago has certainly been mooted, and has met with surprisingly little opposition from the Chicago trading community who appear to put a low value on the time they spend away from the trading floor.

Partly because of disappointment about its link with SIMEX, the CME announced in September 1987 its plans to develop with Reuters a 24-hour trading system initially called Pre- (Post-) Market Trading, but later given the less ungainly name of Globex. This system would allow the CME's contracts to be available for trading on computer screens for every hour of the day when the open outcry trading pits are closed. The idea of screen-based trading is straightforward; instead of shouting bids and offers at one another in a noisy and crowded pit, traders input their bids and offers on computer terminals. A computer matches the trades and reports executed prices on the terminals. This type of trading is widely used in stock markets, and is beginning to find favour with futures markets.

The first fully computerized futures market was INTEX, a Bermuda-based exchange which began trading gold and silver, and later introduced contracts on a freight rate index and a stock market index. The New Zealand Futures Exchange (NZFE) also uses a wholly automated trading system and has been successful with it. The NZFE rarely trades more than 2,000 lots per day, however, and although the system's developers believe it can handle up to 20,000, it has not been tested at this level. In 1987 the London Fox introduced a white sugar futures contract which is traded wholly on screens, and its early performance was as good as its more optimistic supporters claimed.

Screen trading has its advocates and its detractors. To its detractors it dehumanizes trading and, more important, cannot generate the liquidity which is essential for a successful market. The argument runs as follows: without a healthy population of aggressive locals, assessing the mood of the pit and prepared to trade large numbers of contracts for small price movements, a market cannot provide the liquidity which is needed to absorb large hedging orders. Screen trading removes the possibilities for arbitrage within the trading pit itself, and thus denies locals some of their best trading opportunities. Conversely, to its supporters it represents the easiest way in which modern technology can be harnessed to provide 24-hour trading. Since local traders are entrepreneurs, the fact that one set of opportunities will be removed does not matter because new opportunities will be opened up. Moreover, it allows more detailed records to be kept about the minute-to-minute progress of trading.

The CME's plan to keep its open outcry trading pits but to make the contracts available for screen trading for the rest of the day is a novel combination of the two types of trading, and confirms the position of the CME as the most innovative futures exchange. Its trading pits will provide the liquidity to ensure that the bulk of trading goes on during open outcry hours, but the flexibility will exist to allow 24-hour trading for those who need it. The system is scheduled for launch in 1989 and will be closely followed by everyone with an interest in the future of futures markets.

The fear that must haunt exchanges outside the USA, and particularly outside Chicago, is that the CME's Globex system will increase the dominance held by the two Chicago exchanges over world futures trading. This issue of concentration is an important one, and it has two dimensions. At one level, Chicago is the centre of futures trading and shows no sign of loosening its grip. At another level, almost all futures exchanges outside the USA have found that the bulk of their success is accounted for by a small number of contracts. Thus Liffe, for example, is undoubtedly one of the success stories of the 1980s, having become one of the ten most active markets in the world within five years of its inception, but about one-third of its total volume is accounted for by one contract, the 20-year gilt.

Strategic planners in the major exchanges must consider ways in which this concentration can be diluted, at least in terms of their own contracts since the position of Chicago is unlikely to be threatened. They have every incentive to do so, given the low levels of profitability which are associated with low levels of trading volumes. This concern over profitability is a keen one in the futures business as a whole, especially outside the USA and Japan. Financial deregulation has brought a number of new operators into futures trading, particularly in financial instruments, and the pressure of diminished profitability is likely to lead to further concentration of brokerage houses. Those with bases in the profitable US and Japanese markets are the ones most likely to survive. As far as agricultural commodities are concerned, Chicago's dominance is, if anything, greater. Two likely developments, however, give reason for thinking that this domination might diminish somewhat in the future.

The first is that the Pacific region is growing in its importance to the world's agricultural economy, as it is to the world's economy as a whole. Yet there is no clear centre of futures trading for this region. Tokyo is the logical candidate, but the Japanese government has taken a deliberately cautious approach to opening its financial markets. Its agricultural markets are even more tightly protected. This has allowed Sydney, Singapore, and Hong Kong to grow in importance. None the less, there are signs of increasing deregulation in Japan, and this will certainly allow Tokyo's importance as a futures trading centre to grow. Any increased liberalization of agricultural trade in Japan, which may be prompted by the Uruguay GATT round, would allow Tokyo's agricultural markets to achieve a greater significance. Certainly, the expansion of South Korea, Taiwan, and Singapore as agricultural import markets and the realization of the agricultural potential of Thailand, Indonesia, and the Philippines, and the growing involvement in agricultural trade of China, all point to the need for an agricultural futures trading facility somewhere in the Pacific Basin.

The second is that growing dissatisfaction with the costs and operations of the EC's Common Agricultural Policy (CAP) and

217

the liberalization of agricultural trade being negotiated under the GATT point to the possibility of a greater role for agricultural futures markets in Europe. London has the expertise and history to step into this role, and Rotterdam is a major centre for cash and forward trading of a wide range of agricultural commodities. Looking forward to the 1990s, the possibility of more active European markets cannot be dismissed. Difficulties which currently stand in the way of London assuming a greater importance, however, are some regulatory issues which are discussed below.

Futures trading and the economy

An effort has been made in this book to show that agricultural futures markets serve a valuable economic function; they are not analogous to horse-racing or a casino. It is therefore fitting to end the book with some observations about this wider economic function and the challenges futures markets face in fulfilling it as well as possible. We begin with some comments about the UK markets, and then consider a major challenge for the agricultural futures markets and the agricultural economy as a whole.

Regulation and taxation in the UK

In Chapter 3 it was claimed that good regulation of futures markets consists of two elements: investor protection, and ensuring that markets are not manipulated or in some other way prevented from performing their economic function. Investor protection is clearly essential to ensure that speculators have sufficient confidence in markets to risk their money and provide the liquidity the markets need. Prevention of market manipulation is also essential to ensure that hedgers are not dissuaded from using the markets. Recent revisions to the regulatory environment in the UK have provided better investor protection, and it is to be hoped that this will lead to an increase in speculative interest in the London markets. The UK authorities continue to believe, however, that the broader regulatory issue is best left to the informal guiding hand of the Bank of England.

It is unlikely that London will be able to benefit from any increased role for agricultural futures in Europe while this remains the case, for the simple reason that the international community cannot be expected to share the faith that the Bank of England will act in the general interest.

This is not simply a matter of conjecture. A recent study[1] examined the coffee, cocoa, and sugar futures contracts in both

London and New York, and considered the impact of changes in the US regulatory environment on volumes of trade in the two markets. One of the conclusions of the study was that a tightening of the US regulatory regime benefited the New York sugar market and allowed it to boost its volume relative to that in London. The mechanism whereby this is effected is the confidence of the trading community. It is not that the tighter the regime, the more the trade, but rather that it was not until 1975 that the so-called 'international' futures markets of coffee, sugar, and cocoa were brought under the authority of the Commodity Futures Trading Commission (CFTC) and thus subject to the same regulation as the Chicago commodities. The New York exchanges initially worried that the regulatory hand of the CFTC would drive business to the 'freer' London markets, but the opposite seems to have happened.

From the broader perspective it would certainly be extremely difficult to defend the position that the CFTC's regulations are a disincentive to speculative or commercial involvement in the Chicago futures markets. Rather they build confidence that the markets are free and fair and hence stimulate involvement. Chicago's position at the heart of the marketing of agricultural commodities is a testimony to the value of the market which is widely accepted as free and fair. Therefore, it would seem that there is a strong case for regulation of the UK markets designed to ensure that they work as efficient price-discovery mechanisms. The exclusive emphasis on investor protection in the current legislation makes it rather lopsided.

The tax treatment of futures transactions in the UK is a further barrier to increased traded volumes. In recent years the rules governing hedging and individual speculation have been clarified considerably, to the benefit of all. The treatment of losses and gains and whether gains are subject to income or capital gains tax are all now reasonably straightforward. Many people are not exactly happy about the way tax is assessed, but there is at least a high degree of transparency about the regulations. Where there remains a problem, however, is the treatment of commodity funds.

The idea of a commodity fund is straightforward; individuals pool their money and the total sum is entrusted to a manager. The managers compete for business by the performance of their funds. This type of approach to investment has been extremely successful in the stock markets of both the USA and UK, where mutual funds, or unit-trusts as they are known in the UK, have flourished. Commodity funds are also extremely important in the US futures markets; they account for a large proportion of the volume of trade and have come to be a valuable component of individuals' investment portfolios. Funds are an obviously attractive option for newcomers to the commodity markets, just as unit-trusts have been attractive for newcomers to stock markets. Within the UK tax laws make it extremely difficult for this type of fund to operate efficiently since there is no consistent ruling by the tax authorities on what constitutes trading and investment (which are treated differently). There are also restrictions on the exposure which funds are able to have on particular markets. The fundamental problem is that the UK tax authorities distinguish between trading and investing, even though there is no clear economic basis for their distinction. Thus an individual who takes a couple of speculative positions a year might be deemed to be investing, whereas someone who takes a few more positions might be deemed to be trading. This problem is particularly acute for investment funds which might seek to hedge a stock portfolio with positions in futures markets; the Inland Revenue would probably fail to recognize this as a hedge, and would penalize the fund for 'trading', even if it were merely rolling over its hedges into more distant months. Again, the USA is well ahead in this area since the CFTC has developed clear and unambiguous definitions of hedging.

The issue of the tax treatment of futures transactions is of importance because of the impact it has on the range of opportunities available to speculators, and thus the ability of markets to provide the liquidity which hedgers need. The UK markets need more liquidity, especially if they are to take advantage of the future opportunities which are identified in the following section.

Developing countries and futures markets

One of the most interesting of recent developments in futures trading is the growth in activity in developing countries. The Kuala Lumpur Commodity Exchange is now well established, and other exchanges are being set up; the latest is the Manila International Futures Exchange. Developing countries play a central role in the world agricultural economy not only through their traditional exports of tropical products, such as coffee and cocoa, but also in their increasingly important imports of a range of other commodities. Imports of grains, vegetable oils, and sugar are growing, especially into populous countries and those with rapidly growing economies. This trend was noted in several of the commodity profiles in earlier chapters. Unstable commodity prices therefore exert a powerful influence on developing countries' economies, affecting both their export receipts and their import expenditures.

Efforts to reduce this influence have concentrated on international commodity agreements, which have sought to stabilize prices through buffer stocks or export quota schemes. For the most part, the experience of these agreements has not been encouraging, and support for them, especially in consumer countries, is waning. Moreover, these agreements were only ever concluded for commodities which developing countries export; hence they offered nothing to countries anxious to reduce the variability of their import costs.

Futures markets represent one way in which developing countries can improve export earnings and reduce imports costs. Indeed a recent study by Gemmill[2] suggests that forward contracting through futures markets may be superior to a buffer stock in terms of the stabilization of export earnings. Of course, developing country exporters and importers would not be able to develop perfect hedging programmes since they would face considerable exchange rate and basis risk. None the less, the markets could certainly help reduce the problems which are faced by commodity exporters and importers.

Current levels of futures market usage by developing countries are low. There are a number of reasons for this. First, commodity marketing in developing countries is frequently in the hands of parastatal organizations, which may not be very sensitive to short-term fluctuations in markets and where there may be little understanding of how futures markets work. Even in developed countries where commodity imports are handled by government agencies, there is limited use of futures, such is the ignorance of risk management among bureaucrats. Second, a distrust of free market systems is quite common in the developing world. Third, developing countries may lack access to the foreign exchange which would be required to open futures positions and to meet margin calls. Fourth, traditional trade channels provide ample opportunity for corruption, and beneficiaries from this may be reluctant to move to a different way of trading.

None of these difficulties are insuperable, and recent history affords some good examples of developing countries overcoming them. In 1980 the sugar market was rising sharply, fuelled by expectations of a growing supply shortage. The chairman of the Philippine Sugar Commission (Philsucom, the parastatal then responsible for sugar exports) correctly perceived that prices were well above those likely to be obtainable on the world market in the following four years. Unable to make his own sales on the futures markets because of foreign exchange constraints, he made forward sales to merchants of half of the probable Filippino exports over the period 1981 to 1984, and the merchants undertook the hedging programme. Philsucom secured a price of over 20 cents per pound by this programme, substantially above the prices of 5–6 cents per pound which prevailed on the market by the time the contract ran out.

The potential for increased developing country usage of futures markets is huge, given their importance in world agricultural trade. Facilitating the realization of this potential is a major challenge for commodity exchanges and the various international agencies. Apart from the greater volume of speculation which would be required to absorb this new hedging, consideration needs to be given to the necessary training and financial and regulatory issues. This is a fitting challenge for the futures industry in the 1990s.

Appendix 1: The chronology of the agricultural year

The seasonal pattern of agricultural production is extremely important in understanding price fluctuations, as the preceding chapters have made plain. The following is a summary guide to the annual cycle of agricultural production, intended as a source of reference to guide trading decisions throughout the year. It should be borne in mind, however, that improvements in agricultural technology and farming practice mean that this can only be a general guide. This summary follows the calendar year, but remember that each crop has its own crop year.

January

In the northern hemisphere winter grain crops are dormant. The weather is of concern, however, especially in the USSR and the USA, where inadequate snow cover can lead to crop damage if temperatures are low. Cold weather can also stimulate demand for feedgrains, and slow rates of weight gain for animals since they need more food simply to generate body warmth. Florida begins to harvest oranges, and the crop is vulnerable to frost damage. Sugar-cane harvesting is at its maximum in India, continues in the Philippines, and picks up pace in the Caribbean and Central America. Harvest of cocoa and coffee continues in regions near the equator, but is approaching its end in Bahia, the main producing region of Brazil. Southern hemisphere grain crops are at a critical stage. Wheat is being harvested in Argentina and Australia; soybean planting in Argentina and Brazil is finished by early in the month, and early-planted beans are blooming by the middle of the month and setting pods by the end. Argentine corn is silking, and South African corn is at the moisture-demanding reproductive stage. In Malaysia production of rubber and palm-oil begins to fall for the 'wintering' period.

February

In the USA land preparation for spring crops may begin towards the end of the month in the southern states; with good weather, cotton planting will begin along the Rio Grande in Texas. Cold weather remains a concern for dormant winter crops and for feedgrain consumption. Winter grains may resume growth in southern Europe. Sugar harvesting continues in the Caribbean, and the cocoa harvest is winding down in regions close to the equator. Brazilian soybeans are podding by mid-month and, in Argentina, the crop reaches that stage by the end of the month. Corn reaches maturity in Brazil, and harvesting may begin in the north. Malaysian rubber and palm-oil production hit their seasonal lows.

March

As the northern hemisphere winter recedes, land preparation and planting begin, with corn, oats, barley, and spring wheat planting getting under way in southern and central US states. Winter wheat emerges from dormancy in the USA and Europe, and in the southern USSR. Sugar-beet plantings also begin in central Europe. India begins harvesting winter wheat, and the cotton crop is planted in China. The great bulk of the West African cocoa harvest has been gathered by early in the month. Brazil begins harvesting soybeans and corn. In Argentina the harvest of corn, cotton, and early-planted soybeans gets under way. By late March Malaysian rubber and palm-oil production is beginning to pick up.

April

The arrival of the northern hemisphere spring quickens the pace of activity in arable farming. In the USA the pace of corn planting picks up, and has reached as far as the southern corn belt by the end of the month. Soybean planting also begins in the Mississippi delta, and cotton planting is almost complete by the end of April. Spring wheat and sugar-beet planting continues across the USA, is beginning in Canada and the USSR, and approaches completion in Europe. Winter grains, which in most of the northern hemisphere are now at flowering and pollination, are vulnerable to dryness and to late frost; this danger is especially acute in the USA. Soybean planting begins in central China, and corn and soybean harvesting continues in Brazil and Argentina. The coffee harvest begins in Brazil, and the temporão cocoa crop is harvested in Bahia.

May

May is the main corn-planting month in the USA corn belt. Delays are quite serious since late-planted corn will be in its heat-sensitive stages during the hottest days of summer. Soybean planting also moves northwards, but its timing is less critical. Cotton planting starts in the Texas High Plains, and the winter wheat harvest begins in Texas at the end of the month. This is the key month for Canadian planting of spring wheat and is also important in the Soviet Union. Winter wheat is planted in Australia, provided conditions are not too dry. In the southern hemisphere South African corn is harvested, and the Brazilian and Argentine corn and soybean harvests approach completion.

June

Corn can still be planted in the USA until the middle of June, but in the southern states the crop will reach the tasselling stage. Soybean planting will be completed by the end of the month. Harvesting of winter wheat moves northwards up to Kansas, and southern Europe and parts of the USSR will also harvest winter wheat. The monsoon moves northwards through India, and the rains will lead farmers to begin planting grains. The sugar harvest is winding down in the Caribbean, but beginning in Brazil. The grain harvest in Latin America is completed, and winter wheat planting continues. Wheat planting is also completed in Australia.

July

July is perhaps the month in which the weather is of the greatest importance. The Brazilian winter brings the frost season, with possibility of damage to the coffee crop, but the bulk of attention is focused on the northern hemisphere spring-sown grain crops, which enter their most critical growth period. US corn goes through the tasselling and silking stage in the corn belt, and late July may see the southernmost states' crop reaching maturity. The last soybeans are planted (on land from which winter wheat has been harvested), but about a quarter of the crop will be podding by the end of the month. Soil moisture levels are critical at this stage for both crops. Winter wheat harvesting continues to move north, and reaches Montana by the end of the month. The cotton crop moves into the important boll-setting stage. The winter wheat harvest is also moving northwards in Europe and the USSR, and almost all the Soviet winter-planted crop will have been gathered in by the end of the month. The weather is still important for the development of the spring-sown wheat, however. In China, as the USA, corn, soybeans, and cotton enter critical periods, and in Brazil the coffee harvest is in full swing.

August

In the USA soybeans are still at a critical stage, with pods filling throughout the month. Early-planted corn in the southern states is harvested at the end of the month, but most of the crop, in the corn belt, only reaches maturity at the beginning of September. Spring wheat harvesting starts in the Dakotas, and the first cotton is harvested in the Rio Grande Valley. In Canada, Europe, and the USSR spring wheat harvesting is under way. The corn crop in Thailand is harvested. The coffee harvest is progressing in most southern hemisphere producers, and the Brazilian sugar harvest is moving north-east through the sugar belt. Australia's winter wheat remains dormant, but some spring wheat planting may begin in northern areas. During August and September Malaysian palm-oil production reaches its seasonal peak.

September

About three-quarters of the US corn crop is mature by the end of the month, and about 10 per cent will be harvested. The crop remains vulnerable to an early frost, however, right up to maturity. In mid-month the soybean harvest begins, and may be 10 per cent complete by the end of the month. The cotton harvest is also beginning to move north-east. Winter wheat planting begins in the High Plains and moves south; as much as half of the crop may be planted by the beginning of October. Almost all Canadian grain is harvested by the middle of the month. European winter wheat planting also begins, and the European sugar-beet harvest gets under way. Wheat planting starts in the Soviet Union, and must be completed quickly to allow the plants to develop a root structure strong enough to withstand the winter. The Soviet cotton and sugar-beet harvests begin. At the end of the month the passing of the peak of the rainy season in West Africa leads to the start of coffee and cocoa harvesting there. The cocoa harvest also starts in Bahia, Brazil's main cocoa-producing region.

October

October brings the major part of the US corn and soybean harvests, and the cotton harvest also progresses. About three-quarters of corn and soybeans and about half of cotton are harvested by the end of the month. It is also the period of the greatest sugar production, with the beet harvest and cane cutting starting. Winter wheat planting is complete by the end of the month. Most of the European winter wheat crop has been planted by the end of the month. Sugar-beet harvesting is at its most active both in Europe and the USSR. The Chinese cotton, corn, and soybean harvests are under way. In Africa the cocoa and coffee harvests pick up momentum. In the southern hemisphere activity is beginning to increase as the spring advances. Brazilian winter wheat begins to be harvested at the end of the month, but in Argentina the crop is emerging from winter dormancy. In mid-month, soybean planting begins in the north of Brazil and moves southwards; corn planting also progresses quickly. Towards the end of the month Argentine planting of corn and soybeans begins. Sugar-cane continues to be cut throughout the northern areas of Brazil, and the Bahia cocoa harvest reaches its peak. Australian winter wheat matures rapidly and the harvest in northern areas may begin by the end of the month. Corn planting in South Africa starts right at the end of the month, but this depends critically on the level of rainfall.

November

The USA soybean and corn harvests are completed, and the cotton harvest will be almost completed by the end of the month. Winter wheat planting is only possible in southern warmer regions since further north there is insufficient time before winter to allow plant germination. As the sugar-beet harvest nears completion, the pace of cane cutting in Florida and Louisiana increases. Cuba and the Philippines begin harvesting sugar towards the end of the month. In Europe, sugar-beet harvesting continues and there is still planting of winter grains. The Soviet winter grain crop enters dormancy as the winter approaches. Cocoa and coffee harvesting in Africa reach their peak, and South Africa corn planting increases as the winter wheat harvest takes place. Brazil harvests its winter wheat crop and plants soybeans. Argentina may harvest some winter wheat late in the month, and corn and soybean planting are almost complete by the end of the month. The Australian winter wheat harvest moves southwards and may reach New South Wales. Sugar-cane harvesting in Queensland comes to an end.

December

Snow begins to fall in much of the northern hemisphere, providing a protective cover for winter grains, Farmers will plough their fields for summer crops before the first deep frosts. Some cotton and corn will remain to be harvested in the USA early in the month in the southern and south-western states. The European sugar-beet harvest may still need to be completed, but most arable farming activity is at a low ebb. In Brazil winter wheat harvesting and soybean planting are completed. The Argentine winter wheat harvest is at its peak, and planting of soybeans continues. Corn enters into its tasselling and silking stages in Brazil early in the month and in Argentina by the end of the month. Australia and South Africa continue to harvest winter wheat.

Appendix 2: Information sources on commodities

There is a great variety of information sources on commodities, ranging considerably in cost, coverage, and quality. Cheapest are daily newspapers, the *Financial Times* and the *Wall Street Journal*, but they are chiefly valuable for general economic news. They carry little about commodities and the coverage of US commodity markets in the *Financial Times*, in particular, is derisory. Two good newspapers offering more specialized coverage are the weekly *Feedstuffs* (published by Miller Publishing, 12400 Whitewater Drive, Minnetonka, Minnesota 55343, USA) and the daily *Public Ledger* (published by Turret Group, P.O. Box 64, Rickmansworth, Herts WD3 1SN, England). The *Summary of World Broadcasts*, published weekly by the BBC, presents the highlights of radio broadcasts from around the world monitored by the BBC's Caversham facilities. The economic news reports are often extremely valuable, especially for information about China and the Soviet Union.

At the other extreme, in terms of both cost and coverage, are the on-line services. These services, of which Reuters is the best-known, provide real-time price information as well as news reports. Others, such as ADP Comtrend and the Reuters 2000 service, allow charts to be drawn as well. Probably the best of the services currently available is the Moneycenter, provided by a US company, Knight-Ridder Business Information Services. The costs of these services vary considerably with the coverage desired. The companies which provide them also have different pricing structures: some charge a large joining fee and low monthly costs; others have high monthly fees. Broadly speaking, however, it would cost at least £500 per month to have an even rudimentary facility.

These costs are substantial, but they are easily justified if one is trading actively. An alternative, which is not currently available in the UK, but is common in the United States and can be expected to arrive in the near future, is the use of personal computers and satellite dishes to receive price data and other information. The running costs of such a facility are likely to be sharply lower than those of an on-line screen service.

Owners of personal computers with communications facilities can gain access to a variety of library services. For example, there are a number of companies which abstract news items and articles from magazines and journals, and store the abstracts on databases. It is then possible to search through the database, looking for the recent information on a particular development. Obviously, these services do not compete with on-line news agencies, but they do make it easy to compile background information on matters of interest. Costs vary widely; the more comprehensive, up-to-date, and easy to use a system is, the more expensive it is likely to be. A typical monthly charge for someone using a system two or three times per month, however, would be unlikely to exceed £50.

There are two main types of good printed sources about individual commodities: those which are primarily concerned with futures markets, and thus concentrate on providing views on likely price movements; and those which are addressed to a wider audience, and thus concentrate on matters affecting supply, demand, processing, and transportation as well as short-term price movements. This latter category will be considered first.

An excellent background to the supply and demand fundamentals of each commodity market is provided by the annual *Commodity Yearbook* (published by Commodity Research Bureau Inc., 75 Montgomery Street, Jersey City, New Jersey 07302, USA). This publication, which costs less than $100, is an excellent source of reference and is good value for money.

The main source of information on supply of and demand for agricultural commodities is the United States Department of Agriculture (USDA). It produces a wide range of weekly, monthly, and quarterly reports, covering almost every commodity and every region of the world. The USDA's information tends to be most highly thought of, particularly for those commodities which the US produces and exports, but the overall standard is very high. Many USDA reports are crucially important to short-term price movements, especially its monthly Crop Production reports.

All USDA reports are available at only a nominal charge; the major expenditure is airmail postage, which can be quite substantial given the sheer weight of documents produced. Alternatively, summaries of the reports are available on an electronic news network which can be accessed using a personal computer and British Telecom's Packet Switching Service. Full details of USDA's printed and electronic publications are available from USDA, Economic Research Service, Information Division, Room 228, 1301 New York Avenue N.W., Washington D.C. 20005-4788, USA.

The various International Commodity Organizations produce statistics on their commodities. This applies even to those which have no price stabilization role. The International Wheat Council produces a monthly report which covers wheat and coarse grains. There are also regular bulletins available from the International Sugar, Cocoa and Coffee Organizations. Again, the costs of these services are low, typically less than £50 per annum. (The IWC and ISO are both located at 28 Haymarket, London SW1Y 4SS, England; the Cocoa and Coffee Organizations are both located at 22 Berners Street, London W1P 4DD, England.)

There are a number of private organizations which sell information about, and analysis of, various commodities; many of them have a very good reputation and their comments are followed closely. Among them are F.O. Licht (P.O. Box 1220, D-2418 Ratzeburg, West Germany) who publish reports on sugar and coffee; Landell Mills Commodities Studies (14–16 George Street, Oxford OX1 2AF, England) who publish reports on sugar, coffee, cocoa, rubber, and oilseeds; and *Oil World* (published by ISTA Mielke GmbH, 2100 Hamburg 90, P.O. Box 90-0803, West Germany) which covers all vegetable oils and meals. Subscription prices vary from firm to firm, but a typical price would be around £400 per commodity per annum.

There is an even greater array of information geared specifically to futures markets. Most brokerage houses produce some kind of newsletter, and these are normally distributed free to clients. Large trading companies and commission houses produce daily telex reports which are available to clients. The US weekly *Consensus* (published by Consensus Inc., 1737 McGee, Kansas City, Missouri 64141, USA) reprints many brokers' newsletters in addition to other useful information, such as highlights of USDA reports and the Index of Bullish Market Opinion. A year's airmail subscription costs $595; it is probably the single most valuable publication which a speculator can receive.

There are a number of chart services, which, in addition to providing up-to-date charts, provide technical analysis of markets. Two such services are Investment Research of Cambridge Ltd (28 Panton Street, Cambridge CB2 1DH, England) and Chart Analysis Ltd (37–39 St Andrews Hill, London EC4V 5DD, England).

There is also a huge number of newsletters and tip sheets

produced by companies and individuals, each of which has its own approach to market analysis and its own brand of fervent adherents. Few have a wide circulation.

Finally, there is an excellent guide to information sources on the markets, which also includes details of many of the above-mentioned news and analysis services: David Nicholas's *Commodities and Futures Trading: A Guide to Information Sources and Computerized Services*, London: Mansell Publishing, 1985.

Notes

1 Futures markets and agriculture

1. The available evidence suggests that the existence of a futures market improves the quality of the information flow about a product. See C.C. Cox, 'Futures trading and market information', *Journal of Political Economy*, vol. 84, no. 6 (December 1976), pp. 1,215–37.
2. Selling a futures contract is known in the market as 'selling short' or 'going short' or 'shorting'. Buying a futures contract is 'going long'.
3. Empirical examination of the US grain futures markets confirms that the structure of premiums in futures quotations closely reflects the costs of storing grain. Ordinarily, however, the premiums are slightly less than the full costs of storage because of hedging.
4. The distinction between speculation and hedging is also important for regulatory reasons. Margins required by exchanges from traders classified as hedgers are generally lower than those classified as speculators. Moreover, the Commodity Futures Trading Commission, the body which regulates futures trading in the USA, only approves the introduction of futures contracts which meet a genuine hedging need.
5. See Cox, op. cit.
6. Among studies which have analysed this question are the following: T.A. Kofi, 'A framework for comparing the efficiency of futures markets', *American Journal of Agricultural Economics*, vol. 55, no. 4 (November 1973), pp. 584–94; R.E. Just and G.C. Rausser, 'Commodity price forecasting with large scale econometric models and the futures market', *American Journal of Agricultural Economics*, vol. 63, no. 2 (May 1981), pp. 197–208; L. Martin and P. Garcia, 'The price-forecasting performance of futures markets for live cattle and hogs', *American Journal of Agricultural Economics*, vol. 63, no. 2 (May 1981), pp. 209–15.
7. Congressman Conte, 93rd Congress of the United States, 1st Session, House of Representatives, Hearings before the Subcommittee on Special Small Business Problems of the House of Permanent Select Committee on Small Business, 25 July 1973.
8. For wheat see R.H. Hooker, 'The suspension of the Berlin produce

exchange and its effect upon corn prices', *Journal of the Royal Statistical Society*, vol. 64 (December 1901), pp. 574–604; W.G. Tomek, 'A note on historical wheat prices and futures trading', *Food Research Institute Studies*, vol. X. no. 1 (1971), pp. 109–13. For cotton see S.J. Chapman and D. Knoop, 'Dealings in futures on the cotton market', *Journal of the Royal Statistical Society*, vol. 69, no 2 (June 1906), pp. 321–73; H.C. Emery, *Speculation on the Stock and Produce Exchange of the United States*, New York: Columbia University Press, 1896. For onions see R.W. Gray, 'Onions revisited', *Journal of Farm Economics*, vol. 45, no. 2 (May 1963), pp. 273–6; A.C. Johnson, *Effects of Futures Trading on Price Performance in the Cash Onion Market, 1930–68*, US Department of Agriculture, Economic Research Service Technical Bulletin No. 1470, Washington DC (February 1973); H. Working, 'Price effects of futures trading', *Food Research Institute Studies*, vol. I, no. 1 (1960), pp. 1–30. For pork bellies see M.J. Powers, 'Does futures trading reduce price fluctuations in cash markets?', *American Economic Review*, vol. LX, no. 3 (June 1970), pp. 460–4. For live cattle see Powers, op. cit. pp. 460–4; G.S. Taylor and R.M. Leuthold, 'The influence of futures trading on cash cattle price variations', *Food Research Institute Studies*, vol. XIII, no. 1 (1974), pp. 29–36.

9. D.J.S. Rutledge, 'Trading volume and price variability: new evidence on the price effect of speculation', *International Futures Trading Seminar Proceedings* (Chicago Board of Trade), vol. 5 (1978), pp. 160–74. Reprinted in Barry A. Goss (ed.), Futures Markets: their Establishment and Performance, London, Croom Helm, 1986.

10. R.W. Gray, 'Price effects of a lack of speculation', *Food Research Institute Studies*, supplement to vol. VII (1967).

11. For Keynes's views see J.M. Keynes, 'Some aspects of commodity markets', *Manchester Guardian Commercial*, European Reconstruction Series, section 13, 29 March 1923; and J.M. Keynes, *A Treatise on Money*, London: Macmillan, 1930, Vol. 2. Elaboration of these ideas is provided in J.R. Hicks, *Value and Capital*, Oxford: Clarendon Press, 1946, Chs 9 and 10.

12. C.O. Hardy, *Risk and Risk Bearing*, Chicago: University of Chicago Press, 1940.

13. A testable assertion of the Keynes–Hicks view that futures prices tend to rise until expiry is that futures prices are biased forecasts of spot prices; hence the references in n. 6, above, are relevant here. The issue and evidence are well summarized by Gordon Gemmill, 'The forecasting performance of commodity futures markets', City University Business School, London, November 1981, mimeo.

14. Katherine Dusak, 'Futures trading and investor returns: an investigation of commodity market risk premiums', *Journal of Political Economy*, vol. 87, no. 6 (December 1973), pp. 1,387–406.

15. Zvi Bodie and Victor I. Rosansky, 'Risk and return in commodity futures', *Financial Analysts Journal*, vol. 36, no. 3 (May–June 1980), pp. 27–39.

16. H.S. Houthakker, 'Can speculators forecast prices?', *Review of Economics and Statistics*, vol. XXXIX, no. 2 (1957), pp. 143–51.
17. C.S. Rockwell, 'Normal backwardation, forecasting and the returns to commodity futures traders', *Food Research Institute Studies*, supplement to vol. VII (1967), pp. 107–30.
18. Blair Stewart, *An Analysis of Speculative Trading in Grain Futures*, US Department of Agriculture Technical Bulletin No. 1001, Washington, DC, October 1949.
19. Ray L. Ross, 'Financial consequences of trading commodity futures contracts', *Illinois Agricultural Economics*, vol. 15, no. 2 (July 1975), pp. 109–18.

2 Agricultural options

1. Options were traded outside the USA on rather illiquid markets, throughout the 1960s and 1970s, but large-scale development was impossible while the US ban was in place.
2. In both Figures 2.1 and 2.2, and in the examples in the text, the profitability of the option position is evaluated at expiry; i.e. only the intrinsic value of the options is considered. Of course, options also have extrinsic value, but that is so variable that considering it would complicate the graphical exposition enormously. Ways of trading extrinsic value are considered in Chapter 5.

3 Commodity futures exchanges

1. A pork belly is a piece of flesh peeled from the lower central section of a hog, with one taken from each side; bellies are sliced into bacon.
2. Leon Walras, *Elements of Pure Economics* (trans. W. Joffee), Homewood, Ill.: Irwin, 1954.
3. An interesting discussion of the history of onion and potato futures trading is contained in R.W. Gray, 'Onions revisited', *Journal of Farm Economics*, vol. 45, no. 2 (May 1963), pp. 273–6; A.C. Johnson, *Effects of Futures Trading on Price Performance* in the Cash Onion Market, 1930–68, US Department of Agriculture, Economic Research Service Technical Bulletin No. 1470, Washington, DC (February 1973); R.W. Gray, 'The futures market for Maine potatoes', *Food Research Institute Studies*, vol. II, no. 3 (1972), pp. 313–41.
4. L.C.B. Gower, *Review of Investor Protection*, Cmnd. 9125,: London: H.M.S.O. 1984.
5. A recent paper which compares the two systems is R.W. Anderson, 'Regulation of futures trading in the United States and the United Kingdom', *Oxford Review of Economic Policy*, vol. 2, no. 4, Winter 1986, pp. 41–57.

4 Approaches to price analysis

1. The long-term trend in commodity prices has received a lot of
    attention from economists. There are those who claim that the
    downward trend since the Second World War is nothing more than a
    statistical result of the commodity price boom caused by the Korean
    War. Certainly, measuring a trend requires a starting-point – and the
    choice of a starting-point can seriously affect the trend. In addition,
    there are good reasons for expecting that the price of wasting assets,
    i.e. non-renewable commodities, such as minerals, will rise as reserves
    are depleted. Malthusian visions of ever-growing demand for food
    have created the impression in some minds that agricultural prices
    will follow the same path. Nevertheless, the fact that consumers
    spend a lower and lower proportion of the increments to their income
    of agricultural goods does have implications for farm income and
    prices. Moreover, few people who have examined price trends over
    the long term (and some commodity price series are available from
    the early nineteenth century) have much doubt that agricultural
    commodity prices have shown a steady decline. Of course whether
    this will continue is another question.

    A closely related issue is the so-called terms of trade arguments.
    Since developing countries, on the whole, export commodities and
    import manufactured goods, the path of commodity prices affects
    their terms of trade. Economists have long debated whether
    developing countries' terms of trade are subject to a long-term
    decline. Statistical evidence has tended to support the view that there
    is a decline, although the picture varies considerably from one
    historical period to the next and from one country to the next
    (depending on which commodities are exported). The issue and
    evidence are reviewed in A.I. MacBean & D.T. Nguyen, *Commodity
    Policies: Problems and Prospects*, London: Croom Helm, 1987,
    especially Chapter 3, pp. 41–64 and Chapter 7, pp. 346–7.
2. For poor people basic grains account for a large percentage of
    expenditure; hence lower grain prices will stimulate consumption
    through the effect on income.
3. Raymond M. Leuthold and Peter A. Hartmann, 'A semi-strong form
    evaluation of the efficiency of the hog futures market', *American
    Journal of Agricultural Economics*, vol. 62, no. 3 (August 1979),
    pp. 482–9.
4. A review of the issues in commodity modelling and a bibliography of
    models in the public domain are contained in Walter C. Labys and
    Peter K. Pollack, *Commodity Models for Forecasting and Policy
    Analysis*, London: Croom Helm, 1984.
5. For a detailed analysis of this issue see *Variable Exchange Rates and
    Trading on Commodity Markets*, Commonwealth Economic Papers
    No. 20, Commonwealth Secretariat, London, January 1986.

7 Oilseeds, oilmeals, and oils

1. Strictly speaking, the soybean is a legume and therefore distinct from both grains and oilseeds. In so far as the soybean produces both meal and oil, however, no harm is done by this rather loose usage of the term 'oilseed'.

8 Livestock and meat

1. One of the difficulties in defining a contract for live animals was setting delivery terms, given the dispersal of the major cash livestock markets around the country. The live cattle contract specifies certain stockyards and defines discounts for delivery at other stockyards, but reservations have been expressed about this delivery system. The feeder cattle contract has a cash settlement procedure, and introducing this for live cattle has been suggested.
2. Consumer preference for fresh meat is an important factor limiting international trade in meat. Most internationally traded meat is frozen and therefore occupies a rather different segment of the market.
3. The term 'pig' is usually taken to refer to all types of pigs, whereas the term 'hog' is confined to young animals being raised for slaughter as prime pork animals; an alternative to the term hog is 'porker'.
4. The cobweb phenomenon drew its name from the path drawn by price as it converged to, or diverged from, equilibrium in simple diagrammatic representations of different supply and demand conditions. It is now widely used in economic models where demand is a function of current price, but supply is a function of lagged price; the time lag prevents the market from moving quickly to equilibrium and generates the 'cobweb'. A full treatment of the issue is given in N.S. Buchanan, 'A reconsideration of the Cobweb Theorem', *Journal of Political Economy*, vol. 47, no. 1 (February 1939), pp. 67–81.
5. Hogs are simple stomached, like humans, and therefore must be fed complete diets. Cattle are ruminants, and since they generate proteins by microbial synthesis in the rumen, can be fed on carbohydrate diets. Cattle are only fed protein at critical stages of their growth, or to produce especially rapid weight gains.

11 The future of futures

1. Betsey A. Kuhn, Frieda N. Shaviro, and Margaret M. Burke, 'Market regulation and international use of futures markets' (paper presented at the 1985 Meetings of the American Agricultural Economics Association). *American Journal of Agricultural Economics*, vol. 67, no. 5 (December 1985), pp. 992–8.
2. Gordon Gemmill, 'Forward contracts or international buffer stocks? A study of their relative efficiency in stabilising commodity export earnings', *Economic Journal*, vol. 95, no. 378, (June 1985), pp. 400–17.

Index

238

Index

Printed in the United States
by Baker & Taylor Publisher Services